1973 Nervous Breakdown

1973
Nervous Breakdown

Watergate, Warhol, and the
Birth of Post-Sixties America

Andreas Killen

BLOOMSBURY

For Henry, Nicholas, and Marie

Published by Bloomsbury USA, New York
Distributed to the trade by Holtzbrinck Publishers

All papers used by Bloomsbury USA are natural, recyclable products made from wood grown in well-managed forests. The manufacturing processes conform to the environmental regulations of the country of origin.

The Library of Congress has cataloged the hardcover edition as follows:

Killen, Andreas.
1973 nervous breakdown : Watergate, Warhol, and the birth of post-sixties America / Andreas Killen.—1st U.S. ed.
p. cm.
Includes bibliographical references.
ISBN-13 978-1-59691-059-1 (hardcover)
ISBN-10: 1-59691-059-3 (hardcover)
1. United States—Civilization—1970– 2. United States—Social conditions—1960–1980. 3. Nineteen seventy-three, A.D. 4. Nineteen seventies. 5. Watergate Affair, 1972–1974. 6. Vietnamese Conflict, 1961–1975—Peace. 7. Israel-Arab War, 1973—Economic aspects. 8. Petroleum industry and trade—Economic aspects—United States. I. Title.

E169.12.K463 2005
973.924—dc22
2005023661

First published in the United States by Bloomsbury in 2006
This paperback edition published in 2007

Paperback ISBN-10: 159691-060-7
ISBN-13: 978-1-59691-060-7

1 3 5 7 9 10 8 6 4 2

Typeset by Hewer Text UK Ltd, Edinburgh
Printed in the United States of America by Quebecor World Fairfield

CONTENTS

Introduction

The 70s are very empty.

—Andy Warhol

Will the seventies never end? The question asked recently by a pundit in the *New York Times* is a valid one. The seventies are, indeed, the decade that refuses to end—despite the fact that, for a long time, they barely counted as a decade, so completely were they obscured by the long shadows cast by both the sixties and the eighties and by the noisy clamor of their respective partisans. While the former were claimed by the Left and the latter by the Right, the seventies remained the foundling of recent American history, claimed by no one. Despite the current wave of seventies nostalgia and revisionism, these years still need to be liberated from the two decades that bracket them. More than simply the aftermath to the one and the prelude to the other, this decade should be considered on its own terms, as a distinct cultural moment, a moment of rupture and discontinuity in American history but also of tremendous creativity.

Not least among the reasons for reconsidering the seventies is the fact that this most enigmatic of periods in recent American history, this "un-decade," was an incubator for many of the developments that now define our contemporary political and cultural zeitgeist. Just one example among many is *Roe v. Wade*, the landmark abortion rights ruling, which gives 1973 a strong claim to be considered Year One of the Culture Wars—the ongoing conflict that continues to convulse American society. More generally, as the war in Iraq deepens with no prospect of an end in sight, it becomes clear that a specter is haunting our society: the specter of the 1970s, a decade that has entered the historical lexicon as a virtual synonym for weakness, confusion, and malaise. The constant presence of Vietnam in the 2004 elections and the talk of quagmire represent simply one aspect of this sensibility. These days, it seems, scarcely a week goes by without some further reminder of that era: the recent revelation of Deep Throat's identity; *Time* magazine's capitulation to a special prosecutor investigating leaks of classified government information, a case that awakens memories of the Pentagon Papers; rising oil prices and the threat of inflation; abortion and the role of the Supreme Court in legislating morality; the debate over gay marriage. The decade that, in 1973, invented reality television programming has in our time become itself a kind of reality television show, available for endless replay, its melodramatic narratives and images endlessly looping through our current divided red state/blue state consciousness.

This book tells the story of that decade's pivotal year, a year of shattering political crisis and of remarkable cultural ferment. In 1973 America was jolted by three shocks, following on one another in rapid succession. First, the war in Vietnam ended in the first-ever military defeat for the United States. Second, the Watergate cover-up unraveled, and the presidency of Richard Nixon became engulfed in scandal and, by year's end, calls for impeachment. Last but not least, Americans were hit hard by a collapsing economy: 1973 was also the year of the Arab oil embargo and the beginning of the long slide into stagflation that lasted until the 1980s. Any one of these events alone would have challenged America's image of itself; together they shook the national psyche to its very core.

This year marked the true end, too, of one of the most turbulent decades in American history, the sixties. Nixon's landslide victory in 1972, coupled with the war's conclusion, finally closed the book on the antiwar movement that had agitated that decade. By 1973 the wave of student uprisings and radicalism had run its course. One by one the leaders of the counterculture fell off the radar screen: "cultural revolutionary" Abbie Hoffman went underground; former Student

Nonviolent Coordinating Committee leader H. Rap Brown was convicted for armed robbery; Black Panther Huey Newton fled to Cuba; and drug guru Timothy Leary, dubbed by Nixon "the most dangerous man in America" following his escape from a California jail, was captured in Afghanistan and returned to the United States. The nation was rocked by isolated acts of violence, including the standoff between members of the American Indian Movement and the FBI at Wounded Knee and the first "action" by the Symbionese Liberation Army (SLA). But rather than marking a continuation of the insurrectionary impulses of the sixties, the terrorism of the SLA and organizations like it represented the tragic dead end of that decade's contestations.

The end of the greatest prolonged boom in the history of capitalism and, with it, the political and economic constellation that had given birth to President Lyndon Johnson's Great Society also claimed another significant casualty: the progressive liberalism that had attempted to turn America's cities into laboratories of social reform. By the early 1970s these cities were beset by crime and decay on a scale that defied amelioration. A new punitive, neoconservative mood descended over the country in 1973, the immediate fruits of which were the passage of the Rockefeller drug laws and calls for the reinstatement of the death penalty by the Nixon administration, both coming in reaction to an epidemic of drug-related crime. Nixon also began dismantling many of the social programs launched during the Johnson administration's War on Poverty. The crumbling of the built environment of America's great cities was matched by the collapse of the modernist architectural movement that had once promised to use enlightened planning to solve the problems of those cities. Modernism's symbolic death was heralded by the demolition of the landmark St. Louis housing project Pruitt-Igoe and, on a larger scale, by the mounting crisis of the nation's largest city, New York.

Taken as a whole, these events make 1973 a cultural watershed, a moment of major realignments and shifts in American politics, culture, and society. This year marked not just the end of the sixties but the onset of a debate, one that continues to this day, about the legacy of that turbulent decade. At the same time this year was alive with a sense of new possibilities and openings to the future, harbingers of an emerging new postmodern cultural configuration. This book peers into the American mind at a deeply schizophrenic moment. It offers a psychogram of a country that was dealing with the consequences of Vietnam, Watergate, and economic meltdown—a profile of a year of uncertainty and disorientation but also of tremendous vitality and creativity.

By any standard 1973 marked a genuine low point in U.S. history. Yet what looked to some like unequivocal signs of crisis looked more ambiguous to others, a shift in the tectonic plates in American society that released tremendous energy. Seen from this perspective, 1973 represented a year of breakthroughs and of new possibilities. While the generational and oedipal conflicts of the sixties remained, for the most part, politically stillborn, they found new avenues of expression. What survived the sixties was the cultural revolution—the revolution in music, film, sensibilities, and lifestyles. And while the passing of sixties utopianism would be duly recorded in much of the culture of this period, the seventies revolution of everyday life—for all its awareness of being a time of crisis—was not without its own genuinely visionary aspects.

This was certainly true, for instance, in the case of the film industry. In Hollywood, 1973 was a veritable annus mirabilis, a breakthrough year for the new directors' cinema, marked by the release of films like *Mean Streets, Badlands,* and *The Exorcist. The Godfather* won the Oscar for best picture, and its star, Marlon Brando, won best actor. And just as the general public ate up Erica Jong's bawdy novel *Fear of Flying,* so too did it flock to films such as *Deep Throat* and *Last Tango in Paris,* whose popularity served notice of the extent to which the sexual revolution had established its place in American society. At the same time, the hugely successful *American Graffiti,* with its chaste treatment of a more sexually innocent time, tapped into nostalgia for pre-sixties America and prefigured the later advent of the age of the blockbuster.

Musically, 1973 marked a brief yet important interlude between the 1960s and the advent of corporate rock, a moment of incubation that gave birth to the new sounds of punk and disco. In Manhattan two venues opened that contained the seeds of those musical movements: the gay discotheque Le Jardin, a harbinger of the later Studio 54 scene; and the landmark Bowery bar CBGB. One of the early progenitors of punk, the New York Dolls, became darlings of the New York music scene, parading an outlandish camp aesthetic that combined elements of transvestite culture with the sound of 1950s rock-and-roll bands. Both music and film were energized by the larger cultural shifts of the early 1970s and moved to fill the new space of uncertainty, experimentation, and play opened up by the crisis of established institutions—even if that space was already beginning to close down by the mid-1970s, with the advent of the blockbuster and of corporate rock.

One of that year's most remarkable experiments came with the airing of *An American Family*, the first-ever reality television series. This twelve-part series, which documented the disintegration of the Loud family of Santa Barbara, California, marked the convergence of two major postwar developments: the perceived crisis in the nuclear family and the media's invasion of everyday life. During the 1960s innovations in television technology, like the introduction of videotape and direct satellite transmission, had greatly expanded the scope and immediacy of broadcast news. Vietnam became the world's first televised war, beamed to the vast new audience for which pop media theorist Marshall McLuhan coined the label the "global village." At the same time the stresses that had begun to appear in family life during the sixties found their way into a new brand of television sitcom, exemplified by the series *All in the Family*, which its producers conceived of as a response to the anodyne images of family life offered by shows like *The Brady Bunch*. *An American Family* represented the logical culmination of this tendency—a response to a "reality deficit" that TV had itself produced and that America as a whole seemed to be suffering from. In 1973 reality itself seemed to be up for grabs, as one of Nixon's supporters indirectly acknowledged when he affirmed that the president, at the November press conference at which he had announced to

the nation "I am not a crook"—held, significantly, at Disney World—
had achieved "a great deal of verisimilitude." Yet in the two landmark
media events of that year—the Watergate hearings and *An American
Family*—television discovered a new seriousness of purpose that promised to restore Americans' grip on reality.

The reworking of the sixties theme of revolution found its way into
many other parts of American life and was taken up in many
unpredictable ways. When Abbie Hoffman announced that the "modern revolutionary group headed for the TV station, not the factory," he
was registering the changes noted above. Much of the success of the
antiwar movement had derived from its ability to exploit the new
conditions of the global village. This movement reached the peak of its
strength following the Nixon administration's invasion of Cambodia
in 1970. Yet by 1972 or 1973 it had completely disintegrated, as a
result both of external pressures and shifts and of its own self-
destructive tendencies. The final spasm of the sixties came with the
guerrilla organizations of the early 1970s, exemplified by the SLA, the
tiny band that formed in 1973 and that gained notoriety with its
kidnapping of heiress Patty Hearst in early 1974.

By the early 1970s much of the New Left had either degenerated into
self-parody or turned inward to meditation and experiments in communal living. Prior to marrying Jane Fonda, icon of Hollywood radical
chic, in January 1973, New Left activist Tom Hayden lived in a
Berkeley commune called the Red Family, whose members admired
the North Korean leader Kim Il Sung. The comrades of the cult of Kim
reportedly were fond of singing, to the sound of "Maria" from *West
Side Story*: "The most beautiful sound I ever heard / Kim Il Sung, Kim
Il Sung, Kim Il Sung." The playful intent here signals the advent of a
new kind of revolutionary kitsch, for which Hearst, whose image—
garbed in a jumpsuit, beret, and carbine—was flashed across the
nation's consciousness following her participation in a bank holdup,
would become the poster girl.

Another variant of this imagery exists in the series of Mao paintings
that Andy Warhol began to produce in late 1972. This transformation

of a hero of the New Left into an ambiguous new kind of celebrity image offers a comment on the fate of the sixties culture of radicalism. Even in the throes of crisis capitalism was still capable of swallowing all revolutionary impulses. Among other things, Warhol's image attests to what Thomas Frank has termed the "commodification of dissent" that has been a signature of post-sixties American culture—a process that may well have reached its nadir with the recent marketing, by former members of the Black Panther Party, of a new barbecue sauce with the name "Burn Baby Burn," an homage to the incendiary phrase chanted by sixties rioters.

In 1968 Students for a Democratic Society leader Mark Rudd, who would soon disappear into the radical organization the Weather Underground, had captured the sixties' faith in change with the warning he issued to the older generation: "We will take control of your world . . . and attempt to mold a world in which we and other people can live as human beings." Yet in 1973, at a moment seemingly highly propitious for the radical change promised by the New Left—a moment when the movement's fantasy of collapsing authority seemed close to realization— the disarray within the Left rendered it incapable of taking advantage of these conditions. Although the Left celebrated the end of the war and the deposing of Richard Nixon, the larger social transformation that it expected would follow remained blocked—a blockage symbolized by Gerald Ford's assumption of the presidency and his hasty pardon of Nixon. The New Left's critique of American society remained stillborn. Indeed, by 1973 the very language of critique seemed hackneyed, drained of meaning, when it did not seem utterly histrionic, as in the slogan with which the SLA signed off its media communiqués: "Death to the fascist insect that preys on the life of the people!" What took the place of the sixties critique was a new, disenchanted form of social analysis: the pop paranoia that pervaded American culture in Watergate's aftermath. The publication that year of Thomas Pynchon's *Gravity's Rainbow* served notice of the extent to which conspiracy theory had become one of the master narratives of post-sixties culture.

Paranoia also became a response to the cultural fragmentation of the moment, the sense that, psychologically speaking, everything was up for grabs. The political crisis of the republic found echoes in the personality crises of countless Americans, not least that of the president himself. Many Americans, riveted by reports of Nixon's increasingly erratic behavior as the Watergate scandal deepened, suspected him of having suffered a nervous breakdown. Though Nixon's psychiatrist tried to squelch the rumor, the mere fact that the president's doctor felt compelled to engage in such damage control attests to the intense public interest in the year's biggest psychodrama. What, after all, was the spectacle unfolding on American TV screens, if not an oedipal one, culminating in the symbolic killing of the nation's "father"?

Whether it was seen as a terrible moral crisis or as an opportunity, the perceived collapse of established institutions necessitated a rewriting of the basic national storyline. For author Joan Didion, the principal legacy of the 1960s was that she "began to doubt the premises of all the stories I had ever told myself" growing up in the 1950s, leaving her with the conviction that "the narrative on which many of us grew up no longer applies." If the 1960s generation had failed to realize their revolutionary dreams, they had nevertheless subverted the self-satisfied story of success and fulfillment of 1950s America. In 1973, indeed, it seemed to many Americans that history itself had become unhinged from any master narrative or enterprise with a secure outcome. Amid the wreckage, Americans discovered that instead of a chosen people they had become a nation of survivors, and because, to cite Didion once more, "we tell ourselves stories in order to live," they began telling themselves new stories.

Not surprisingly, in a nation coping with, or celebrating, the symbolic death of the father, women emerged as central voices and symbols of the new cultural configuration. From Jong's Isadora Wing, in search of the mythical "zipless fuck," to the speaking-in-tongues of *The Exorcist*'s demon-possessed Regan O'Neill, to the female private investigators that peopled blaxploitation pictures like *Cleopatra Jones*, evidence of disarray in the old American gender order could be found across the cultural spectrum. Further evidence could be seen in the movements for sexual liberation that emerged from the sixties. The women's movement, for one, counted several major victories, none bigger than *Roe v. Wade*. And for gays, the decade between the Stonewall riots and the onset of the AIDS epidemic represented, at least in retrospect, a golden age. Despite these developments, the seventies have entered popular consciousness burdened by Tom Wolfe's label "the Me Decade"—when political transformation was exchanged for personal transformation—a label that may owe more to the fact that Wolfe, as a straight white man, was not inclined to grant legitimacy to these movements or their political struggles, than to anything inherently shallow and narcissistic in them.

Nevertheless, Wolfe did put his finger on an important aspect of post-sixties culture: its promise of a new, radical kind of individualism. As Paul Berman has observed, the self became the answer to the question: What was left to revolutionize after the 1960s? Some felt this task to be particularly urgent given the extent to which Americans were perceived as remaining hostage to older images, stereotypes, and fears and thus were responsible for having failed to measure up to the utopian ideals of the 1960s. Others saw it rather as a continuation, by other means, of those ideals, an effort to cultivate, on a more local or personal scale, values that society at large was not ready to embrace. Many took their attempts to revolutionize the self to astonishing extremes: hence the proliferation of the seventies cults that Wolfe catalogues; hence too the conversion of Patty Hearst from society girl into the urban guerrilla "Tania."

To still others, a major part of the appeal of the seventies promise of new identity lay in the spectacle of acting it out on a public stage, whether in the innumerable encounter groups to which people flocked during this period, or on television, or in the pages of a magazine like Andy Warhol's *Interview*, which emerged as the leading chronicle of the celebrity culture that was a hallmark of this decade. Some commentators felt indeed that the desire for celebrity had begun to outstrip the desire for money or power as the central animating force in American life, and they invoked this desire to account for a wide range of contemporary phenomena that seemed to otherwise defy comprehension: the graffiti that began appearing on New York City's subway trains; the reality television series *An American Family*; and psychotic loner Arthur Bremer's attempted assassination of presidential candidate George Wallace. Stardom, as rock critic Lester Bangs argued, had become a virus infecting everything in American culture, from pop music to politics.

The title *1973 Nervous Breakdown* is borrowed from Bangs's review of the Rolling Stones album *Goat's Head Soup*. Published in December 1973 in *Creem* magazine, Bangs's review panned the Stones' latest offering. Never one to mince words, he was unusually savage in his appraisal of this album. Coming from a band that had once epitomized the energies of the rock-and-roll generation, this album, he felt, offered evidence that the Stones' brand of outlaw chic had worn itself out.

But Bangs's review was more than simply a comment on a lesser album by a band that now seemed to be going through the motions; it was an epitaph for an entire decade. If the Stones had once symbolized the sixties, their performance at Altamont in 1969 had—along with the Manson murders—marked for many the symbolic death of that decade. The demons and insurrectionary impulses conjured up by the Stones had finally unleashed forces they could not control. The spectacle of flower children being beaten up and, in one case, killed by Hell's Angels, recorded in the Maysles brothers' documentary *Gimme Shelter*, became a testament to the broken dreams of a decade.

Rock music had subsequently entered a period of drift for which the Stones' recent performances offered the most telling proof. Reduced to a series of gestures and poses that were emptied of conviction, the band members had become trapped in their role as superstars. The Stones' most recent American tour, Bangs wrote, "carried a mood that left you with the feeling that the artificial hysteria had finally tumbled past the overload, and strained nerves were not just visible but were twitching all around." Mick Jagger seemed to be visibly preparing for his role as "society creep" alongside his new wife Bianca (who'd appeared on *Interview*'s cover in January 1973), while Keith Richards's well-known problems with drugs earned him first place in a music industry poll of the rock musician most likely to die (followed closely by Lou

Reed). To Bangs, the Stones were looking like has-beens. The New York Dolls, the paragons of the new drag sensibility that was sweeping the music world in "the year of the transsexual tramp," as *Creem* called it, represented the "next true mania."

In a later review, Bangs—who is affectionately portrayed in Cameron Crowe's recent homage to the rock scene of 1973, *Almost Famous*—would expand on this analysis of the pathology that the music industry, as a microcosm of the larger society, now seemed to harbor within itself. McLuhan, he wrote, had missed the truly significant thing about the contemporary era: "We're not a global village, we're a global OUTPATIENT CLINIC, and the life force itself is most fully embodied in a frenetically twitching nerve."

The ironic fact that now, three decades after Bangs's cranky post-mortem on the Stones, they continue to perform at huge, sold-out arenas does nothing to lessen the basic force of his judgment. Ever since the constellation of traumatic events that took place in 1973, contemporary American culture has been marked by deeply neurotic undercurrents. Taking its cue from Bangs, this book treats the culture of that moment as a collection of symptoms, as signs to be included on the fever chart of a year in which an illness was eating away—not just, as John Dean famously put it, at the presidency but at the entire American body politic. Like all fevers, this one produced moments of lucidity and flashes of brilliant insight, and one purpose of this book is to highlight those. While many Americans were having a hard time locating themselves in an increasingly disorienting political, social, and economic landscape, they could turn for guidance to the signposts found in music, movies, and novels. *1973 Nervous Breakdown* assembles these signposts into a road map of a moment and of a collective sensibility that in many ways is still ours.

Fear of Flying

> It is not an overstatement to say that the destiny of the entire
> human race depends on what is going on in America today.
> This is a staggering reality to the rest of the world; they must
> feel like passengers in a supersonic jet liner who are forced to
> watch helplessly while a passel of drunks, hypes, freaks, and
> madmen fight for the controls and the pilot's seat.
>
> —Eldridge Cleaver, *Soul on Ice*

JANUARY 1, 1973: *New Year's Day wire services report that Roberto Clemente, star outfielder for the Pittsburgh Pirates, has died in a plane crash off the coast of Puerto Rico on the final day of 1972 while en route to Nicaragua to bring relief to the victims of a recent earthquake that had leveled much of Managua.*

Clemente's take off had been delayed for several hours due to mechanical difficulties, problems assembling a crew, and the pilot's lateness. His wife Vera expressed concern that the plane seemed old and overloaded and pleaded with him to call off the trip, but Clemente was determined to deliver the relief supplies. The pilot finally arrived, and following another short delay to resolve further mechanical problems, the plane, a four-engined DC-7 cargo plane, taxied down the runway. As millions of Puerto Ricans prepared to celebrate the New Year, the plane lifted into the air over San Juan International Airport shortly after nine P.M. Moments later it crashed into the sea a mile and half from shore. Clemente's body was never recovered.

With the death of Clemente at thirty-eight, major league baseball lost one of its greatest talents. Over his eighteen-year career he had compiled a brilliant record, and just two months before his death, on the last day of the 1972 baseball season, Clemente had collected his three-thousandth hit, becoming only the eleventh player in history to do so. The previous year he had batted .417 in the World Series and was named Most Valuable Player as he led the Pirates to the world championship. A fearsome hitter and skilled outfielder who electrified fans with his fielding exploits, Clemente was perhaps the most complete player of his generation.

Clemente was also a figure of enormous personal dignity, who battled prejudice throughout his career even as he lived out the American dream. Breaking into major league baseball in 1956, ten years after the color barrier had been breached by Jackie Robinson, and at a time when Latin ballplayers were still a rarity in the big leagues, he had to contend with a double stigma: being black and speaking English as a second language. In addition, as a result of injuries that plagued him throughout his career, he became known as a hypochondriac. His combative relationship with the press earned him a reputation as a "touchy Latin." It was not until the latter stages of his career that Clemente shed this label and received the recognition that he deserved. He used it to speak out against the second-class status of Latin ballplayers and to criticize club owners for failing to hire black managers.

Clemente's death plunged his native Puerto Rico into grief. Three days of mourning were declared, while in Hispanic neighborhoods across America huge crowds turned out to pay tribute to him. A song, "The Ballad of Roberto Clemente," was released in his honor. Later that year Clemente became the first Latin American player to enter Baseball's Hall of Fame, after the normal five-year wait was waived. To millions, Clemente's untimely passing turned him overnight from baseball hero into tragic figure. In death he joined a pantheon of youthful icons—James Dean, Marilyn Monroe, Buddy Holly, Otis Redding, Jimi Hendrix—who embodied a sense of promise cruelly snuffed out. His death served notice both of the fragility of the American dream and of the hazards surrounding one of its most myth-laden symbols: air travel.

developments that helped usher in the modern age of mass air travel. The nation's tremendous postwar economic expansion fueled a new prosperity. As incomes rose, the businessmen who once made up the bulk of airline passengers were joined by growing numbers of ordinary Americans. Growth, measured in air passenger traffic during the years 1955–72, exceeded that in any other industry. While some of these passengers were enjoying new opportunities for travel to tourist destinations like Las Vegas, many were part of a huge population shift that brought millions to the Sunbelt and the West Coast. The aerospace industry became a leading edge of America's postwar industrial expansion and a key player in the Sunbelt's emergence as an economic rival to the Northeast. The growing ease of jet travel helped transform the scale of corporate operations and created, as the vanguard of the globalization process, a new class of global workers.

The airline industry made extensive use of marketing campaigns to highlight the glamorous, sexy aspects of air travel. Once upon a time the American romance with flying had been fueled by the barnstorming exploits of Charles Lindbergh and Amelia Earhart; now it crystallized around the alluring figure of the stewardess. Ads drove home the notion that air travel welcomed passengers into a new world of movement and sexual adventure. To board a plane during the 1960s, as one former stewardess later wrote, was to enter an airborne fantasy world in which male passengers were ministered to by a phalanx of sexy yet subservient women who had taken their place "right next to the Playboy Bunny in our national psyche."

By the 1970s a decade of expansion had altered the face of the commercial aviation industry, which was beginning to chafe at the restrictions imposed on it by the federal government back in the days of its infancy. During this decade the industry became transformed from one of the nation's most heavily regulated into one of the most competitive, the leading edge of a streamlined new form of capitalism that would emerge in the 1980s following deregulation and the smashing of the air traffic controllers' union. While these changes still lay ahead, the seeds for them had been planted in the 1960s. The introduction of the Boeing 747 in 1970 helped further democratize air travel. Yet the coming of the 747 was not without its risks; aviation giant Pan Am, which staked its future on the jumbo jet, was eventually bankrupted by saddling itself with debt incurred through purchasing a new fleet of 747s.

The huge new jets, which required more taxiing space on runways and more distance between gates, heralded a new era of bigness in airport design. The biggest of all the new terminals was Dallas/Fort Worth Airport, dedicated in the fall of 1973. Dallas/Fort Worth was designed to be the largest airport in the world when it opened—larger than the island of Manhattan and able to handle more traffic than LaGuardia, Kennedy, and Newark airports combined. Hailed by its developers as "the biggest public works project since the pyramids," the new megaterminal represented a radical departure from all previous airport projects.

Dallas/Fort Worth was designed as if in answer to the questions posed by Burt Lancaster in his role as manager of a small midwestern airport in the 1970 picture *Airport*, the prototype of a new genre of disaster films that became popular during the 1970s. Navigating his way through an escalating series of crises—a snowstorm, a stowaway, the breakdown of his marriage, a bomb-carrying passenger—Lancaster finds time to spell out his vision of the future of aviation for his obstinately old-fashioned employer. Pointing to a scale model of the airport in his office, he asks, "What are we going to do about these jumbos that seat five hundred people? And how are we going to get them to and from the airport?" Lancaster harangues his boss about "congested air traffic, stacked up in holding patterns," and about "tired, overworked, underpaid traffic controllers." Yet his plans for expansion are opposed by his employer, who is cowed by a group of local citizens concerned about noise and environmental impact. The lesson is plain: in the old days air travel was the exception that had to be fitted to society's needs; now air travel is the norm, dictating its own conditions to which society itself must adapt. This lesson holds true for the family as well: Lancaster's wife's lack of sympathy for the demands of the job results in their separation; her place is quickly taken by his pretty assistant, ready to sacrifice everything to the needs of her man and his airport. The airport, the film suggests, is a microcosm of the larger society, where all the issues of the day (the environment, breakdown of the family, abortion, terror) are played out. There is room here for dreamers and big projects, but ultimately such projects take a backseat to the need for survival in the face of disaster. Such "Ark films," as Vincent Canby called them in a review in 1973, served a necessary function by binding the audience together as a community of survivors.

Situated on seventeen thousand acres located midway between the two cities, Dallas/Fort Worth was designed to eliminate the problems of congested airspace that plagued older airports across the country. The resulting airport was so huge that it required its own internal transport system, a fully automatic, pilotless train that conveyed passengers from one terminal to the next. Local authorities celebrated the gargantuan scale of the project and dismissed talk of overdevelopment and environmental degradation. The spirit of bigness prevailed at the dedication ceremony, attended by more than two hundred thousand people, who witnessed the first U.S. landing by the supersonic Concorde as well as performances by popular entertainers Willie Nelson and Doc Severinsen.

Project coordinators predicted that the new airport would become part of an economic tributary area embracing all of Texas and Oklahoma as well as parts of Arkansas, Louisiana, and New Mexico and would further catalyze a larger shift in the nation's economic center of gravity toward the Southwest. Erik Jonsson, founder of Texas Instruments and a key figure in the project's genesis, enthused that Dallas/Fort Worth would open new markets to the region: "The planet shrinks about as fast as the plane develops."

While Jonsson referred primarily to economic issues, his statement alludes to a development of more general significance: air travel's impact on the coordinates of time and space that traditionally structured man's mental geography, a phenomenon that social scientists have dubbed "space-time compression." The planet's shrinking through the new technologies of globalization, mirrored in the acceleration of the news cycle and in the shortening of transatlantic travel time, brought about a profound shift in sensibility. Air travel was becoming more than just the experience of getting from one place to another; like the automobile before it, it was creating its own culture and psychogeography—including the well-known phenomenon of delusional individuals who took up residence at airports.

Nowhere was this more evident than at Dallas/Fort Worth. A virtual city in its own right, dubbed by one journalist a "Los Angeles of transportation," the terminal was a world unto itself, lacking nothing, from restaurants and retail shops to fitness centers; its design even included on-site "spiritual centers" to help passengers cope with feelings of anxiety. To be sure, there were nay-sayers, like the New York art critic who visited Dallas/Fort Worth and came away lamenting the "unending repetition of bland geometry" and worrying about the "inner life of the people who must inhabit it, as well as those who pass through." Yet although the terminal's design evoked little of the bygone romance of air travel, the boldness of its conception invited bold cultural statements as well. In the initial stages of planning, the projects' engineers hired as a consultant Robert Smithson, a young star of the New York art world who would soon go on to become a leading figure in the Earthworks movement. Smithson, as he later wrote, used the project to reflect on the opportunities that presented themselves to the artist interested in a form of art that used the "land as a medium." As part of this conceptual leap, Smithson placed himself in the imaginary position of a satellite, suggesting that such projects could rely on television to be transmitted around the world. "Just as our satellites explore and chart the moon and planets," he wrote, "so might the artist explore the unknown sites that surround our airports."

Like the film *Airport*, but also like two works of fiction that appeared in 1973—Erica Jong's *Fear of Flying* and J. G. Ballard's *Crash*—Smithson's work takes for granted the power of air travel to work on the inner life of those (increasingly, everyone) affected by it, to become an object of fascination, sexual excitement, and fear. The airport was no longer purely a material but also a mental construct, one that demanded, in Smithson's words, "an esthetic based on the *airport as an idea*, and not simply as a mode of transportation." Smithson's contribution to this new aesthetic, though never adopted by the project developers, laid the groundwork for a seminal moment in the history of modern art. He suggested a series of designs visible only to the airborne traveler, including one he described as "a progression of triangular concrete pavements that would result in a spiral effect" that could be built as large as the site would allow and could be seen from approaching and departing aircraft. In thus exploring the aesthetic possibilities opened up by air travel, Smithson stumbled upon the form that would become the basis for his masterpiece, the Spiral Jetty, a fifteen-hundred-foot-long causeway extending in the shape of an enormous coil into the Great Salt Lake, large enough to be seen from space.

But if Smithson's "aerial art" explored the poetic possibilities of air travel, his death in a plane crash served notice, like Clemente's, of its tragic risks. On July 20, 1973, while surveying a desert lake in western Texas for a new project, the small plane in which he was flying along with a photographer and pilot crashed, killing all three men.

Air Travel and Its Discontents

Like the assassinations of the sixties, the deaths of Clemente and Smithson, and later that year of pop singer Jim Croce—whose "Bad, Bad Leroy Brown" reached number two on the charts for 1973—served as reminder that the promise of American society was fragile indeed. The mystique surrounding aviation technology had its dark side as well. By the early 1970s the symbolism that equated air travel with American technological and imaginative prowess had begun to break down.

This crisis in the symbols by which Americans ordered the world was brought home by the war in Vietnam. In more ways than one, Vietnam had complicated the narrative of American supremacy through technological genius. The air war in Indochina reflected a prime article of faith among American military planners: that technological superiority dictated military outcomes. No person epitomized this faith more than Robert McNamara. The talents he first revealed in his work for the air force, organizing the fire-bombing of Japan, and then in the postwar reorganization of Ford Motor, he brought to the war in Vietnam during his tenure as secretary of defense, when he became architect of a new kind of "war without death" waged from the air. The price of this new kind of war would turn out to be very high on both sides even while its value as military strategy was nullified by what General Maxwell Taylor famously called the Vietcong's Phoenixlike "recuperative powers." Yet even after McNamara had left the stage, American leaders continued his bombing strategies. Indeed the air war was intensified after 1969; over the next two years the United States dropped more bombs on Indochina than it had in all of World War II. As late as Christmas 1972 Nixon, in a final demonstration of his "madman theory"—a form of aggressive brinksmanship by which he hoped to frighten the Communist world into backing down—ordered a savage B-52 bombing campaign against North Vietnam, hitting Hanoi virtually around the clock for twelve days. Less than a month later peace accords were signed that left the North Vietnamese positions in South Vietnam essentially unchanged from those they had occupied in 1968.

While America's awesome industrial capacity had once, as David Halberstam suggested, fueled a myth of omnipotence, by 1973 that myth seemed to have come crashing to earth. The failed project in Vietnam suggested that history, and technology along with it, were turning against America; history, as any number of 1960s manifestos declared, seemed to be on the side of those waging wars of national liberation. Not only was massive firepower ineffectual against this new force, but its use stripped America of any claim to virtue. American technological genius was no longer, as it had been in World War II, a force for good; much of the world regarded the Christmas bombings as little short of state terrorism. The fate of hundreds of American POWs, most of them pilots shot down and languishing in North Vietnamese prisons, further drove home the fact that American mastery of the skies could no longer be considered a birthright.

If, as Frances Fitzgerald suggested in *Fire in the Lake*, her 1973 Pulitzer-winning account of the war, Americans tended to conceive of history as a straight line, then Smithson's spiral forms conveyed a sense that history's linear trajectory was broken, turned back on itself, reverting to preindustrial temporal schemas. The Spiral Jetty, which its creator envisioned eventually subsiding beneath the rising waters of the Great Salt Lake, invited the viewer to contemplate the effects of entropy, the winding down of history, environmental catastrophe. These themes were echoed in a novel written by one of Smithson's favorite authors, Ballard's *Crash*, which linked entropy with eros through its characters' twin obsessions with technological disaster and sex. While *Crash* takes car culture as its ostensible subject, recalling Warhol's serial prints of car accidents, its setting is the landscape created by the highways that ring London's airport and its action unfolds beneath a sky filled with planes taking off and landing. The narrator convalesces from a car accident in a hospital ward reserved for air disaster victims, then moves for the rest of the novel through this landscape in a dreamlike, eroticized repetition of his accident, which itself evokes the traumatic vehicular deaths of James Dean, Jayne Mansfield, and John F. Kennedy. Published in the year when the American love affair with the car fell under the shadow of the OPEC oil shock, *Crash* depicts an advanced technological society haunted by the possibility of its own breakdown.

Fatalistic in the extreme, Ballard's meditations nevertheless could not have failed to strike a chord within an American public whose nerves were growing increasingly jangled where air travel was concerned. According to a lengthy article in the August 12, 1973, *Times*, 25 million Americans were now afraid to fly. The list of those suffering from this condition was a long and growing one and included such luminaries as Joan Crawford, Tony Curtis, Carly Simon, and Ronald Reagan (who, it was reported, believed the only thing holding the plane in the air was his own willpower). Surprisingly, the list also extended to several figures noted for their excursions into the realms of daredevilry and science fiction: Evel Knievel, Ray Bradbury, Isaac Asimov, and Stanley Kubrick. (A later article documented Martin Scorsese's debilitating fear of plane travel. The director of the just-released *Mean Streets*, which dealt with—among other subjects—his ambivalence about the Catholic Church, admitted that every time he boarded a plane he was forced to concede that he was not an atheist: " 'Oh God, dear God,' I say the minute the plane takes off. 'I'm sorry for all my sins—please don't let this plane crash.' ")

Statistically, the article pointed out, air travel was safer than almost any other means of travel, including cars and buses. Indeed, it was safer to be on a plane than in your own bedroom, where most homicides occurred. But such reassurances tended to get lost on those prey to fears of crashes, hijackings, or mere turbulence. In fact the real problem, according to one psychiatrist, lay deeper. Flying symbolized achievement, power, and sex; those who were afraid of it had issues with all three and needed treatment on that basis. Another expert cited in the article was Nathan Cott, author of the self-help manual *Fly Without Fear* (1973), whose list of recommended techniques for conquering fear of flying—yoga, meditation, biofeedback, relaxation exercises, medication (especially Valium)—reads like a compendium of Me Decade faddism. Cott created the first self-help group to combat fear of flying in 1973. The founding, that same year, of the Institute for the Psychology of Air Travel in Boston further testified to the heightened public awareness concerning the stresses of air travel.

In 1973 Americans had many reasons to be afraid of flying, including turmoil within the commercial aviation industry itself. Years of expansion had led to excess capacity, a situation only worsened by the new generation of supersize jets. Coupled with FAA fare restrictions, this was leading to an industry-wide shakeout, whose biggest victim was Pan Am. While deregulation still lay ahead, a constellation of factors—bankruptcy, contentious labor relations, and safety concerns—was taking the wind out of the sails of America's flagship industry. And by year's end the most serious threat of all had emerged: rising fuel costs caused by the oil crisis were forcing the airlines to cut service. The embargo—declared by OPEC in response to U.S. support of Israel during the Yom Kippur War—opened up a new front in the Middle East crisis and exposed the American economy's Achilles heel: its shocking dependence on Arab oil. With six percent of the world's population, the United States consumed 30 percent of the world's oil, a sizable portion of it from the Middle East. By cutting off this supply, the embargo, although it lasted only five months (from October 16, 1973, to March 18, 1974), altered the course of modern economic and political history. Along with the growing inflation that was a legacy of the Vietnam War, the oil crisis plunged the U.S.

economy into a recession that lasted the rest of the decade. The immediate effect was to produce panic among the public and to force Nixon, who had hitherto ignored the signs of a looming energy crisis, to order a host of measures designed to manage the fallout, including a ten percent reduction in air travel. More extreme measures were also contemplated: recently released documents have revealed that at the height of the crisis Nixon and his secretary of state Henry Kissinger considered seizing oil fields in the Middle East.

Paradoxically, by triggering an economic meltdown, the oil crisis helped accelerate the process of organizational change that swept American business during the 1970s. Nineteen seventy-three was a key moment in the history of globalization, which emerged as the reigning new ideology to fill the vacuum left by the end of the postwar boom. Deregulation and privatization became the new mantras of American corporate life, with the airline industry leading the way. A wave of bankruptcies and mergers swept the industry, making the decade a very unstable one for the airline business and contributing to the erosion of public trust.

As if all this were not enough, a serious blow was being dealt to one of the industry's mainstays. The marketing of air travel through sexualized imagery (symbolized by Braniff's "I'm Cheryl, Fly Me" campaign) was confronted with a feminist revolt against the airlines' fantasy world and its "imagery of the virile pilot and his submissive geisha girl." In her book *Sex Objects in the Sky* (1974), ex-stewardess Paula Kane charged that the airlines bore a large share of the blame for the fact that men still clung to outdated, degrading myths of femininity. The airlines, according to Kane, exploited the fact that men get physically aroused at the thought of flying, using stewardesses "to create a flying dream machine," in which "male customers can indulge their fantasies instead of feeling afraid or insecure in the air."

But, Kane went on, the objects of these fantasies can live in this "never-never land" only for so long: "Then they become disillusioned, angry, rebellious." Portraying herself as someone in recovery from extensive brainwashing—she described flight training school as boot camp for a Miss America pageant, a total immersion in a "paramilitary regimen of hairdos and precise shades of lipstick"—Kane recounted her growing unhappiness with the job, a debilitating series of psychosomatic illnesses, and her decision to quit in 1973 in order to write an exposé of the "myth of the stewardess as carefree and glamorous sex symbol." Kane documented at length the physical and emotional costs of the job: jet lag, job insecurity, lack of a permanent home or family relationships, and the inability to live up to passengers' expectations of the myth. The beguiling, airbrushed fantasy of the jet-fueled economy painted by the airlines' stewardess-centered marketing strategies concealed sickness, the psychosomatic precipitate of space-time compression. Citing a psychiatrist who'd studied several hundred stewardesses, Kane wrote, "The script that airline stewardesses are supposed to play is a neurotic one."

By the early 1970s discontent had come to a head, culminating in 1973 in the formation of two organizations, Stewardesses for Women's Rights and Mary Poppins. Spearheading what Kane called a "giant battle of the sexes in the skies" their formation reflected changes sweeping through the industry, including growing union militancy and lawsuits charging the airlines with discriminatory hiring practices. Two changes in particular threatened to undo the gender order in the skies. In February 1973 the first female copilot joined men in the cockpit; that same month the first male flight attendants entered the main cabin. As Kane put it: "The American psyche received a jolt in its sex stereotypes in 1973."

Kane also leveled another charge at the airlines. Conspicuously absent from the flight schools' crash course in the feminine ideal was any basic training in safety preparedness. Safety, she wrote, was simply not a big concern of an industry fixated on the bottom line. This was a serious accusation, given public concern over safety as well as the dark picture Kane painted of flight crews plagued by jet lag, mental fatigue, and neurotic disorders. Taking a page out of Ralph Nader, she depicted American capitalism as out of control, sacrificing safety concerns to the myths by which it generated profits.

Safety was indeed uppermost in the minds of many air passengers. The biggest concerns cited in the *Times* article were crashes and hijackings, and 1973 was a dramatic year in both respects. The most lethal of that year's air disasters occurred on July 31 at Boston's Logan Airport, when Delta Airlines Flight 723, a DC-9, crashed attempting to land in thick fog, killing all eighty-nine passengers aboard. Confusion and visibility on the ground was so bad that it took ten minutes before airport authorities even realized something was wrong and the wreck-age was discovered. When rescue workers finally located the plane, they found, according to the *Times*, a scene of "incredible horror." A representative of the National Transportation Safety Board (NTSB) reported that she'd "never seen an accident where the plane was so thoroughly disintegrated."

What caused the accident? Apart from the less-than-ideal weather conditions, the causes of the crash remained unclear. The NTSB's report shrouded them in a thicket of technical language as dense as the fog on the runway. It determined that:

> [T]he probable cause of the accident was the failure of the flightcrew to monitor altitude and to recognize passage of the aircraft through the approach decision height during an un-stabilized precision approach conducted in rapidly changing meteorological conditions. The un-stabilized nature of the approach was due initially to the aircraft's passing the outer marker above the glide slope at an excessive airspeed and thereafter compounded by the flightcrew's preoccupation with the questionable information presented by the flight director system. The poor positioning of the flight for the approach was in part the result of nonstandard air traffic control services.

Was it the weather? The flight crew? The instruments? Air traffic control? The answer remained unclear, although two factors stood out. The first concerned Delta's merger with a smaller airline—one of several such mergers reshaping the face of the industry—and subse-quent complications in switching the instrumentation of the other airline's planes (of which Flight 723 was one) to Delta specifications. The second factor concerned problems with air traffic control, whose instructions to Flight 723 had been delayed while it attempted to prevent a collision between two other aircraft. In the end a series of minor problems with instrumentation, communication with air traffic control, and visibility had all cascaded out of control. The accident, concluded the report, "demonstrated how an accumulation of discrepancies, none of them critical, can rapidly deteriorate, without positive flight management, into a high-risk situation."

The crash of Flight 723 fits the profile of what some sociologists have termed a "normal accident." Accidents like this are "normal" in the sense of being predictable features of life in a highly technological society; as the French theorist Paul Virilio has put it: "To invent the ship is to invent the shipwreck, the train the derailment." This axiom had been demonstrated with the harrowing 1970 flight of Apollo 13, recounted in Henry S. F. Cooper's *Thirteen: The Flight that Failed* (1973). Cooper's account, which was a kind of epitaph for the now-discontinued Apollo program, described the circumstances surrounding the explosion of the spaceship's oxygen tank, the crew's return to earth, and the disarray into which the accident had thrown the entire space program. Such accidents are, as William Langewiesche writes, science's "illegitimate children, bastards born of the confusion that lies within the complex organizations with which we manage our dangerous technologies."

Flight 723's crash was far from an isolated occurrence. There were at least ten other major crashes around the world that year, including a Libyan commercial flight that wandered off course and was shot down by Israeli jets, and a Boeing 707 that crashed in Nigeria, killing 176, the worst aviation death toll at the time. None, however, was as horrifying as that of a small Uruguayan plane bound for Chile that came down in the high Andes in October 1972. The plane was carrying a rugby team plus assorted other passengers (forty-five in all) over mountains in blizzard conditions when the pilot lost control and crashed at twelve thousand feet. Sixteen survivors clung to life for seventy days until, in what came to be known as the Christmas Miracle, they were finally rescued on December 21, 1972. This story of triumph in the face of extreme adversity appeared in the January 1, 1973, edition of the *New York Times* under the headline "A Chronicle of Man's Unwillingness to Die." But the triumph was clouded by the discovery that it had come at the cost of violating one of civilization's fundamental taboos: those who survived had been able to do so only by eating the flesh of the dead passengers. The survivors justified their "unspeakable" acts by finding solace in the thought of Christ giving his body and blood to save mankind: "What we did was really Christian. We went right back to the source of Christianity." Representatives of the Catholic Church later endorsed this view.

Within hours of the rescue dozens of media representatives had descended on the remote site where the survivors were gathered. Their story became one of the biggest media spectacles of the new year. In interview after interview the survivors traced their endurance to their faith. Public interest in the details of the survivors' ordeal, and testimonies of their faith, remained high: that year alone no fewer than four books were published, featuring titles like *Survive* and *They Lived on Human Flesh*. The publishing frenzy reached a new pitch with the publication in 1974 of British author Piers Paul Read's account of the story under the title *Alive*. Read's book was a huge best seller, ultimately being translated into fourteen languages and made into a film. A Catholic himself, his account highlighted the faith of the surviving members of the Old Christians rugby team and suggested that once civilization's thin veneer had been stripped away, only the Church stood between man and barbarism.

As media spectacle, this story served a function similar to *Airport*, binding readers together in a community of survivors; as morality play, it served as a cautionary tale for a region engulfed in civil strife. The crash and rescue occurred in a Chile deeply divided by President Salvador Allende's socialist experiment, less than a year before he was overthrown. Moreover, early suspicions about what had happened to the missing plane focused on the possibility that it was brought down by left-wing Uruguayan hijackers, caught up in their own struggle against a repressive regime. This struggle was depicted in Costa-Gavras's *State of Siege*, a film that, upon its release in 1973, stirred intense debate over the alleged anti-Americanism of its portrayal of U.S. involvement in Uruguay's internal politics. Read's story gained its full meaning of redemption through faith against a backdrop in which, as Costa-Gavras's film makes plain, Uruguay's ruling clique (armed with American assistance) saw itself defending "Christian civilization" against a "godless plague"—the urban guerrillas known as the Tupamaros.

Learning to Love the Hijacker

The initial suspicions concerning the role of the Tupamaros in the Andes crash testified to the extraordinarily high level of public anxiety about hijackings. Statistically, in fact, Americans stood a much better chance of being victims of a hijacking than of a plane crash. As air travel underwent exponential growth during the 1960s, so too had incidents of air piracy. From 1968 onward hijacking became an increasingly popular tool of radical political groups who exploited the conditions of the global village by using the power of a planeload of hostages to generate media attention for their cause or as leverage for obtaining the release of prisoners. This was above all true in the Middle East, where pro-Palestinian commandos discovered that the value of jetliners and the sheer numbers of passengers (a 747 cost $20 million and carried four hundred passengers) made them ideal targets. By the early 1970s Palestinians could count on the assistance of a network that spanned the globe. The rash of political hijackings underscored the perverse realities of globalization. On December 17, 1973, members of the Black September group, who had first come to the world's attention during the dramatic and bloody events at the Munich Olympics in September 1972, which culminated in a televised airport shootout, staged another action at Rome's airport. They set fire to a Pan Am jetliner and killed thirty passengers, then commandeered a Lufthansa flight that they threatened to crash into the center of Athens. According to one British terrorism expert, however, most Arab governments stopped cooperating with Palestinian terrorists after 1973, when they discovered the superior effectiveness of the "oil weapon" in exerting influence on the United States and Europe.

In the United States, political motives played a somewhat lesser role in hijackings, though gaining the release of imprisoned Black Panthers remained a frequent objective. Beginning in 1968, attempted hijackings rose dramatically, with 1969—the peak year—seeing eighty-two attempts. By the end of 1972, 159 American aircraft had been successfully hijacked, the majority to Cuba. Hijackings to Cuba became so routine that U.S. airliners began carrying approach plans for the Havana airport. But by the 1970s Cuba's status as a hijackers' paradise was creating problems for Castro, who had no wish to antagonize his American neighbor over this issue any further.

After a slight drop-off in the number of incidents, the problem escalated again in 1972, prompting the *Times* to suggest in January 1973 that it was reaching "epidemic" proportions. In one particularly harrowing incident that took place in November 1972, an escaped convict and two associates held the passengers of a Southern Airways flight hostage for twenty-nine hours while they crisscrossed the country negotiating a ransom and repeatedly threatening to crash the plane into the nuclear facilities at Oak Ridge, Tennessee. Finally making it to Havana, they were arrested by Castro and later turned over to American authorities. Alarmed by such incidents, experts probed the vulnerability of the airline industry and the propensity for what the author of one study called "the intense communicability of the images surrounding skyjacking" to generate apparent copycat incidents. That the hijacker could even become a kind of folk hero was illustrated by the public reaction to one highly publicized incident in which a mysterious figure named D. B. Cooper hijacked a plane, demanded and received a ransom, and then parachuted to safety. Cooper's exploits were celebrated in song and prose, and the so-called parachute hijack subsequently became fashionable in the United States.

By 1973 some experts were arguing that the typical profile of the American hijacker had changed. No longer was he someone with a radical agenda; indeed, according to Dr. David Hubbard, a Dallas psychiatrist, most had no political motivation at all and were simply criminals or mentally unstable. Hubbard, author of the influential study *The Skyjacker*, was interviewed in the *Times* in January 1973 in connection with the case of Francis Goodell, a Vietnam veteran gone AWOL who'd hijacked a flight en route from Oakland to Burbank. On the basis of interviews he conducted with more than fifty hijackers,

Hubbard argued tendentiously that the hijacking problem should be viewed not in political terms but through the lens of generational conflict. The hijackers he interviewed tended to be the sons of deeply religious and authoritarian parents, suffering from sexual insecurities and social problems, who turned to hijacking out of a desire to realize some fantasy of achieving manhood.

Goodell was certainly a cipher, remembered by all who knew him as shy and introverted. His parents recalled that he was too awkward to ask girls for dates. But they were seemingly unaware of the medical history of fainting spells and insomnia that he recited to the examining physician upon being drafted into the military. The army ignored Goodell's requests for psychiatric help. The first signs of real trouble came in letters he wrote back to his parents from Vietnam, in which he told of how he and his fellow recruits wanted Nixon to "get us out of this hellhole" and of his firm belief that he was "in Vietnam to receive punishment for past sins." He met and fell in love with a Vietnamese girl, but his parents advised against a hasty marriage and the army blocked his plans. Upon returning to the States for leave, his parents later recounted, he vegetated in front of the TV, watching detective shows like *Mannix* and *Ironside*. He made repeated efforts to contact the Pentagon by phone in order to "tell the Army brass off." After eventually returning for duty, he went AWOL, phoning his father on at least two occasions from Las Vegas, where he'd gone to gamble.

Finally, at the end of June, Goodell went AWOL again. On July 6, 1972, with a gun in hand, he seized a Pacific Southwest flight bound for Burbank, presenting a note to the pilot demanding $455,000 for two unspecified organizations involved in the crisis in the Middle East. After flying to Los Angeles, where all but one of the fifty-eight passengers were let off and Goodell collected the money and a parachute he'd also demanded, the flight returned to Oakland. Nine hours of negotiation ensued before he was talked into surrendering.

The trial centered on Goodell's psychological condition. His family was convinced that the retiring son they had once known had become emotionally unbalanced during his tour of duty in Vietnam. After visiting Goodell in jail, his father reported him saying, "It's like I'm at home watching *Mannix*, and all these exciting things are happening to other people." Despite the findings of a psychiatrist who believed him incompetent, the judge ordered him to stand trial. His lawyer argued that Goodell had suffered an acute schizophrenic episode at the time of the incident and could not be held responsible for his actions. On January 18, 1973, however, the jury heeded the prosecution's argument that the defendant was simply after money and convicted him of air piracy. The judge sentenced him to thirty years in prison.

A footnote to this episode concerned Goodell's hostage, the passenger who stayed on board for the return flight to Oakland. This was a California highway patrol officer named Lloyd Turner, to whom Goodell poured out his personal history and his problems with the army. Goodell seems to have found a sympathetic listener in Turner, who testified on the defendant's behalf and told the press that he had children Goodell's age and that he knew some of the problems they faced. While surprising on the face of it, Turner's apparent sympathy for his captor was far from unique, as Tom Wolfe suggested in his article "The Perfect Crime," published in *Esquire* in December 1973. Surveying a series of recent high-profile crimes—airplane hijackings, the prison riots at Attica in 1971, the kidnappings at the 1972 Olympics, and recent bank robberies, including one incident in Stockholm in the summer of 1973 in which four hostages were kept in a bank vault for six days (the incident that gave birth to the diagnosis Stockholm syndrome)—Wolfe concluded that taking hostages had become the ideal crime of the 1970s.

What was the common thread in these incidents? The hostage takers had been people "at the end of their ropes" in struggles against "the system." Though the ostensible purpose was to achieve a concrete goal, usually political, this was often merely a pretext; the real purpose, according to Wolfe, lay elsewhere: "With one stroke, the Hostage Taker creates his own society, his own system: in the bank vault, in the Olympic quarters, in the airplane, in the prison courtyard." Their success could be measured in the often unpredictable nature of the hostages' responses. Two months before Patty Hearst's kidnapping by the SLA, Wolfe was noting, "It is astonishing how often hostages come away from their ordeal describing the Hostage Taker as 'nice,' 'considerate,' even 'likeable.'" The Hostage Taker, he concluded, "may soon have the hearts and minds of his subjects."

Wolfe offered up this theory as a lesson in the topsy-turvy realities of a world in which groups like the Palestinians and the Tupamaros seized whatever means were available to strike out against "the endless exfoliations of American power." The logic was like something out of *Alice in Wonderland*: "All at once I am not the lowliest subject but the head of state," forcing chiefs of police, mayors, and governors to negotiate: "I finally cut through the red tape." It gave the Hostage Taker the "ultimate certification" that "in the most modern sense [his] class position is secure: *I am a celebrity!*"

The Hijacker and His Audience

The unstable psychology of the hijacker was once again placed at center stage in the strange case of Garrett Trapnell. Trapnell's trial in Brooklyn on hijacking charges ended in a hung jury on January 15, 1973, when a lone juror voted to acquit, apparently convinced by the defendant's claim that he suffered from schizophrenia and that his alter ego, "Greg Ross," had been responsible for commandeering a TWA Boeing 707 bound from Los Angeles to New York the previous January. The incident had ended dramatically: after demanding a ransom of $306,800, a pardon from President Nixon, and the release of Angela Davis from prison in San Jose, and then threatening to crash the jetliner into the TWA terminal at Kennedy Airport, Trapnell had finally been overpowered and shot in the arm by an FBI agent as the plane sat on the tarmac waiting to be refueled. This denouement came after lengthy cockpit negotiations between FAA authorities and Trapnell, who evidently was counting on a live broadcast of the proceedings. An additional party to these negotiations was Dallas psychiatrist David Hubbard, who conversed with Trapnell by radio. Hubbard had previously interviewed Trapnell for *The Skyjacker*, following an earlier incident in which he had been arrested for carrying a gun on a flight.

As reported in the *Times*, the lone holdout on the jury of twelve was one Gertrude Haas, an unemployed psychiatric therapist and social worker. Had Haas been influenced in her decision by factors other than the evidence presented at trial? Had she, in her sympathy with the perpetrator, even suffered a vicarious form of Stockholm syndrome? Six days before the case went to the jury, Trapnell hinted at such an interpretation of events when he predicted to a reporter that the trial would end in a hung jury and also who the holdout would be. The presiding magistrate, Judge Rosling, was so enraged by the result that he directed a tirade at social workers for their "preconceptions"; at Trapnell's retrial, he screened the panel of prospective jurors for possible associations with psychiatrists. Rosling, in fact, seems to have gone a little mad himself during the trial, first threatening Haas with investigation, then denying making any such threat, blaming the media for distorting his words, and saying of Haas that "she and Freud are siblings." He was finally forced to recuse himself from the retrial but not before launching an ad hominem attack against what he called the "Liberal Thinker," a figure to whom "there is no such thing as a crime, there are only a lot of sick people, until you get your purse snatched." In Rosling's overheated imagination—expressing itself here in a virtual paraphrase of neocon maxims—shrinks, social workers, liberals, and the media were all part of an unholy alliance conspiring to undermine the social order.

The star witness at the trial had been Hubbard. By this time he was serving as an expert consultant to the FAA on skyjacking-related matters and had become closely identified with the position Rosling was attacking: namely that hijacking was a medical problem and should be treated as such. According to his book, the skyjacking impulse was rooted in a sense of "masculine failure" and the threat of emergent homosexuality. In an interview recorded in Johan Grimonprez's fascinating documentary history of hijackings *Dial H-I-S-T-O-R-Y*, Hubbard described the typical hijacker as a man with no sexual experience: "He looks at an air hostess as a sexual symbol and when he sticks his gun into her belly and says, 'Honey, we're going all the way—to Cuba,' he may very well be making the first sexual gesture of his life." In other words, skyjacking was a desperate assertion of manhood, and the perpetrator deserved to be treated not as a criminal but as a sick person who required help—a belief that put Hubbard at odds with an increasingly punitive society.

The effort to psychologize the hijacker, and with him the sixties culture that had ostensibly produced him, reached its apotheosis with Hubbard's speculations. He offered both a diagnosis of American society at a moment of profound social convulsion and an elaborate revision of Freudian thinking. In a series of case studies, he defined hijacking as a highly symbolic act that combined defiance of society with defiance of the physical environment and, in particular, of the laws of gravity. Bizarrely, Hubbard attached great value to gravity as a psychiatric construct, seeing it as the missing element in Freud's theory. Its true importance had been revealed only by modern man's increasing mastery of the skies since the invention of aviation and more recently the space program. From the perspective of the second half of the twentieth century, wrote Hubbard, it was plain that the fear of gravitational pull (the first thing a baby is aware of at the moment of birth) served as the paradigm of all other fears, and that under some circumstances it could be linked to severe "ego strain" and even schizophrenia in infants. In his view, gravity replaced the father as the focus of the child's complexes; the Oedipus complex had been superseded by a Newton complex—a complex that, in the form of the antigravity experiments being conducted aboard Skylab, might stand at the threshold of a historic resolution.

All this helped explain the intense symbolic importance that, in Hubbard's estimation, many Americans ascribed to the space program. In his case histories of skyjackers Hubbard found that several seemed to be in the grip of a profound obsession with this program. One such patient, "Dick," described being "very much stimulated by the news of Sputnik" and swept up in the ensuing rocket craze that swept America. "Dick" was Hubbard's pseudonym for Trapnell, whose case had first drawn his attention because of his history of restless nomadism, which included manic episodes of crisscrossing the country by car and plane. Hubbard's interest in what he called "wave-types" of human behavior led him to wonder in passing about what sort of tools the government had to measure the "internal temperature" of the population: "Were there 'probes' by means of which one could actually measure the level of unrest as shown by the movement of citizenry within the body politic?" Closer study of cases like "Dick's" might shed light on the possible connection between social unrest and skyjacking incidents.

What emerges from Hubbard's book is a picture of the skyjacker as the most vivid symbol of a profoundly agitated nation. (He also cited burning cities, occupied campuses, and assassinations.) Taken together, these phenomena were indicative of what Hubbard described as a phenomenon peculiar to the second half of the twentieth century: the emergence of a new kind of public for which he proposed the name "disparate mob"—a mass of people without direct contact among themselves: "The reactive mass would be the entire population tied together by our nearly instant news media." By virtue of the "intense communicability of the images surrounding hijacking," such acts could inflame an entire population.

What was more, Hubbard believed, the agitation spreading throughout this disparate mob increasingly blurred the distinction between hijacker and hostage. He enumerated common passengers' responses to hijackings:

> "History is being made and I'm part of it."
> "Gosh, wonder what I'll see in Cuba."
> "If they put us in a hotel, will there be any women?"
> "That guy [the hijacker] has really got guts."
> "That damned pilot was the boss 'til a minute ago, now all of a sudden he's nothing."

Such responses testified to the extent to which hostility to authority, delight in iconoclasm, and admiration for the outlaw had become widespread in the wake of the sixties. "The skyjacker," Hubbard concluded, "speaks for the mob, i.e., all of us, in his sick moment. Since the public knows the rules of the game . . . they sit quietly by for a free ride to Cuba. They know that the game, correctly played, makes them celebrities too."

Such blurring of the boundaries was of course anathema to the defenders of law and order, for whom Trapnell was to serve as a test case. Hubbard had testified at the trial that in his view Trapnell was a paranoid schizophrenic (a diagnosis he blithely extended to approximately eight percent of the total population). Nevertheless he undercut his argument when he admitted that there was some doubt in his own mind as to whether Trapnell was having a schizoid episode at the time of the hijacking. Evidence presented at the retrial, held later that spring, only added to the confusion by revealing that there were good reasons for doubting both Trapnell's mental stability and the authenticity of his insanity defense. Testimony about the defendant disclosed a broken family and a fantastic fifteen-year trail of robbery, forgery, and false identity across many states. Indeed, Trapnell's story had many romantic elements, including a claim that he had spent time running guns to Fidel Castro before being expelled from Cuba by the Batista government, a tendency to style himself after cinematic outlaws (he signed his holdup notes "Butch Cassidy"), and the fact that he'd been married six times. Trapnell would eventually be made the subject of a sympathetic biography, *The Fox Is Crazy Too*, by author Eliot Asinof, who likened the tall, cool, good-looking figure to a kind of guerrilla at war with an oppressive system.

Testimony also uncovered the defendant's talent for avoiding serious jail time by claiming mental illness. Several witnesses came forward to reveal that Trapnell had repeatedly boasted of his skill in deceiving psychiatrists. The defendant, it turned out, had read extensively in the field of psychiatry and had perfected a technique for mimicking the symptoms of schizophrenia, a technique he tried to impart to at least one former cellmate. While at least five psychiatrists testified at his trial that he was mentally ill during the hijacking, two others argued that he was malingering. Sifting through all this conflicting psychiatric evidence severely taxed the jury's abilities, but in the end a taped interview that Trapnell had granted to a freelance journalist several years previously proved to be his undoing. On it he boasted of his expertise in feigning the symptoms of mental illness and of the ease with which he slipped into his schizophrenic persona. He was finally convicted on May 16, 1973, and later that year sentenced to life in prison, though not without protesting what he saw as a conspiracy between the judge and the prosecution—a charge that at least some observers felt was warranted by the circumstances.

From the outset, in fact, the Nixon administration had followed the case closely. At first the U.S. Attorney's Office had considered sending Trapnell to a psych ward, but the 1972 election and its law and order theme dictated a trial and the need to convict. Along with drugs, pornography, and crime, hijacking became one of the fronts in the war that the administration was waging against the 1960s. In the State of the Union address that he delivered in January 1973, in which he called for reinstating capital punishment, Nixon singled out the hijacker as one of those criminals who risked incurring the final penalty for his actions: death at the hands of the state. The fact that the hijacking problem loomed large within Nixon's thinking about the pathologies confronting post-sixties America, however, did not prevent him from making strained attempts at public levity; at one press conference he was heard to suggest: "If it hadn't been for science we wouldn't have had airplanes, and if we hadn't had airplanes we wouldn't have had hijackings, so we could therefore argue that it would have been better if we didn't have science."

FAA officials were also worried that if insanity were established as a defense for hijacking, it would trigger another wave of hijackings. Trapnell's case was to serve as Exhibit A in the administration's efforts, as part of its tough new criminal code, to abolish the insanity defense. The White House submitted legislation to Congress in the spring of 1973 asking it, in addition to reinstating the death penalty, to overturn the century-old insanity defense. An editorial in the July 8 *Times*, written by psychiatrist David Abrahamsen, who testified for the prosecution at Trapnell's trial, laid out the government's case against the insanity defense, which according to Nixon had been "unconscionably abused" by hijackers and other criminals. Abrahamsen cited extensively from the trial, suggesting that Trapnell had used his high IQ and his knowledge of psychiatry to fool, over the course of his criminal career, more than forty psychiatrists as well as several lawyers and judges—indeed, to perpetrate "one of the greatest hoaxes in the annals of psychiatry." Yet Abrahamsen still wanted to preserve the insanity defense, and strove to defend it and his professional turf against both the administration's attacks and abuse by criminals. If only Trapnell had been examined by a "well-trained psychiatrist," Abrahamsen lamented, "the skyjacker would never have been able to get away with his undaunted criminal behavior by feigning insanity." But this was exactly the issue: as Trapnell himself pointed out repeatedly at his trial, and as his own history of deceptions eloquently testified, psychiatry was not an exact science.

Amid charges of conspiracy and counterconspiracy, the Trapnell trial exposed deep rifts in American society over the causes of and remedies for social maladies. It shone a light on numerous hot-button issues: the uncertain border between sanity and insanity and the role of psychiatrists in policing this border; the propagation of criminal or antisocial impulses through the media; the mood of national vulnerability; efforts to restore order through tough-on-crime policies; and ultimately the contested memory of the 1960s. Though Hubbard's strained attempt to rewrite that decade in the language of psychopathology betrayed signs of intellectual confusion, his profession still wielded considerable cultural authority. In the end the Nixon administration failed to strike the insanity defense from the legal books, a failure that would resonate eight years later in the success of would-be assassin John Hinckley in pleading not guilty by reason of insanity for trying to kill President Ronald Reagan. But the Hinckley case dramatized the copycat scenario that had worried Nixon administration authorities. Found in Hinckley's room at the Park Central Hotel after the shooting were, in addition to the screenplay of *Taxi Driver* and love letters to the movie's star, Jodie Foster, a hijacking note ("This plane has been hijacked! I have a bomb"), and copies of *The Fox Is Crazy Too* and Hubbard's *The Skyjacker*. Trapnell's many other admirers included a mother-daughter team that staged two separate hijacking incidents in 1978 in an effort to free him from prison. Trapnell eventually died in a federal penitentiary in 1992.

Among the many ironies of the Trapnell case, the parallels between the defendant and Nixon himself are amusing to consider. Just as the case against the trickster figure "Dick" turned on a tape recording, so too "Tricky Dick's" downfall became inevitable following disclosure, two months after Trapnell's conviction, of the existence of the White House tapes by Nixon aide Alexander Butterfield. Moreover, like Trapnell's, Nixon's madman pose, perfected as part of his Indochina strategy, ultimately raised doubts within his inner circle as to whether it was more than a pose. The title of one *Times* article about Trapnell—"Sane or Insane?"—echoed the question many had begun asking about the president.

Though the administration's efforts to combat hijackings by blocking the insanity defense were stymied, its efforts to shore up airport security met with greater success. By early 1973 the hijacking problem had generated pressure for a complete overhaul of airport security. On January 5 of that year new legislation took effect designed to tighten and standardize security at airports across the nation: all airlines were required to carry out electronic screening to search for guns and knives. Magnetometers were installed, followed shortly by X-ray scanners. Psychiatric profiles devised by Hubbard were deployed to help security officers single out suspicious passengers. Later that month, after many previous abortive efforts, an agreement was finally reached between the United States and Cuba, with Castro formally agreeing to extradite hijackers back to the United States. Success was immediate; from a peak of eighty-two in 1969, the number of hijacking attempts dropped to three in 1974, none successful. One of these was the botched attempt, in February 1974, by a disgruntled salesman named Samuel Byck to hijack a plane and smash it into the White House to kill Nixon. Byck's story was later told in the 2004 film *The Assassination of Richard Nixon*.

Shrinking the Planet

"There were 117 psychoanalysts on the Pan Am flight to Vienna and I'd been treated by at least six of them. And married a seventh. God knows if it was a tribute either to the shrinks' ineptitude or my own glorious unanalyzability that I was now, if anything, more scared of flying than when I began my analytic adventures some thirteen years earlier." The opening lines of Erica Jong's *Fear of Flying* place us squarely within the liminal cultural space whose contours we have been tracing and set the stage for the antic tale that lies ahead.

Published in the fall of 1973, *Fear of Flying* was hailed by John Updike and Henry Miller as one of the publishing events of the year, while Paul Theroux reacted with visceral disgust, calling Jong's heroine Isadora Wing a "massive pudenda." The book became a cultural phenomenon, tapping into a deep vein of discontent with its exploration of the dilemmas to which women's lib had delivered American women and of Isadora's struggle to find her own voice. The story begins with Isadora accompanying her husband Bennett to Vienna for a Freud conference, and from there it moves on to explore a psychological landscape defined by the mythical pleasures of the one-night stand (the so-called "zipless fuck"), the war between the sexes, madness, and the perils of authorship. Isadora is a woman in thrall to a series of men, most of them older, professional scientists of the soul (psychiatry represents for her the world of male authority), as well as to her own neuroses. She identifies herself as liberated, yet she still craves the safety and validation of marriage; her "blocked rebellious-ness" expresses itself in elaborate phobias and in a morbid fascination with fiery plane crashes (she rhapsodizes about "the excitement of the Kamikazes"), as well as in a tendency to identify, in her literary endeavors, with the male narrator because she assumes no one would be interested in a female point of view.

If fear of flying serves as Jong's metaphor for the terrors of Isadora's quest for authenticity, then this quest ends when she finally assumes her own voice. By turning her fear of flying—a fear shared by millions—into her raw material, Isadora is able to conquer it and to liberate herself from the male voice and its claims to authority. While the terms of her quest conform to Tom Wolfe's definition of the Me Decade—personal trans-formation replacing political transformation—Jong's book also an-nounces the advent of a new kind of cultural politics.

As she commits her reminiscences to paper, we learn that the beginning and apparent end of Isadora's marriage to Bennett coincides with the beginning and end of the war in Vietnam. She projects onto this war a paranoid historical consciousness informed by her identity as a Jew. Early in the marriage Isadora finds herself stuck in Heidelberg, Germany, where her husband works as a psychiatrist at a U.S. Army base. Feeling trapped, she begins conducting research on the Holocaust as an outlet for her feelings of helplessness and victimization. Yet it is a limited outlet at best, just as her analogy between the war of the sexes and the war in Indochina has its own limitations. Even as the Christmas bombings in Vietnam were prompting comparisons between Americans and Nazis in the European press, Isadora must confront the fact that the easy distinction between victims and perpetrators has been scrambled, in her case, by her own complicity. Hostage to her fantasies, fears, and false images—"Fly Me, I'm Isadora" she jokes at one point— she is in the grip of a kind of Stockholm syndrome, identifying with the masochistic female narrator of *The Story of O* and invoking Sylvia Plath's line "Every woman loves a fascist."

Ultimately she needs to undergo a form of deprogramming before she can be freed from the grip of this masochistic form of self-victimization. "Growing up female in America," she writes. "What a liability!" Her mind overflowed with cosmetic ads, love songs, advice columns, the rubbish of American consumerism: "What litanies the advertisers of the good life chanted at you!" It didn't matter, she continues, whether "you had an IQ of 170 or and IQ of 70, you were brainwashed all the same." Her neuroses were the products of the cultural narratives of the 1950s, whose power prevents her from authoring her own narrative. Moreover, psychoanalysis—a science that once promised deliverance from the hypocrisy of middle-class society—had simply become a part of the establishment; its members exuded squareness and unquestioning acceptance of the social order, a social order constructed according to the specifications of the American male and his claims to global mastery. Yet this social order, as Isadora notes, was crumbling: "The symbol of the apocalypse: the atomic warhead prick which self-destructs."

Her own personal deprogrammer arrives in the form of Englishman

Adrian Goodlove, a radical analyst and disciple of R. D. Laing, for whom schizophrenics are a kind of new folk hero, "the true poets of society." Adrian idealizes madness as a form of sanity within an insane world and tempts Isadora with visions of a commune for schizos, poets, and radical shrinks. He cultivates a form of schizo chic as a strategy for remaining authentic in a world that prefers self-betrayal and dishonesty. While Isadora eventually leaves Adrian—whose limpness as a lover reflects what she comes to see as a generalized crisis of male virility— their relationship is crucial to her passage to authorial independence.

Jong's challenge to the 1950s gender order may be contrasted with another of that year's best sellers, Richard Bach's *Jonathan Livingston Seagull*. First published in 1970, Bach's book wove a childishly simple story out of a bird's quest for liberation from the limitations of his existence. An outcast among his conformist fellow creatures, Jonathan is a poetic soul who yearns for escape from the struggle for mere survival. The pathos of his condition boils down to a simple statement: "More than anything else Jonathan Livingston Seagull loved to fly." Bach restores to his reader a myth of freedom uncomplicated by history or sexuality. (None of the gulls in the story are female.) His book's version of the mass society critique is grounded in nostalgia, in the naïve dream of flight of simpler times, the infantile wish to escape gravity.

While the blockbuster success of Bach's book testified to the American public's yearning for restoration of a basic myth, now reworked to fit the requirements of the Age of Aquarius, Jong's book suggested that the myth was beyond repairing. *Fear of Flying* testified to a deep crisis in the narrative and symbols by which Americans ordered the world. The preoccupation with air travel and its risks that overtook the nation in 1973 reflected anxieties about the larger catastrophes overtaking the American ship of state. These catastrophes, in Jong's telling, had their counterpart in the breakdown of customary relations between men and women. Portraying the old myths and the gender order underlying them as having reached an advanced, perhaps terminal state of crisis, *Fear of Flying* charted the new territory opened up by this symbolic disaster.

Reality Programming

Television ate my family.

—Lance Loud

JANUARY 18, 1973: *PBS airs the second episode of its twelve-part reality television series* An American Family, *which follows the daily lives of the Louds, a family of seven who live in Santa Barbara. Ten million viewers tune in to watch Episode 2, in which Pat Loud visits her oldest son Lance in New York City. Having recently come out of the closet, Lance has taken up quarters in the Chelsea Hotel, where he mingles with members of Andy Warhol's entourage. In subsequent episodes, the Louds' marriage fell apart, and Lance would later observe: "The Andy Warhol prophecy of fifteen minutes of fame for any and everyone blew up on our doorstep."*

The press release for *An American Family* introduced the Louds to viewers as a model family. But if they were chosen as latter-day Ozzies and Harriets, shaped (in the words of the release) "by the national myths and promises, the American dream and experiences that affect all of us," the Louds came instead to symbolize the unraveling of those myths and promises. By the early 1970s severe fraying had become visible in the fabric of American family life. Infidelity, divorce, and a widening generation gap were the common themes of a drama being acted out in households across the country: the meltdown of the American nuclear family. *An American Family* documented the impact of this social upheaval and showed that the center, as one reviewer noted, citing Joan Didion citing Yeats, no longer held.

Year One of the Culture Wars

The forces reshaping family life were many: they included the sexual revolution launched by the Pill, the growing influx of women into the workforce, and the *Roe v. Wade* decision. One of the most vivid signs of the perceived crisis in family life could be found in divorce statistics. Between 1965 and 1975 the number of divorces each year in the United States doubled. The passage in many states of "no-fault" laws allowing couples to divorce without bringing charges lightened the stigma of the broken marriage. In a lengthy article accompanying its review of *An American Family*, *Newsweek* reported that at current rates, four out of every ten couples who wed that year would not live happily ever after. The shattering of the fifties' domestic ideal also reflected the fact that, for the first time in U.S. history, a majority of women were working outside the home. Their growing economic independence from men was liberating women from what Betty Friedan, in *The Feminine Mystique*, had called the "comfortable concentration camp" of the suburban home. Writing in the *Times* in March 1973, Friedan struck a Jong-like note in proclaiming that, while she had once been deathly afraid of flying, she was no longer. Signs of the emerging new gender order were many: with more women devoting themselves to their careers, and new contraceptive methods readily available, birth rates reached their lowest level in U.S. history in 1972.

Many welcomed these developments. Futurologist Alvin Toffler, speaking to *Newsweek*, speculated that American women were caught up in a revolution of rising expectations. Toffler predicted that more sequential coupling—four or five marriages per lifetime— would become the norm and would be accompanied by the emergence of a new class of professional parents to raise the children of people who chose not to shoulder their parental duties. Anthropologist Margaret Mead dismissed talk that marriage was obsolete, saying that the only thing that was obsolete was the nuclear family. She foresaw a return to a preindustrial model of the extended family, arguing that three-generational networks were needed to help manage child-rearing duties.

More radical feminists went further, calling for the outright abolition of the family. Arguing that the political and social crises of the sixties had their underlying roots in the "patriarchal sex caste system," militants such as Shulamith Firestone wanted to scrap marriage and the family as institutions altogether. Firestone harnessed her critique of patriarchy to calls for an "androgynous society" in which women would be liberated from pregnancy and motherhood by technology. Variations on such themes abounded; in a somewhat jaundiced article on the women's movement written in 1972, Joan Didion captured such sentiments with the remark: "If the family is the last fortress of capitalism then let us abolish the family." Far out though such demands may have been, it is nevertheless the case that the only truly successful protest groups to survive the 1960s were those challenging sexual mores, and these groups defined the battleground on which the new culture wars would be fought.

Among other things, the sexual revolution, launched in the sixties, entered middle-class America in the early seventies. In Rick Moody's novel *The Ice Storm*, set on Thanksgiving weekend 1973, Connecticut suburbanites dabble nervously in a new form of socially sanctioned infidelity: wife-swapping. Nineteen seventy-three was also a breakthrough year for more permissive attitudes toward materials hitherto defined as obscene: Bertolucci's *Last Tango in Paris* was released in the United States, while *Deep Throat* played to packed houses, despite the efforts of judges to ban the film and despite a landmark Supreme Court ruling that summer that gave local communities the right to ban pornography. Meanwhile advocates for gay liberation were able to count a significant victory when in December 1973 the American Psychiatric Association (APA) announced that it no longer considered homosexuality a mental illness and removed it from the list of disorders in its *Diagnostic and Statistical Manual*. At one stroke, several million people defined as sick became well. Explaining that the APA had not been taken over by "wild revolutionaries or latent homosexuals," Columbia professor of psychiatry Robert Spitzer nevertheless defended the decision as a reflection of the zeitgeist: "Psychiatry, which was once regarded as in the vanguard of the movement to liberate people from their troubles, is now viewed by many, and with some justification, as being an agent of social control." If history was on the side of those waging wars of sexual liberation, then it behooved the scientists of the soul to position themselves on the right side of the conflict.

No single issue more fueled the general reexamination of the sexual contract on which the family was based than did the abortion ruling handed down by the Supreme Court on January 22, 1973. Abortion rights activists had been pressing for changes in the state laws that criminalized the procedure throughout the 1960s, pointing to statistics that showed that more women died of illegal abortions each year than Americans were killed in Vietnam. When it finally came, the court's surprise 7–2 decision became the most controversial constitutional ruling of the era. Pitting a woman's right to privacy against the unborn fetus's "right to life"—a right strongly backed by President Nixon—*Roe v. Wade* also became a flashpoint for larger debates over the changes in sex roles that had swept America during the 1960s. This mainstreaming of the feminist agenda, greeted by supporters as a landmark ruling acknowledging women's right to control their own bodies and sexuality, sparked an angry "family values" backlash that would make abortion rights a battleground for decades to come. A *Times* editorial expressed the hope that the Court's decision might resolve a debate that had divided America too long: "As with the division over Vietnam, the country will be healthier with that division ended." Rather then settling the issue, however, the decision only energized forces on both sides of the debate. One psychiatrist explained the intensity of the reaction in terms of castration anxiety, speculating that the termination of pregnancy represented a threat to a prime symbol of male potency. In August, thirty-nine CBS stations refused to carry a rerun of an episode of the sitcom *Maude*, a spin-off of *All in the Family* starring Bea Arthur, in which the lead character finds herself pregnant and eventually opts for abortion. Deluged with seventeen thousand protest letters, the stations finally bowed to pressure brought by the U.S. Catholic Conference and by corporate sponsors. NOW organized protest campaigns in cities where anti-abortion groups had forced cancellation of the TV show. The controversy ensured a huge audience: CBS estimated that as many as 65 million people watched at least one of the episodes, either first run or in the rerun.

The First Family and the Media

In the unfolding national drama of domestic crisis, it was the fate of the Nixons to serve as Exhibit A. As the Watergate scandal deepened, every dinner invitation, interior decoration decision, and Christmas photo issuing from the White House was scrutinized for clues as to the stability both of Nixon's mind and of his marriage. Despite closely guarding his privacy, Nixon had invited such scrutiny throughout his career by his history of erratic behavior. Rumors of problems with drugs and alcohol, as well as his proclivity for taking out his anger on his wife Pat following political setbacks, had circulated in the press since his loss to Kennedy in 1960. During his 1968 campaign he was dogged by stories about his secret visits to New York psychiatrist Arnold Hutschnecker. Even as he was riding his new "silent majority" to victory, allegations concerning Nixon's addiction to sleeping pills and amphetamines were raising doubts in some quarters as to whether he was the right man to have his finger on the nuclear trigger.

These concerns about the president's mental stability reached a new pitch during the Watergate crisis. Deep Throat informed Bob Woodward that Nixon was in the throes of a "dangerous depression," while author Theodore White concluded that the men in the White House were involved in "the management of an unstable personality." Psychiatrists had a field day with Nixon's increasingly strange behavior; after one particularly disjointed public appearance in the summer of 1973, one doctor thought he discerned signs of incipient schizophrenia in the president's speech. During that summer Hutschnecker penned a *Times* op-ed piece titled "A Suggestion: Psychiatry at High Levels of Government," in which he argued that the public had a right to know that the president had a clean bill of mental health. Nixon suffered further indignity when the *Washington Star-News* ran a piece that summer asking what would happen if a U.S. president suffered a mental breakdown.

Throughout this ordeal, Pat worked hard to keep up appearances. She paid close attention to her duties as First Lady, diligently answering all mail sent to her (up to three thousand letters a week), often enclosing photographs, birthday and anniversary cards, and family recipes in her responses. She took seriously her responsibility of maintaining a reassuring ideal of domesticity, giving the first public tour of the Rose Garden in April 1973 and later posing for pictures in the newly redecorated White House (a redecoration, it was revealed, carried out at great cost to taxpayers). Pat was fond of saying, "There is no generation gap in our family," and she claimed Tricia and Julie preferred having dinner with their family to going out to parties. Yet the growing pressures enveloping the White House exposed cracks in this carefully cultivated image of unity. Whereas in 1971 the First Family had released their traditional Christmas photo, during Christmas 1972, with the bombings in Vietnam under way and the kids holidaying in Greece—the first time the Nixon family had ever spent the holiday apart—Dick and Pat simply vanished from the public eye for eleven days, and, according to the *Washington Post*, left millions of Americans wondering about "their President's very sanity."

As the Nixons' world began to implode, there were growing signs that the scandal was taking its toll on Pat. Throughout her husband's second term Pat was rumored to drink heavily and, it was alleged, to consider divorce. The leaks that plagued the Nixon administration provided endless fodder for the Washington rumor mill. Presidential press aides continually fended off questions about whether Nixon was using drugs or seeing a psychiatrist, as well as open speculation about Pat and Dick's marriage. As Julie Nixon Eisenhower wrote in her biography of her mother, "In the ugly climate of Watergate, dissection of the Nixon marriage was considered fair game by some."

The contrast between Pat's efforts to uphold a reassuring image of domesticity and the siege mentality in the White House lent a surreal air to the twice-weekly briefings to which correspondents covering the First Family had been treated since 1971. Reporters' questions at these briefings ranged from Pat's views on important subjects to what the Nixons were giving each other for Valentine's Day. But efforts to manage the accelerating news cycle became increasingly hopeless; these briefings only opened the door to ever more personal and awkward questions. By the end of Nixon's administration reporters questioning the First Family's use of federal money to finance improvements on their homes in California and Florida were, Julie complained, tossing around completely absurd figures. (Some estimates, later confirmed as correct, were as high as $17 million.)

Just as Pat's expenditures would become a subject of scrutiny, so too would her husband's obsession with and large expenditures on surveillance equipment. The secret recording system Nixon had installed in the Oval Office in the summer of 1971 was, unlike that of previous presidents, voice-activated. Lacking a control system, the mikes simply picked up everything. "Nixon," in the words of one biographer, "had created a monster." This would become startlingly clear with the release of the transcripts, whose "moral tone," as Julie Nixon called it, appalled listeners: discussion of hush money, anti-Semitic slurs, and perhaps most of all, X-rated language. Her famously secretive father was now exposed to the nation as no president had ever been before. His daughter offered the following explanation for these indiscretions: "Once the decision was made to tape, my father seemed to forget that the system existed, accepting it 'as part of the surroundings,' as he expressed it." Yet this was only partly true. The White House taping system had a decidedly bizarre effect on intimate discourse; according to one account, Nixon routinely played to an invisible audience: "In the midst of supposedly private conversations Nixon would begin declaiming."

The question raised by the tapes was: why did he do it? His supporters took at face value Nixon's explanation that he had done it for the sake of the historical record, while critics preferred to believe that the archconspirator had become entangled in the coils of his own paranoia. But these answers raised a further question: just who was the real Nixon? Julie Nixon assured her readers that "the Richard Nixon on the tapes was not the Richard Nixon the family saw every day." His critics, on the other hand, were convinced that the tapes showed the public the true Nixon for the first time. Pat was torn: appalled at what she heard, yet strenuously insisting that the tapes were "like private love letters, for one person only." The protestations of the Nixon family were thick with irony, given the administration's assaults on other Americans' privacy, starting with the burglary of Daniel Ellsberg's psychiatrist's office and ending with the Watergate break-in itself, which prompted Senator Sam Ervin to claim hyperbolically that the burglars were "in effect breaking into the home of every citizen of the U.S."

Nixon had indeed unleashed a monster, even if it was only partly of his own making. The president's famous paranoia about the media, which he saw as part of an East Coast liberal conspiracy to unseat him, was partly hypocritical, given the fact that many of his closest advisers came from the worlds of advertising and television and that his career had from the beginning been closely intertwined with the mass media, especially television. When in 1952 Nixon made his career-saving "Checkers" speech on television, he spoke to the largest audience any politician had ever commanded. Yet in constructing his own personal demonology of the media, Nixon was also tapping into a fear shared by many concerning the awesome new cultural authority it had come to enjoy.

As a result of innovations in technology and programming, and its role in reporting Vietnam, the mass media had assumed an increasingly prominent place in public life over the preceding decade. This was particularly true of television: according to a poll conducted shortly before the Watergate hearings began, 48 percent of Americans considered television the most believable form of major media (over newspapers and radio). Statistics like these fueled anxieties that televised images were beginning to undermine the public's hold on reality. Critic Harold Rosenberg noted that the media was bringing about a strange mutation in notions of what was "real": "On TV POWs returning from Hanoi were shown passing the time by watching POWs returning from Hanoi on TV," a fact he took as emblematic of a larger truth: "We have entered an epoch in which nothing is real until it has been reproduced. With events and their copies standing in for each other . . . the objective form of modern culture has become the farce of mistaken identity. Facts no longer enjoy any privilege over various renderings of them."

In making this point, Rosenberg was echoing a lament that had become standard since the appearance in 1961 of historian Daniel Boorstin's *The Image, or What Happened to the American Dream*. Addressing what he took to be the most important question of the day—"namely, what we believe to be real"—Boorstin pessimistically analyzed the effects of the media's invasion of American politics and everyday life. Within the media echo chamber, real events were increasingly replaced by "pseudo-events," or staged happenings that became news only because of the attention paid to them by the media, while heroes were replaced by celebrities, or human pseudo-events. Everyday experience became increasingly "programmed," resulting in a crisis of authenticity and a hunger for "reality" that could be satisfied only by media events of high drama, like Kennedy's assassination, the moon landing, and the Watergate hearings. The ascendance of image culture was connected in Boorstin's mind with the decline of traditional forms of authority, both cultural and political.

The primal scene of this new image-saturated culture had been the televised Nixon-Kennedy debates of 1960. It was partly as a result of his loss to Kennedy—later chalked up to his sweaty appearance in those debates—that Nixon's relations with the media became increasingly antagonistic. Yet as David Greenberg documents in *Nixon's Shadow*, Nixon had from the beginning of his career attended carefully to the craft of image-making. This orchestration of imagery extended to his family and domestic life. He presented himself as an exemplary family man, patriarch of a model postwar family. Like other First Families before them, the Nixons, once they occupied the White House, took with utmost seriousness the task of projecting an image of familial harmony. An important part of the campaign carried out by his image-makers was the fashioning of an "imperial presidency." The Nixons cultivated a self-consciously grand style, marked by huge expenditures on planes, communications systems, and houses. Tricia Nixon's White House bedroom was decorated in a Louis XV style, complete with figurines made of Dresden and Meissen china, and her wedding was a TV spectacle seen by 60 million viewers. At one point Nixon had White House Secret Service agents outfitted with new uniforms with epaulets and Beefeater hats resembling those worn by the British royal family's palace guards.

Nixon's efforts to craft a presidential image included trying to strike a Kennedyesque pose by having himself photographed walking on the beach at San Clemente. The attempt was a failure; choosing to keep his wingtips on as he strode along the sand, he succeeded only in looking stiff and awkward. But this failed effort holds a clue to Nixon's presidency. In many ways he was haunted by the posthumous aura acquired by his erstwhile opponent, a far more naturally gifted image-maker than he was. According to Henry Kissinger, Nixon was deeply jealous of Kennedy's popularity and craved a similar kind of public adulation. From the day he assumed the presidency Nixon strove to fill the void left by JFK's assassination, to create a countermyth to replace that of Camelot. But try as he might, Nixon could not do so, either by his own efforts to look Kennedyesque or by the increasingly imperial trappings with which he surrounded his presidency. Caricaturists predictably savaged Nixon's royalist style, depicting him as Louis XVI on the eve of the revolution, while underground filmmakers circulated pornographic films about Tricia's wedding, and painter Philip Guston, punning on his name, portrayed him as a giant penis and testicles.

Historians have often pointed to the centrality of "narratives of the family" to the constitution of most forms of political authority and social order. During earlier periods of social upheaval such as the French Revolution, the king's overthrow was experienced as a symbolic "loss of the father." The beheading of the French king inflicted a symbolic decapitation on the larger body politic, unleashing a generalized crisis of the familial model of politics that reverberated through-out the entire nation. This breakdown of traditional patriarchal authority shook the foundations of French society, opening the door to confusion in traditional family relations and gender norms and necessitating far-reaching revisions to the old social contract.

While the analogy is imperfect, it was not far from the minds of some observers of the Watergate hearings. In an advertisement that appeared in the *Times* on July 29, 1973, one of Nixon's supporters wrote that "viewing the proceedings one thinks more of 1789 than of 1973. The noisy claque that makes up the caucus room audience resembles nothing more than the Parisian mob cheering and shouting as the tumbrels deposit their victims before the guillotine." As in the French Revolution, the extraordinary disarray within the most powerful institution in America produced confusion and uncertainty at every level of society, a sense that conventional relations between leaders and citizens, men and women, parents and children, were up for grabs. It was against this backdrop that, in the winter of 1973, *An American Family* reached the national airwaves as an unprecedented experiment in what its makers called "television vérité," documenting both the sense of crisis within the familial order and the larger crisis of authenticity.

Television's First "Real" Family

The producers of *An American Family* were able to achieve an unprecedented degree of intimacy and realism in their portrayal of the Loud family by taking advantage of several technical innovations, including new lightweight cameras and tape recorders and wireless mikes, that allowed portable synchronous shooting. Presenting itself to the public as a radical step forward for television, the series offered viewers what an ad in the *Times* called the drama of "Television's first 'real family.'" In its prime-time Thursday-evening slot, the series became one of the year's biggest media spectacles: Pat Loud would later claim that those who weren't watching the Watergate hearings were watching *An American Family*.

The show was the brainchild of producer Craig Gilbert, who had worked for over a decade for WNET, a precursor to PBS, producing programs such as Margaret Mead's *New Guinea Journal*. In the early 1970s Gilbert's marriage had fallen apart, and he became increasingly pessimistic about the future of family life. As he told Pat Loud the first time they met, his motive was partly anthropological in that he conceived of the series as an opportunity to document the family before it became obsolete. Coupled to this motive was another, rooted in Gilbert's commitment to the so-called "observational style" developed by documentary filmmakers during the sixties. Observational films like Albert and David Maysles's *Gimme Shelter* strove to keep the directorial presence as unobtrusive as possible so as to allow the material to speak directly to the viewer. Gilbert's commitment to this style was wedded to a critique of television and the "false images" it purveyed, particularly those of family life. Conceived of as the antithesis to shows like *The Brady Bunch* and *The Partridge Family*, *An American Family* would puncture the anodyne reality created by standard television fare and depict "the politics of everyday life."

As Jeffrey Ruoff has shown in his study of the series, *An American Family* was partly inspired by Gilbert's reading of Ross McDonald's recently published *The Underground Man*, a crime novel whose setting—upper-middle-class Santa Barbara—seemed to Gilbert to represent the American dream in its most idealized form, albeit one that harbored genuine pathology. To demystify the TV image of the family, Gilbert wanted a family that closely matched this image, at least superficially. The clan ultimately chosen for the series, the Louds (to whom McDonald reportedly helped steer Gilbert), seemed, as many reviewers noted, to be starring in their own sitcom version of the good life. The parents, Pat and Bill, and their five children, Lance, Kevin, Grant, Delilah, and Michelle, lived along with assorted pets (including a horse) in a large house with swimming pool, recording studio, and four cars in the beautiful coastal hills above Santa Barbara. Bill Loud was the owner of a company that manufactured parts for strip mining machinery, while Pat was a housewife.

For seven months filmmakers Alan and Susan Raymond and their crew enjoyed complete access to the Loud household. Shooting the series was an intricate technical feat involving lightweight cameras and tape recorders, fast lenses, and light-sensitive film stock that allowed shooting with available light. Coincidentally, the installation of this equipment in the Loud household in the summer of 1971 occurred shortly after the installation of the White House taping system. In effect, shooting the series entailed an extensive bugging operation—from telephone taps to the mikes installed throughout the house (one was placed in the chandelier over the dining-room table) to the numerous cameras, all positioned to provide maximum coverage—in order to record with absolute fidelity daily life in the Loud household. The purpose was to make the technology, and those operating it, as invisible as possible, to reach a point where the Louds accepted it as part of the surroundings, even, as Pat later said, as part of the family. And although consensual, the imperative to record everything took on a logic of its own, forcing the Louds to continually renegotiate the threshold of disclosure they had initially consented to and allowing the Raymonds ultimately to film even the most intimate and painful interactions between family members. Eventually three hundred hours of film were distilled into twelve one-hour episodes covering the seven-month period. While much of the resulting footage simply recorded the everyday minutiae of their lives—eating breakfast, feeding the dogs, attending classes—there was plenty of drama as well.

Beneath the outward appearance of enviable privilege and happiness, of course, lay a rather different reality. In the course of filming, long-simmering tensions between Pat and Bill came to the surface until, in the climactic episode, she asked him to move out of the house. By the time the series aired in the winter of 1973, the two were divorced and Pat had become a single working mother. Once the tensions between the two came into the open, they were quickly seized on as the series's main storyline. The first episode gave the plot away by introducing Pat and Bill in their postmarital state and setting up the following eleven episodes as an extended flashback. Thereafter this framing device was condensed into the title montage that preceded each episode: head-shots of each family member were followed by the title, with the word "family" set off by fracture lines. Episode 2, in which Pat Loud visits her eldest son, Lance, in New York, revealed the second main "point of tension." The story of Pat and Bill's failed marriage was perhaps straightforward enough in what it suggested about the problems of the contemporary family, but the Lance storyline opened up an altogether more complicated Pandora's box: issues of generational conflict, sexual orientation, and not least, the medium's claims to realism. Lance and his mother quickly emerged as the series's central characters—hardly surprising, given that it was their actions that brought the traditional family most sharply into question.

In brief introductory remarks he offered at the beginning of Episode 1, Gilbert attempted to map some of the historical and cultural coordinates of the Loud family story. Standing against a backdrop of densely vegetated coastal mountains that functioned ironically to signify Santa Barbara's status as a Garden of Eden, he sketched the family's genealogy: "The Loud family has a history, moving, like the frontier, westward. What were their forebears looking for? Better business opportunities, a better place to raise a family . . . Their search took them to Eugene, Oregon. Unlike their parents, the younger generation could no longer move west. The frontier was gone. So they moved south to Santa Barbara." This reference to the disappearing frontier located the Louds within the mythic space charted by Richard Slotkin in *Gunfighter Nation*, which documents the immense symbolic importance of the frontier within American history and the feared moral decay connected with its loss. Certainly some such fear animated the questions that, as Gilbert went on to explain, provided the series with its starting point: "What is the current American dream? Why has marriage become something less than a permanent arrangement? What is left of the parent-child relationship? Where are America's children going?"

Over the course of the series the Louds emerged as members of what Nixon had hailed as the silent majority, an affluent, white middle class forged by the combined forces of the baby boom, suburbanization, and rising affluence. Yet although the Louds were eminently a product of the fifties, the sixties had also left their mark on them, most visibly in

Lance's coming out and Pat's break with Bill, but also in the rock-star
dreams and hairstyles of the younger boys, and in the self-consciously
casual atmosphere of the household. Bill Loud later confessed that he
hoped the series would make them look like "West Coast Kennedys"
or like a hipper version of *ur*-sitcom family *Ozzie and Harriet*.

Yet the pleasant façade was offset by repeated intimations of disaster,
from the brushfire that nearly destroyed their home, to Grant's car
accident, to Pat's offhand remark that "we are due" for an earthquake.
More serious were the signs of the impending collapse of the great
postwar boom. Early in the series a longshoremen's strike held up
delivery of vital parts from Europe, disrupting Bill's business and finally
provoking a serious crisis in his company's fortunes. By the series's end,
Bill was swimming against a tide of bad business news and the family
was financing its lifestyle with credit cards. In one episode Kevin, whom
Bill was grooming for a position in his company, was sent off to look
for business opportunities in Australia and Southeast Asia. As Ruoff
observes, this oblique reminder of the struggle to defend capitalism in
Indochina thus became linked to the fact that capitalism at home stood
at a historic turning point from expansion to contraction.

This sense of vulnerability was heightened by the fraying of the work
ethic that had once provided a solid foundation for middle-class
affluence, evident in Bill's frustration with his sons' unwillingness
to abandon their dreams of stardom and get a job. Meanwhile, the
series's efforts to contrast Pat's secular mores with those of her
churchgoing mother documented the decline of religion as a force
in the Louds' lives. Work, family, and religion no longer provided the
anchorage points they once did. Even the ability to articulate the
American dream seemed lost: in one early classroom scene, Grant,
seated in front of a blackboard with the words "American Dream"
written on it, struggles to define the post–Civil War Reconstruction era
and its efforts to integrate blacks. As the Louds went about their daily
lives—Delilah in dance recital; Bill and Pat at a cocktail party; Michelle
riding the horse; Kevin and Grant in the recording studio—the
audience was invited to dissect the family for signs of impending
collapse.

Making Sense of *An American Family*

From the day it premiered on January 11—the same day the Senate Democratic Caucus voted unanimously to investigate Watergate—the series was a sensation. By the final episodes, an estimated 11 million viewers were tuning in every week to watch the trials of the Louds. The series clearly struck a nerve in the viewing public, crystallizing anxieties about divorce, women's lib, new sexual mores, and the generation gap. Feminists, sociologists, psychiatrists, and magazine columnists weighed in on the Louds, their reactions ranging from fascination to horror. Two questions dominated the coverage: why did they do it? did the cameras affect their behavior? Just as the media would soon be wondering why Nixon had recorded the Oval Office tapes, so they now obsessed over why the Louds had invited the cameras into their lives. Whatever was wrong with this family, the subtext to these questions suggested, was connected with its willingness to expose itself to the camera and in a more general sense with the pervasive role of the media in American society.

At one end of the spectrum stood those who hailed the series as an important, even revolutionary breakthrough in the medium. Anthropologist Margaret Mead gave it the highest accolade, saying that in her estimation *An American Family* was "as new and significant as the invention of drama or the novel—a new way in which people can learn to look at life, by seeing the real life of others interpreted by the camera." She made the obvious reference to contemporary group therapy, whose popularity, she noted, reflected a desire to break the bonds of solitude: "It is related to a strange new willingness to share one's inner life, to perform on a stage before other concerned eyes."

Mead was seemingly untroubled by this "new willingness," perhaps recognizing, as an anthropologist, the relative novelty of modern conceptions of private life. In addition to sharing Gilbert's views on the imminent demise of the nuclear family—though not his pessimism—Mead appreciated the documentary form's representational power. Having herself been the subject of a documentary (produced by Gilbert), she regarded the truth claims of the medium as unproblematic:

> With *An American Family* it is not your imagination but the immediate, the actual, what it is really like, that is there. The closest TV has come to this until now has been the infrequent glimpses it has given us of real life—a father weeping over his son's court-martial, the Kennedy children weeping beside their father's bier, the flickering image of the men who were at that moment on the moon.

What united these seminal moments in the history of television was a public thirst for "real life," satisfied by moments of high tragedy and drama. At such moments TV, as it were, broke through its own limitations, transcending the inauthenticity that Boorstin saw as the hallmark of image culture.

Others were less sanguine. Many critics were predictably appalled at the Louds for turning their lives into a spectacle. *Time* marshaled the opinions of several psychologists who suggested that the Louds were symptomatic of a cultural "compulsion to confess," of desperate people who turned to the mass media in hope of therapeutic relief. Other critics pathologized the Louds as "affluent zombies" mesmerized by the media's promise of celebrity. The divorce, in their eyes, did not hold the larger significance that the show's producers claimed for it but merely signified that the Louds had been a "nonfamily" to begin with, a collection of narcissists whose only allegiance was to their future careers as media celebrities.

Critic Anne Roiphe described the Louds as cultural philistines who had been cast into a "vacuum" in the absence of those "structures of work and religion that used to shape the days." They were like a primitive tribe that had been driven out of its homeland and had lost its power "to create or impose order." Roiphe concluded on a sentimental note by wishing that Americans could return to an earlier time when they enjoyed a greater sense of belonging. Referring to the season's other great portrayal of family life, she wrote, "Maybe it's better to be a Corleone than a Loud, to be tribal and ethnocentric than urbane and adrift." For Roiphe the story of the Louds became an allegory of Americans' fall from a state of innocence. She later reviewed *The Waltons*, a sitcom about a poor yet virtuous family whose reassuring artifice she found infinitely preferable to the more unsettling artifact created in *An American Family*.

Others adopted a more nuanced position, arguing that, however unsavory the Louds' behavior, the refusal to identify with them was simply a form of blaming the messenger. Abigail McCarthy suggested that most viewers tended to come to terms with the discomfort they felt at the series "by blaming the Louds for being themselves, and by patronizing them for being the kind of people who would allow themselves to be the subject of such a television series. This last betrays ignorance of the unique hold of the medium on people today." As the wife of former presidential candidate Eugene McCarthy, McCarthy was in a position to speak with some authority on the media's hollowing out of privacy:

> In public life one learns very quickly that everyone wants to be on television. There are very few private people left. Let a television crew appear to follow a campaigner and a crowd gathers almost at once, pushing each other, pressing close so that they, too, will be on screen. Appear on a talk show and you take on new reality, even for close friends. In recent months we have seen the wife of a prisoner of war allowing her husband's first phone call to be recorded by television sound and camera crew—without his knowledge.

Indeed, as Gilbert reminded critics, he'd interviewed more than fifty families before selecting the Louds, and virtually all had been willing to participate. As Lance would riposte to those who saw his family as freaks: "The series was the fulfillment of the middle-class dream that you can become famous for being just what you are."

Many reviewers remained skeptical of the series's claim to realism. For one crucial episode, Gilbert had gone to great lengths to persuade Pat to let him record the conversation with her brother and sister-in-law in which she informed them of her decision to separate from Bill; though reluctant at first, she eventually consented and later referred to this episode as her "best scene." Such statements inevitably led to mention of the Heisenberg principle, according to which the observed is never wholly independent of the observer, and from there to a detailed inventory of other forms of compromised realism in the Louds' on-camera behavior and remarks. Noting that Gilbert had found inspiration for the series in a novel, some reviewers concluded that rather than depicting reality, the series had succeeded only in relativizing all notions of the real.

The most pessimistic analysis of the series was offered in *The New Republic* by Roger Rosenblatt. Writing in the fall of 1974, at a time when the Louds were beginning to discover how fleeting fame could be, Rosenblatt suggested that their celebrity had in fact been "obliterated, as if by popular demand." In essence, the series had transgressed against audiences' conventional notions of reality. Television, he wrote, "attempts to create its own brand of realism, and to destroy our idea of reality in the process." In doing so, it insists on the integrity (however manufactured) of its own brand of realism. *An American Family*, however, had wound up thoroughly confounding generic distinctions between reality and image: "The Louds' divorce was a real event; it actually occurred. Never was there greater realism on television except in the murders of Oswald and Robert Kennedy." Nevertheless, in Rosenblatt's verdict, the series seemed staged, pure pseudo-event. So contaminated was the family's reality by its televised image, in Rosenblatt's view, that the Louds were in fact "playing *American Family*, not living it, just as they had played *American Family* long before Craig Gilbert hit upon his brainstorm." Ultimately, he felt, "the Louds were born a TV program waiting to be discovered. They had always thought of themselves as a family show."

The Media as Usurper

The somewhat paranoid undertone in Rosenblatt's analysis was spelled out in its closing lines. Writing a few months after Watergate's final denouement, Rosenblatt could not help noting that "there is a curious correspondence here with Richard Nixon, who was the real Nixon on tape, and the fake, the liar, when not on tape. This is one reason we sought those tapes so avidly: to see the real person in the nation's trust. The Louds, however, had more integrity than Nixon. They were equally unreal on and off camera."

The sense that the Louds had transgressed against deeply held proprieties no doubt reflected their role in giving human faces to the increasingly pervasive influence of the media in American life. This, as we have seen, was something that many Americans felt deeply ambivalent about. Throughout the 1960s the media had assumed an increasingly assertive role in questioning the official version of events both at home and abroad. First Vietnam and then Watergate had presented the media with unprecedented opportunities to broaden their public mandate. A decade that had weakened so many other forms of authority had immeasurably strengthened that of the media.

It was precisely this new authority that Nixon railed against in demonizing the "eastern liberal media" and playing it off against his supporters. Nixon's televised address on November 3, 1969, in which he called upon "the great silent majority" to support his Vietnam policy, was followed up by a series of press conferences in which Vice President Spiro Agnew blasted the networks as biased and elitist. Describing them as run by a "tiny, enclosed fraternity of private men elected by no one," in effect Agnew charged them with attempting to usurp the institutions of established authority. This line of attack would culminate with the administration's response to the publication of the Pentagon Papers, which it depicted as nothing less than an attempted media coup d'état.

And yet the Nixon administration was itself deeply implicated in the new realities of image culture, assiduously cultivating relations with select organs of the media deemed favorable to its policies in order to sell those policies to the public. The single greatest sales job, as Joe McGinniss had shown in his *The Selling of the President,* involved the president himself. The handlers brought aboard for his 1968 campaign had undertaken the job of giving their candidate a wholesale image makeover. In their efforts to address Nixon's perceived awkwardness in the public arena, these men drew a distinction first invoked by Marshall McLuhan: "The response is to the image, not to the man . . . It's not what's there that counts, it's what's projected." Once this fundamental separation between man and image had been made, according to one campaign reporter, it became impossible to look at candidates the same way: "From that moment on we had emerged from the Garden of Eden." Yet however successful these efforts to craft a natural-seeming television image were, they never fully resolved Nixon's underlying problem. Garry Wills spoke for many in persisting in calling Nixon "the least authentic man alive."

This perception returned with a vengeance in the scandal surrounding Watergate. Once the Senate Watergate hearings began their televised sessions on May 17, millions of Americans found themselves transfixed by the near-daily bombshell disclosures of the dark machinations emanating from the White House. The Watergate hearings represented a defining moment both in the history of American politics and in the history of the medium. In the days before C-SPAN, live daytime coverage of government affairs was virtually unknown. At the outset, only PBS, which was not beholden to advertisers, offered live, gavel-to-gavel coverage of the hearings. But as the proceedings turned increasingly sensational and the American public began to tune in in ever-larger numbers, the major networks followed suit. Within a week, the hearings had been transformed into a huge media event, complete with a grand setting, the Senate caucus room, a compelling cast of characters—from homespun Senate committee chairman Sam Ervin, to clean-cut special counsel to the president John Dean, to glowering former attorney general John Mitchell—and graphic accounts of the administration's crimes. Watergate burglar James McCord was the first to provide public details of the cover-up, and subsequent testimony tied Mitchell to the cover-up. But it was Dean's testimony that proved most damaging to Nixon, with its revelations of the administration's "enemies list," its plans for a secret domestic intelligence unit, and, most devastating of all, his account of meetings that directly implicated Nixon in the Watergate cover-up from the outset. Dean also hinted at the existence of Nixon's tapes, and this was later confirmed in the testimony provided by White House aide Alexander Butterfield on July 16. Butterfield's revelation that the president had bugged himself was followed by an immediate request from Ervin that the tapes be handed over. Nixon tried to resist the request by invoking privilege, a privilege he compared to that between a husband and a wife.

As the hearings continued, Nixon's paranoia became a self-fulfilling prophecy; the president who, according to Kissinger, wanted nothing more than to be loved by the public lashed out increasingly wildly as the cracks in his carefully manufactured public image were exposed. Now, however, his earlier success at playing off the liberal media elite against the silent majority turned against him. In 1973, as CBS newsman Daniel Schorr would later write, a new kind of journalism was born as reporters who had been demonized by the president's men exacted bloodthirsty revenge from the increasingly beleaguered president. Notwithstanding Daniel Boorstin's fears concerning the diminishing authority of the real—and with it, the hero—the blockbuster success of Woodward and Bernstein's *All the President's Men* testified to the emergence of the investigative reporter as a new kind of folk hero.

Yet the single worst blow to the authority of the office of the president—the Oval Office tapes—was self-inflicted. Once Alexander Butterfield disclosed their existence in July, Nixon's efforts to maintain control over his fate and his public image were damaged beyond repair. Why had Nixon preserved the tapes? Was there a relation between the taping and his obsession with his image? Journalist Shana Alexander later suggested as much in theorizing that Nixon, like an increasing number of Americans, was haunted by a feeling of being onstage; having been forced by television to become an actor, he hoped that the tapes would reassure him of his reality. This widely shared sense of simultaneous entanglement in, and anxiety about, the new realities of image culture is partly what makes Nixon, almost despite himself, a tragic figure. How, lamented Pat, "could any individual survive a public reading of private conversations?"

This may also help explain why the story of the Louds, which played itself out nearly simultaneously with that of Watergate, stirred such intense reactions. Violence had been done to established codes of propriety; someone had to be blamed. As the visible faces of the new mediatized dispensation, the Louds, and in particular Lance, became an inviting target, a "sacrificial spectacle."

This was perhaps especially the case given that, while *An American Family* certainly invites a Boorstinian analysis, with its conviction that a culture predicated on the image suffered a high price—the loss of its sense of reality, history, democracy, authentic experience—it also advances another, more radical reading of image culture. This is connected with the marginal presence of Andy Warhol in the series. Rosenblatt's reaction, in fact, points in this direction; whereas for Roiphe the story of the Louds was an allegory of a fall from a state of innocence, for Rosenblatt the Louds had always been a TV show. They inhabited a Warholian world in which there were no originals, only copies.

"TV swallowed my family" was Lance's verdict on the experiment to which his family had been subjected. It was not by chance that Lance authored this statement, given his emergence over the course of the series as the most trenchant critic both of the values of his family and of their fate within prime-time America. At the heart of Lance's critique of his family and its way of life stood his father, Bill, a figure of deeply compromised authority. Most commentators agreed that, whatever else it revealed, the series offered a picture of fatherhood imperiled. The evidence for this ranged from the near-collapse of Bill's business, to his waning influence over his sons, and finally to Pat's decision to kick him out of the house. There were deeper signs as well: in her memoir Pat hinted that following her own sexual awakening Bill had begun to find her too sexually aggressive, emasculating.

Charming and handsome, Bill was cut in the mold of a rugged individualist. Yet his somewhat roguish persona concealed consider-able pathos. In one early scene Bill is shown describing a recent car accident to friends at a restaurant. Slightly drunk, he speaks as if about a scene in a movie as he enumerates details: the smoke and flames, a wheel flying off: "For a few seconds it's an exhilarating experience, and then you come down, you know your body is safe, and you haven't been cut up, and you've been through a wonderful wreck." The scene conveys a man in mourning for a lost sense of indestructibility and youth. So too do his quite public on-screen flirtations with women, visible signs of the serial philandering that precipitated the final crisis in his marriage. Bill was a man of contradictions: he lamented his sons' lack of a work ethic while chafing visibly at his own paternal responsibilities and sporting fashionably long sideburns and a swinging sensibility. (It was later disclosed that he had encouraged Pat to have affairs.) No less than his sons, Bill did not want to grow up.

By all accounts, next to Lance it was Bill who most enjoyed the experience of being on camera. He described it as like having a "maid in the house." Even as his fantasy that the series would show the Louds as "West Coast Kennedys" crumbled, he continued trying to play by what he imagined to be the rules of the medium, affecting a studied coolness. When in the climactic episode Pat asks him to move out after he has just returned home from a business trip, he responds wearily, yet with a hint of relief, "Fair deal. I won't have to pack." Later, in a letter he writes in response to one of Lance's provocations, he states that he "very much enjoyed your analogy of the 'return of Lance' vs. the 'fall of the father.'" The traditional oedipal conflict has been emptied of its emotional charge, turned into a pseudo-event, by TV. Faced with starting over again in a new apartment after the breakup, Bill hires a decorator, to whom he confides, "You know, I like the French stuff, Louis XV kind of jazz." The decorator responds with a joke: "Like the White House." Later Bill describes the result as "Versailles meets Travelodge." His symbolic dethroning cannot be played as tragedy, only as farce.

Torn between an older image of the paterfamilias and a newer, hipper one, Bill's authority is deeply compromised. In a real sense, allowing the cameras into the house involved a symbolic abdication of authority. This was made explicit in one interview in which Bill said he wished he'd thrown his kids' TV sets into the Pacific Ocean. Once the critical reaction to the series had set in and it became clear that it was not favorable, Bill charged the filmmakers with having deliberately selected the material that showed the family in the worst possible light. Denied his wish of becoming a West Coast Kennedy, he began to sound like Nixon, accusing the filmmakers of having "a preconceived, liberal, leftist view that the American way of life is wrong, that family life is wrong, that our values are wrong. They feel something should be done about it, some sort of new movement like communes or welfare, some socialized way of looking at things." As the now somewhat hysterical voice of the silent majority, Bill Loud charged the media not simply with usurping traditional authority, but with trying to put in its place a society that had distinctly un-American features.

Bill's tendency to blame television for his family's troubles was mirrored in the eagerness with which some critics seized upon rumors of a romance between Craig Gilbert and Pat. The implication was that the filmmakers' presence had hastened the divorce. In the autobiography she published the following year, Pat denied the rumor and explained the camera's influence on her behavior in somewhat different terms, saying that *An American Family* was "what came along to save me . . . from my 46-year-old identity crisis." Twenty years of marriage to a serial adulterer had left Pat without what she called a "real self": "So now, instead of going into analysis or getting my MA or boozing or running off with a beach bum, all in search of my real self, apparently I've acquired a real self just by being on Channel 13."

While Bill hoped the series would provide entry into a fantasy world, Pat hoped it would compensate for a deficit of reality. More than any of the other family members, Pat internalized the filmmakers' view that TV was both sickness and cure. According to series director Alan Raymond, "An entire generation of viewers has been unconsciously traumatized because they could never measure up to the image of family life they saw on the screen." If cultural images could produce sickness, then Pat Loud was living proof. "I had," she wrote, "been programmed for marriage." When confronted with evidence of Bill's cheating, she simply swallowed her pride and stayed in the marriage.

A decisive turn in the marriage finally came in the mid-sixties, a turn Pat linked to the war: "In '66 the whole thing blew up. The Vietnam

War was on and Bill was selling a lot of castings for the paving they did there. (Bill never had any problem with the war because he's a Republican and believed in it, and for a short time I went along with him politically.)" Like Erica Jong, Pat Loud mapped the battle of the sexes onto the war to defend capitalism in Indochina. One night she let herself into his office and rifled his files for evidence of his infidelity. In a scene reminiscent of Watergate, this "Night of the Files," as she called it, finally opened Pat's eyes to the magnitude of her husband's betrayals: "There were ten women to every one I had imagined. It was vast, cosmic." Pat's deprogramming took years to complete, years in which—like her namesake in the White House—she descended into alcoholism, depression, and bitterness. This phase finally culminated with the decision to invite the filmmakers into her house. Why did she go along with it? On the one hand, she wrote, "it seems to give people a kind of permanence or reality if they're on TV"; on the other, she clearly accepted the premise that television vérité would puncture the false reality that had been bequeathed her by fifties sitcoms. Pat's book ends with her, Jong-like, boarding a plane as she is about to leave Santa Barbara for New York to begin a new life: "Once in the air, I can't turn back."

Lance Loud Superstar

Yet if it was Pat who brought about the formal dissolution of the Loud family, it was Lance who became the target of the most visceral reactions in the press. Critic Anne Roiphe set the tone when she expressed shock at Lance's "flamboyant, leechlike homosexuality" and referred to him as the family's "evil flower." Even those sympathetic to Lance could not help but comment on his "damaged" persona—leaving unclear whether they meant his homosexuality or his "pandering" to the camera—and probed for evidence of his treatment and medication history.

Lance's offense to conventional sensibilities is of two kinds. Over the course of the series he undergoes a vivid transformation, evolving from a fairly conventional twenty-year-old with surf-dude good looks and gay mannerisms into a drag queen wearing makeup, jewelry, and scarves. By the time he returns to Santa Barbara in the penultimate episode, the makeover is complete and he is in full drag, a transformation underscored by a scene at the airport in which Lance is depicted alongside a soldier—a scene that reminds us that Lance is not serving. His homecoming (with Bill now out of the household) is followed by a scene in which he parades in a variety of colorful getups and gives both of his sisters makeup tips. With "the fall of the father" having left a symbolic void in the family, "the return of Lance" fills it with campy scenes, black lipstick, and dark background music by the Velvet Underground.

Lance Loud's coming out on television would become one of the landmark events in the medium's history, and his public avowal that he was homosexual would make him a hero in the gay community. Lance eventually parlayed his status as television's first gay icon into a career as a journalist, writing a column for Andy Warhol's *Interview* and performing as lead singer of the punk band the Mumps. His performance had wider ramifications as well: following the publication of Roiphe's article, members of the Gay Activist Alliance met with representatives of the major networks to protest the depiction of gays and lesbians in commercial television, a meeting that marked the beginning of a gradual shift in the American media.

But as scandalous as this challenge to conventional images of masculinity and gender orientation was, Lance's affront to traditional sensibilities went further. He also served as a mouthpiece for a Warholian perspective that called into question television's role in naturalizing such images. In interviews and articles subsequent to the series, the full story of Lance's infatuation with Warhol emerged. At the age of thirteen, after seeing a *Time* article on Warhol and Edie Sedgwick, he had dyed his hair silver and begun sending Warhol lengthy letters. Warhol eventually responded by asking Lance to call him one night. Their subsequent correspondence and late-night phone calls continued until Warhol was shot in 1968 and he became more reclusive. By the time *An American Family* went into production,

Lance had developed a well-honed Warholian sensibility that he used to great effect on camera: "When the cameras were on me," he wrote, "I was really thinking, you know, *Chelsea Girls*." In a real sense Lance was now living out a wish that Warhol had once expressed concerning his desire to make a movie of a whole day in the life of Edie Sedgwick. Ironically, in the series's final segment, Lance and Edie briefly crossed paths, the very night that the former Superstar died in her sleep.

While the performances of the other family members reflected a controlled self-consciousness that both denied and unconsciously reflected the camera's presence, Lance's was pure artifice, overacted burlesque. It is impossible watching Lance not to be reminded of the presence of the camera, not least because of his preoccupation with clothing, makeup, and hair. In Lance's scenes, reality television took on increasingly surreal qualities, no more so than in those moments in the Chelsea Hotel in which Warhol Superstar Holly Woodlawn appeared, or in the performance of *Vain Victory*, the transvestite variety show ("The ultimate in underground!" in Lance's breathless description) starring Jackie Curtis and Ondine, to which Lance took his mother. Many reviewers expressed shock at these moments and sympathy with Pat's own evident discomfort at this collision between two worlds. Yet Pat's own consciousness was hardly unmarked by Lance's preoccupations. In one scene, as the two stroll through Central Park, she asks, "Where does Jackie Onassis live? Your grandmother is still fascinated with the events of her life. She and her friends buy all those supermarket magazines." Lance's knowing response is to say, "The great American pastime." Pat's rejoinder: "The great American dream." (Several critics, moreover, noted her resemblance to Jackie.)

But at least Pat still spoke a shared language, one in which the crisis of authenticity experienced by many Americans was linked to its desired recuperation—even if many critics felt she placed too much faith in the power of television to effect this. Lance, on the other hand, represents a point of view in which there is no loss to be mourned, no "reality" prior to the image. Following Bill's eviction from the Loud household, Lance takes to referring to the "breakup" in a highly stagy voice, at one point mentioning that this scene has happened several times already, and that his parents have been rehearsing for this moment for a long time.

In Lance's world authenticity holds no privileged place; there is only imitation, the serialization of images without origin. The latter point is made clear when Lance takes Pat to the Whitney Museum to see a Warhol retrospective. Pat and the audience are treated to multiple images of soup cans, Elvis and Marilyn, car accidents, and Warhol's own visage. In an interview given several years later, Lance would underscore the cultural shift hinted at in these scenes when he described Warhol as "the greatest father figure . . . [of] that generation," and said, "He was always parental." Lance radicalized the familiar lament that the media had usurped the family's place in the socialization of American youth, and he put a name to the condition that resulted: Warhol.

It was in the person of Lance that the series's contamination by the presence of the camera became most visible. Lance disrupted the series's naturalistic mode of address in numerous ways. Although Pat and Bill were sometimes recorded in voice-over, Lance was the only family member filmed speaking directly to the camera. In one scene, he is interviewed on the roof of his apartment building in New York musing, "I love to live with a style and a certain phony, put-on elegance . . . I guess I want to be a superstar. I wish I was Peter Pan." The decision to allow Lance to break the frame by speaking directly to the camera was just one of many that endowed him with authority. In several scenes Lance was filmed watching TV; as the audience became aware of itself watching a TV image of Lance watching TV, it became implicated in a kind of vertiginous reflexivity that was at odds with the series's professed "realism."

In the end, Lance called into question both the naturalism of the family arrangement and the naturalism of the televised image. Perhaps this constituted the real scandal of the series, the real reason the Louds' celebrity had to be "obliterated, as if by popular demand." In the person of Lance, the series had the effect of scrambling all the generic codes governing the family, gender orientation, and not least, television's role in shoring up those codes. The unraveling of the Loud family seemed to tear open the fabric of the media product called "reality." By the common consent of the critics, Lance was damaged goods, the pathological offspring of an unholy marriage between TV and an underground culture that was suddenly erupting into mainstream America. Alternately fascinated and repelled by Lance, the critics finally wound up making him the scapegoat for the perceived crisis of traditional values associated with the breakup of the family and the rise of the mass media. If many viewers shared the concern articulated at the end of Abigail McCarthy's article—what is TV doing to the family?—then Lance seemed to flaunt the answer: ending the comfortable manhood that had once upon a time been the customary birthright of the American male, and opening the door to a grab bag of alternative identities.

Television, the Schizophrenic Medium

Pat Loud later described being in front of the camera every day as akin to being "split in half." Symptomatic of the dual consciousness that resulted from this experience were her contradictory attempts to come to terms with the series's effects on her life. On the one hand she was angered by her family' transformation into a "freak show"; on the other she welcomed the "reality" that television seemed to confer on her. Helping compensate for her own felt lack of a "real self," the series broke the emotional dam in the Loud household and gave her the courage to bring about the long-postponed break with her husband. Bill too was "split in half," torn between being a square and being a swinger, raging against his kids' addiction to TV and lamenting their "unrealistic" dreams of stardom, yet wanting to be in on the joke (he obligingly calls Lance "Superstar") and entertaining his own Kennedyesque dreams. During one of their arguments Pat accuses him of being "schizophrenic." Perhaps only Lance seems to escape this divided relation to television. It is for this reason that Pat, in her more optimistic moments, calls Lance "the future" and sees him, ironically, as "so real."

The underlying condition to which these ambivalent responses refer has to do with the invasion, or—to use Lance's term—swallowing, of private space by the mass media (a condition, it must be noted, that in the case of the Louds predated the onset of filming, given the proliferation of devices in the family's household, from TVs to Super 8 cameras to recording studios). It is an ambivalence that marks the form and reception of the series itself. Was *An American Family* a milestone in media realism, the birth of a new kind of video vérité? Or was it simply one of the major pseudo-events of 1973? Did television take away the Louds' reality and make them characters in a television show no different from, say, *The Brady Bunch*? Or did it, in exposing some of the destructive myths of American family life, perform a strange alchemy that restored the family members' reality to them?

These questions have continued to mark attitudes toward the series, which has been both embraced and demonized by critics since it first aired in 1973. The series has become a touchstone for gay culture and an object lesson in the rules governing what Jean Baudrillard called the society of the simulacrum. It is seen as the prototype of today's reality television programming and is compared with shows like *Big Brother* and MTV's *The Osbournes*. On both ends of the cultural spectrum, the series has fed into long-standing critiques of the medium: among conservatives, who accused TV of undermining traditional values; and among liberals, who criticized it for trafficking in "false images" and "unreal" representations of the family. In blaming the messenger, both sides attributed causality to the camera. But both also tried to use it to counteract those destructive effects, just as the makers of *An American Family* attempted to do in trying to undo the media construct "family." Televangelists, who had already begun using the medium as a pulpit to decry abortion and call for a return to tradition and "family values," would welcome a new addition to their ranks in 1973 with the introduction of Jim and Tammy Faye Bakker to the public as the "first family of televangelism."

Perhaps the most compelling frame of reference for the series is the other great drama being acted out on television sets across the country that year, namely the Watergate hearings—described by Hollywood producer Julia Phillips (winner of an Oscar that year for *The Sting*) as the "greatest miniseries ever." The extraordinary crisis unfolding in the White House reverberated throughout the nation, unleashing confusion and moral panic and inviting more than a few critics to view the series through a Watergate lens. One result of the convergence between the two media events, Watergate and *An American Family*, was the discovery that Americans seemed to be under a strange compulsion to place themselves (as well as others) under surveillance. Yet while both involved unprecedented invasions of privacy, there were important distinctions between the two events. The seamless integration of surveillance technology into the everyday lives of the Louds represented a kind of inversion of the Big Brother methods emanating from the White House. If Nixon's crimes awakened fears of an Orwellian future, then *An American Family* pointed to a Warholian future, one presaging today's experiments in reality television.

While both media events aroused anxieties about the hollowing out of private space, they also sounded the alarm about the breakdown of traditional authority. Over both the Watergate hearings and the series hovered the ghost of John F. Kennedy. Both Bill Loud and Richard Nixon aspired to look Kennedyesque, with unhappy results; when the media refused to cooperate, both men hinted darkly of a conspiracy masterminded by an eastern liberal elite. But if Bill's wish was symptomatic, so too was Lance's: that, once the camera was on, he saw himself acting in a Warhol film. In the end, the warnings about image culture sounded by Boorstin were too pessimistic: as the Watergate hearings showed, television could effect real change. And as *An American Family* showed, pseudo-events could as well. The story of the Louds suggested that the "fall of the father" did not simply usher in a new tyranny, that of the "image": by helping end the stalemate in their household, the series opened up a space within which Pat and Lance could emerge as hero-celebrities of a new cultural dispensation.

Operation Homecoming

The name of the game is air.

—American pilot involved in bombing of Laos

The traumatic experience came from the complete comfort
and home of that cockpit . . . a minute later you're in a
savage world . . . you know all is lost.

—Thomas Kirk, POW

Those who remember the past are condemned to repeat it too,
that's a little history joke.

—Michael Herr, *Dispatches*

FEBRUARY 12, 1973: *The first POWs land at Clark Air Force
Base in the Philippines following their release from North Vietnamese
prison camps. After being debriefed, undergoing medical examina-
tions, and dining on steak, beer, and ice cream, this group of twenty
pilots finally sets foot on American soil three days later. Some of them
have been in captivity for up to eight years.*

By the end of March a total of 591 POWs had returned from prison
camps to scenes of joyful reunion across the United States. Their return
was the immediate dividend of the Paris peace accords signed on
January 27, formally bringing an end to the war in Vietnam. But with

more than thirteen hundred MIAs still unaccounted for, Operation Homecoming, as the POWs' repatriation was called, did little to satisfy the American public's need for closure on the war. The returning men soon found themselves caught up in the competing narratives of the war. To some Americans, they were heroes of a nation desperately in need of reminders of its essential virtue and innocence. To others, their heroism was very much in question: at the very least, their transformation into heroes served to obscure and distort the truth about the war, to say nothing of their own role in it. Given that many of the POWs were bomber pilots and had played instrumental roles in the campaign of airborne destruction waged against Vietnam, some Americans felt they deserved their treatment as war criminals in the prison camps.

At the same time, most POWs found that the homes to which they returned were no longer the same. Everything, in fact, had changed. Confronted with the sexual revolution, the countercultures spawned by the antiwar movement, and an increasingly bleak economy, many of the men experienced intense culture shock. Yet their return home was relatively less traumatic than that of most Vietnam veterans, who were denied the hero's welcome accorded the POWs in the elaborate ceremonies of Operation Homecoming. After World War II a grateful government had invited veterans to participate in that miracle of social engineering, the GI Bill, which helped turn millions of Americans into homeowners for the first time. Most Vietnam veterans, however, returned to find no such gratitude awaiting them for their role in the nation's first-ever military defeat. Their homecoming was further complicated by the antiwar sentiment that permeated the veterans' organizations, a sentiment that would be scapegoated in some quarters for defeat. The POWs, on the other hand, remained with few exceptions committed to the war as a just cause. It was for this reason that they were destined to play a key role in shaping the memory of the war—a role that has reverberated throughout American political life up to the present day.

Culture Shock

The spring of 1973 marked the end of the longest war in U.S. history, its dispiriting conclusion obscured by the rhetoric of "peace with honor." A large part of the honor claimed by Nixon was based on the release of the POWs, negotiations over whom had been ongoing since 1969. By the time of their return these men, who had spent more time in captivity than any other Americans in history, had become national obsessions. The majority of the returnees were career officers and fighter-bomber pilots who had been shot down over North Vietnam (some as recently as the Christmas bombing of 1972). They included some of the cream of the American campaign in Indochina, among them senior officers like James Stockdale, Robinson Risner, and Jeremiah Denton. All three men were among the first Americans shot down and had been held in captivity since the war's early stages. They were part of a contingent of men held at the notorious prison known as the Hanoi Hilton, where many had been tortured. A second contingent had been captured and held in the jungles of South Vietnam, before being moved, in the war's latter stages, to North Vietnam. Unlike the Hanoi prisoners, this second group was for the most part made up of ground troops. While most had not undergone torture, the conditions they faced in the jungle camps had been if anything even worse, and far fewer of the jungle POWs survived captivity.

As symbols of the war's end, the POWs returned home to wildly enthusiastic welcomes. Large crowds turned out to greet them at the military bases where they landed, and millions watched the proceedings on television, following their every move as they were welcomed back into civilization like a population of wild children: reunited with their families, then plied with pizza and beer, taken shopping, and invited to movie premieres and baseball games. Throughout the spring the nation continued to show its appreciation in a series of gala celebrations held across the country: Bob Hope hosted one event at the Cotton Bowl; another was held at Shea Stadium in New York; while in Dallas four-hundred POWs were honored in a parade and banquet sponsored and organized by Ross Perot, one of their most ardent champions. This outpouring of feeling culminated at a major event hosted by Nixon at the White House in late May.

As the men filtered back to the States, the public's appetite for details of prison life was fed by a barrage of media coverage. The faces, biographies, and family histories of the men became engraved in the public mind. Captain Harry Jenkins, a prisoner for six years, was greeted with a cake on which the words "Welcome Home. We're a Whole Family Again" were spelled out in icing. Air Force Major Joseph Abbott, enjoying Easter with his wife and seven-year-old daughter—only a week old when he left for Vietnam—admitted to feeling like a stranger in his own home at times. A stream of memoirs, biographies, and interview collections appeared, detailing the horrors and routines of camp life: scenes of deprivation and torture, but also more mundane details like the fact that a POW poll taken in 1968 had selected Liz Taylor as the world's most beautiful woman, or that Muhammad Ali had been the most controversial sports figure in the camps for his outspoken position against the war. Americans could not get enough of these prison stories, with their details of secret communication codes, sadistic guards, and testimonials of faith in God, country, and family.

Public interest in accounts of prison life was matched only by curiosity about the POWs' reactions to American society. Invoking the Rip Van Winkle motif that would become a standard trope of the media coverage, Robinson Risner observed: "It's like we've been asleep for seven years." Virtually all men noted that women seemed sexier, more independent, and uninhibited. But for some men the joy of the homecoming experience was tempered by dismay over the changes in American society. "I was amazed by the divorce rate," said one. "I've been visiting friends in Los Angeles, and most everybody is divorced." Sounding the religious note that would become a prominent feature of many POW memoirs, Air Force Major Jay Jensen, whose wife had divorced him while he was in prison, stated, "I feel that I have spent six years in hell and that I have been resurrected and I'm going to start a new life." He went on to observe that although he had been informed by men shot down more recently than he of changes in hair and style, they still came as a shock. Particularly for some of the senior officers, like Jeremiah Denton, the shock was profound. In his memoir Denton wrote of his outrage at the new "permissiveness" he found awaiting him, whose symptoms included "group sex, massage parlors, X-rated movies, the drug culture"—all signs, he felt, of a new "weakness in the national character." For those prisoners who had clung to an idealized picture of American society the awakening was a rude one.

There were other shocks in store as well, as the sister of one POW, Lieutenant Commander Everett Alvarez, predicted. The first of the Hanoi prisoners, Alvarez had been shot down in 1964, at a time when the world looked very different. "There was complete faith in the Government, the Government knew best. The military and the uniform were looked upon with a tremendous amount of respect," his sister Delia explained. Eight and half years later, she noted, "all that has changed considerably." Ms. Alvarez went on to say that initially she had shared her brother's views: "I believed in the domino theory." As the war dragged on, however, her views had undergone a transformation, and eventually she had turned to full-time antiwar activism. She predicted that her brother would have a hard time adjusting to the new cynical attitude toward government.

The problem of adjustment to post-Vietnam America was a major concern for military authorities. To ease the men's transition, the Pentagon set up programs to reintegrate them into a society convulsed by eight years of social change. At Maxwell Air Force Base in Alabama, for instance, the air force held classes for 235 ex-POWs designed to bring them "up to date on world and cultural affairs." Class subjects covered matters that were bound to seem strange to many of the men who had left a world governed by the moral absolutes of the cold war and the traditional gender and race relations of prewar America: Nixon's visit to China, women's liberation, race relations, and drug use. It was evidently felt that such classes were needed to offset some of the cognitive dissonance caused by what Frances Fitzgerald called "the spectacle of a President, Richard Milhous Nixon, who with one hand engaged in peaceful negotiations with the Soviet Union and the People's Republic of China, and with the other condemned thousands of Americans and Indochinese to die for the principle of anti-Communism."

The return of the POWs became an occasion for all Americans to take stock of the changes of the preceding decade. The *Times* editorial page ran a helpful glossary of terms to acquaint the POWs, as well as any squares who had somehow missed out on the sixties, with slang expressions now in use (*acid, afro, bad scene, bummer, gay, vibes*). In *Time* magazine Stefan Kanfer employed the trope of time travel to describe the homecoming experience and suggested that the rest of the nation would benefit from looking at itself through the "returning POWs' fresh, hungry eyes." Surveying the contemporary cultural landscape from their perspective, he highlighted X-rated movies, *Ms.* magazine, men sporting high heels and long hair, liberation movements of all kinds, the World Trade Center, blaxploitation films, and Andy Warhol.

Most experts agreed that while outwardly healthy, the POWs might bear the scars of "invisible wounds" that could take years to heal. The shock of capture, suggested a psychoanalyst interviewed for a *Time* article called "The Psychology of Homecoming," could produce feelings of helplessness and extreme stress, in response to which men developed a common syndrome: "the emotional anesthesia of captivity." Back in the outside world they retreated into a "zombie reaction." Problems of impotence and overidealization of loved ones might also haunt the returnee. Anticipating such difficulties, in early June a Pentagon health official issued a statement warning that the returned POWs were likely to experience "serious adjustment problems," including "stress reactions" and "depression," and that they would be closely monitored for several years to avoid the high violent death rates that had plagued POWs following the Korean War.

As if on cue, two days later Air Force Captain Edward Brudno was found dead after committing suicide at his in-laws' home in upstate New York. Brudno, a captive since 1966, was described as despondent since his return. "He was a very, very disturbed guy, another tragic victim of the war," observed one family acquaintance. Brudno's story was indeed tragic: married only two months before he was shot down in 1965, he had idealized his young wife to the point of writing an epic poem for her over the course of his seven-year captivity. On his return home, however, he found that the object of his idealization had developed from a young, immature woman into a "very strong person." The discovery that the traditional relationship between man and woman could no longer be taken for granted precipitated a crisis evidently worse than anything he'd endured in camp life.

Homecoming, as the POWs learned, could be as traumatic as the war they had left behind. Many of the men discovered that their wives' faithfulness had been seriously tested by the long years of absence. While older wives, like Sybil Stockdale, went out of their way to preserve an image of tranquil domesticity, many younger wives found it difficult to pretend that time had stood still since their husbands' departure. Out of a need for companionship or security, or simply out of a desire to sample some of the sexual freedom that had swept the country, they had moved on to new partners. In many cases, these women had gone for years without knowing whether their husbands were dead or alive, whether they would survive captivity, or when they would be released. Some feared their husbands would be impotent. A dozen wives had gotten divorced while their husbands were in prison, and one wife interviewed in the *Times* predicted more to come. A later *Times* article reported in June that 39 of the 420 married POWs were now divorced or in the process of obtaining a divorce. Some put the number far higher.

Perhaps the biggest challenge facing the POWs was coming home to wives whose ideas about relations between men and women had changed. "After so many years of forced independence," concluded one *Times* piece, "few wives remain subservient homebodies." If changes in hair and style came as a shock to many, one POW confessed that "most shocking to me is the sexual revolution." Six years of captivity had turned him into a sexual relic. Some wives spoke openly of "knowing themselves sexually much better." Alvarez pointedly asked his sister Delia if she was a women's libber, and then, when she tried to engage him in a conversation about it, seemed turned off by the subject. Many POWs, according to one study, felt "that military failure in Vietnam, antiwar protests and social unrest, and their own family upheavals were related symptoms of a moral collapse represented by the figure of an unfaithful, defiant, or simply different woman."

Dismayed by this perceived "collapse," many POWs, particularly the senior officers, cast about for explanations. The view that something had gone terribly wrong back in America was reflected in one POW's statement that the high divorce rate proved "that the wives have been running things for so many years." Some POWs used their new status as heroes to offer sharp critiques of the moral drift they sensed in the society to which they had returned. Having framed their captivity in essentially religious terms, they often invoked God in their critiques. The best known of the POW memoirs had titles like *With God in a POW Camp*, *When Hell was in Session*, and *Six Years in Hell*. These POWs believed that captivity had bestowed on them authority as moral leaders. But there were significant differences within the POW community itself. If the clash between outdated images of gender relations and current realities could prove difficult and even fatal, so too could the clash between the military ethos of the hard-line POWs and the view of those who had come to question the rationale for the war.

Torture, Collaboration, Brainwashing

The conclusion of the first televised war in history was marked by an elaborate media blitz orchestrated by the Pentagon. So concerned was the military with getting the homecoming story right that it assigned a team of nearly eighty military public relations specialists and information officers to act as what the *Times* called "a filtering screen between the press and the story." Nothing was left to chance; each POW was also assigned his own escort, whose function was to act as "buffer between past trauma and future shock." They were instructed to handle the men with kid gloves, making sure that questions on controversial topics like collaboration were avoided. Access to the POWs was carefully screened, and their public appearances carefully managed. At the outset these appearances were generally led by spokesmen for the Hanoi contingent, whose statements proved to be so remarkably similar that some journalists began to suspect that the POWs had been coached beforehand. Indeed by early March the Pentagon found itself in the embarrassing position of denying charges that the POWs' appearances had been scripted. Playing on one of the prevalent fears surrounding the POWs, Izvestia, the Soviet news service, accused the Pentagon of brainwashing the men, and of using them to brainwash the American public: "If one puts aside the emotions and touching scenes of family reunions, one feels at once the director's guiding hand—a giant propaganda and psychological campaign prepared by the Pentagon."

What lay behind the military's concern with managing the public image of the POWs? Clearly the Pentagon wished to present them to the American public as heroic figures who ennobled an otherwise tragic conflict. To accomplish this feat, it was crucial that the POWs speak with one voice; according to one senior officer, "This was their way of showing that Hanoi had not broken them." Yet this effort at cultivating a unified front could not long survive the intense media attention. As the *Times* was already pointing out in mid-February, the Hanoi contingent was made up of career officers and pilots, men who were probably "the most enthusiastic of American warriors." Unlike large sectors of the American public, as well as many enlisted men, their opinions about the war had remained essentially frozen in the hard-line cold war climate of the war's early years. Eight years in captivity, many marked by torture, had only hardened their views of the North Vietnamese and of the justice of the American cause. On the other hand, those who were held in South Vietnam and were not part of the fighter-pilot fraternity had a significantly different outlook. The horrors of the ground war in South Vietnam had taken its toll on morale and led many of these men to question the war's official rationale.

Once the initial glow created by Operation Homecoming had faded, these differences would surface in allegations that some of the returning POWs had collaborated with the enemy or not done enough to resist pressure to divulge information under torture. These allegations were lodged by members of the fighter-pilot fraternity against the "grunts," and, in a few cases, against pilots captured after 1968, whose doubts about the war reflected the general shift in American public opinion that had set in following the Tet offensive and the revelations of the My Lai massacre.

Accounts of torture were first made public at a press conference held on March 30, following the return of the last group of POWs. While the public had received hints of mistreatment—solitary confinement, beatings, and other forms of abuse—this marked the first confirmation of what had long been suspected: that many of the Hanoi prisoners had been subjected to systematic torture. Detailed accounts followed concerning the methods used, among them the "rope trick" in which the prisoner was tied so tightly into a ball that, after twenty minutes of excruciating pain, circulation in the upper part of his body was completely cut off; being suspended upside down for hours or even days at a time; and episodes of solitary confinement that in some cases lasted months or even years. Antiwar activists like Jane Fonda, who made a highly publicized, and widely criticized, visit to North Vietnam in 1972 during which she met with POWs, expressed skepticism about these accounts. "Hanoi Jane," as she became known, took pains to point out the justifiable anger of the Vietnamese at the pilots, whom they regarded as instruments of an illegal war, war criminals, and "air pirates" who had violated the sovereign air space of North Vietnam to bomb civilian populations. The North Vietnamese argued that the Geneva Conventions did not apply to these prisoners because it was an undeclared war. Other activists reminded the public of the use of torture, conducted with the full knowledge of American authorities, on Vietcong prisoners in the notorious "tiger cages" of South Vietnam.

Such appeals fell mostly on deaf ears. The torture narratives that formed the core of many of the POW memoirs conferred on these men an immense moral authority in the eyes of the American public, seeming to provide an emotional anchorage point in a war whose hallmark had been its pervasive sense of unreality, its lack of a clear mission. That the public hung on these accounts was not surprising, for here at last seemed incontrovertible evidence of the demonic "Other" depicted in American propaganda. Torture stories offered a glimpse into what *Newsweek* called "the mystery of the enemy"; they justified the war in a way that the abstract threat of the domino principle could not. "This shows how humane and just they are" was one POW's comment. Another confessed that when he was shot down, he wasn't entirely certain what the war was all about. Captivity had erased this uncertainty. "A few years of living with the Communists," he said, "gave me a better understanding of why we were fighting the war." The prison camps became a symbol of the totalitarian society the North Vietnamese allegedly wished to impose on the rest of the country.

Yet though most people did not share Hanoi Jane's outright dis-belief, questions continued to be raised about these torture accounts by dissidents, antiwar activists, and some POWs. They pointed out that the Pentagon's information officers had tended to spotlight the senior officers, who had led the resistance and had the most dramatic stories to tell about captivity, but that this emphasis had to some extent distorted the real picture of camp life. They also suggested that a variety of motives—hatred for their captors, ideological fervor, a desire to enhance their own status among the other prisoners—might have compelled some POWs unconsciously to embellish their stories. For most, however, the authenticity of the stories was less in question than their use to manipulate public sentiment about the war.

By the end of the spring, the façade of unity had broken down. The conflict between the Hanoi hard-liners and the other POWs was forced into the open when charges were filed in June by hard-liner Colonel Theodore Guy against eight enlisted men alleged to have collaborated with the North Vietnamese. The members of this so-called "Peace Committee," all ground troops, were accused of making antiwar statements and refusing to obey orders from senior American prison-ers. Weighing the charges, an editorial in the *Times* suggested that the eight accused men had probably not received enough training to resist their captors and that their views had been radicalized by having seen the horrors of an "unjust" war at first hand. Guy, on the other hand, was described as a "lifer," a "true believer," who had fought the war "from several thousand feet up" and saw it "second-hand."

Ultimately the Pentagon, under pressure from the White House, which did not wish to reopen the divisions of the war, declined to prosecute the men. It was a bitter pill for the Hanoi hard-liners, strengthening their conviction that the country they'd fought for had drifted away from its own ideals. Most who had been tortured attributed their endurance to strict adherence to the military Code of Conduct that lay at the heart of Guy's allegations. This code was a set of rules for POWs that had been drafted by the Pentagon in the mid-1950s, in the wake of widespread charges of collaboration and brainwashing among the several thousand POWs of the Korean War. These rules specified that captured soldiers should divulge only name, rank, and serial number and make no disloyal statements unless tortured. While most POWs admitted that at some point they had been broken, Guy's position was that the eight charged men had given in too soon. But, as the *Times* editorial pointed out, what is too soon when the soldier lacks conviction in his cause?

The affair ended tragically when one of the accused men, Sergeant Larry Kavanaugh, committed suicide at the end of June. Kavanaugh, who faced five charges of collaborating with the enemy, killed himself with a gunshot to the head. His pregnant widow later blamed his death on Guy and the Pentagon and filed a lawsuit against them. It was later reported that eight members of the so-called Peace Committee had earned the animosity of their fellow prisoners by making statements against the war and developing "rather friendly" relations with their captors. All eight had been captured and held in the jungle camps of South Vietnam and only later moved to Hanoi. Lower in rank, they also reflected the greater racial diversity of the ground troops: two of them were black, one part Indian, and one part Chicano. These men attributed their preferential treatment in the Hanoi camp not to opportunism but to the fact that they treated the guards as "human beings" rather than "gooks" or "slopes"—that is, racial inferiors. They expressed little interest in the heroic test of resistance that had defined the hard-liners' captivity.

Perhaps most significantly, these men, who had witnessed or partic-ipated in the killing of civilians and the destruction of villages, had been deeply affected by their combat experiences and had been compelled to reexamine their basic assumptions about the war. In a way that was unthinkable for the career officers, they had abandoned their belief in the war as a just cause and had come to regard it rather as a manifestation of American racism, militarism, and imperialism. Some members of the Peace Committee expressed open admiration for the Vietnamese, and a few had embraced Communism: POW John Young described himself as "grief-stricken" over Ho Chi Minh's death and called himself a Communist after leaving Vietnam; his fellow-POW Robert Chenoweth believed Communism "was the answer to the world's ills." Another made a radio broadcast in which he sent a message to Nixon: "I no longer want to fight for you . . . I can no longer support the killing of innocent Vietnamese men, women, and children or the destruction of their beautiful country." For these men, readjustment had been difficult: Kavanaugh, according to his friends, killed himself after being turned into an "outcast" by Guy's charges; another found himself facing divorce and a custody battle; while Alfonso Riate, the part-Indian, was quoted as saying that he was "appalled" by Nixon and Watergate.

For their part, the officers were scornful of the antiwar convictions of the Peace Committee members, calling them "cowards" and "mercenaries who had sold themselves to the highest bidder." For them, the military Code of Conduct was what set them apart, made them superior to the Vietnamese; to violate the code was to break a sacred contract. "These men," said one, referring to the Peace Committee members, "will be marked for the rest of their lives . . . They weren't Americans, as far as I was concerned." Such views, as one Peace Committee member pointed out, reflected the officers' training and their position in the military chain of command: "A pilot flies around and drops bombs. He doesn't ever see the war, he's not watching people get blown away, he doesn't even know what's happening." Another suggested that "the officers have been subjected to the military mentality for a long time, and if there's such a thing as brainwashing, the military does the best job."

The Manchurian Candidate Syndrome

If the POWs' experience would be used to shape the memory of the Vietnam War, their experience was in turn shaped by the memory of the Korean War, in particular by the performance of U.S. POWs during that conflict. As POW John McCain was to write in an article about his imprisonment that appeared in *U.S. News & World Report* in May 1973, "Remember, a handful of turncoats after the Korean War made a great majority of Americans think that most of the POWs in that conflict were traitors."

This image of the Korean War POW fueled the narrative of one of the great political thrillers of the 1960s. *The Manchurian Candidate*, released in 1962, was a chilling tale of a Korean War hero, Raymond Shaw, who was brainwashed while a POW in North Korea and programmed to become a political assassin under the control of his operators back in the United States. The film used a toxic brew of cold war hysteria, conspiracy theory, Pavlovian mind control, and political assassination to introduce into popular consciousness a figure that film critic J. Hoberman calls the "secret agent of history"—a part for which Lee Harvey Oswald would soon be auditioning. Another ingredient in this sinister concoction was the psycho-sexual drama centered on Raymond's relation with his mother, who, in the final paranoid twist, turns out to be the real mastermind behind the plot, which she has orchestrated in an effort to mobilize a "nation of television viewers into hysteria" and sweep her McCarthy-like husband into power. Shaw, in other words, is the perfect patsy for this plot: he is vulnerable to brainwashing because he has already been "unmanned" by his scheming mother. If the film depicts a world turned upside down, in which Communist agents plot to destroy American democracy and women call the shots for their docile men, in the end the natural order of things is restored: the assassination, scheduled for the 1952 Republican National Convention, is foiled when Shaw guns down his mother and stepfather instead of the designated target.

The Manchurian Candidate derived much of its lurid power from the popular image of the Korean War POW. Close to five thousand

U.S. soldiers had been taken prisoner during that conflict and were subjected to abuse and brainwashing, which had become an instrument in the propaganda war waged by the North Koreans. A few had succumbed by releasing antiwar statements. Although most charges of collaboration were uncorroborated, these few cases were enough to cause profound concern to the military high command. The Pentagon issued its new Code of Conduct in 1955 in response to what it perceived as the shocking vulnerability of U.S. soldiers to Communist mind control techniques. The Vietnam POWs were haunted by this earlier episode; they tended to measure their own performance against that of the Korean War POWs, whose supposedly deplorable performance was blamed by some on a failure of childhood and adolescent training. Charges that America's youth were turning soft would later be replayed in the scapegoating of pediatrician and antiwar activist Benjamin Spock, who was attacked for his permissive attitudes toward child-rearing, which were blamed for discipline problems among Vietnam ground troops.

The new Code of Conduct held POWs to an impossible standard—antiwar POW George Smith called it the "Superman Code"—a standard that even the most hard-line prisoners ultimately could not live up to. POW John Dunn, interviewed in the *Times*, marveled at the discovery of his own limitations: "I found myself doing things that I never thought I would, like making statements against my country. I was sure I was a superman." The "continuous high level of pain" inflicted on him had finally broken him, just as it did the rest. As more than one POW noted, those who refused to give anything more than name, rank, and serial number simply didn't come home. Once "broken," the men were forced to sign antiwar statements and make radio broadcasts. Nonetheless the senior officers continued to refuse any compromise on the code; they clung to it in the belief that it vouchsafed their moral superiority in the face of Communist savagery.

The enduring image of the brainwashed POW was to exercise a powerful spell over the Vietnam prisoners, the military high command, and the American public. Given that all the POWs had eventually been broken to some degree, they feared that they would come in for the

same treatment as the Korean War POWs. Such fears were fueled by a
series of high-profile cases. Probably the most iconic image of a
Vietnam War POW was a widely seen picture—it appeared in 1968
on the cover of *Life*—of Colonel Richard Stratton, who had been shot
down in 1967. Taken at a press conference held in Hanoi, the image
showed a gaunt, stooped figure with a haunted expression on his face,
bowing to his captors. Stratton reportedly confessed to dropping
bombs on heavily populated areas of Hanoi to intimidate the population—a confession that the North Vietnamese claimed backed up
charges that the pilots were war criminals and "air pirates." A media
coup for the North Vietnamese, it was a nightmare for the Pentagon
and spurred a series of charges and countercharges on either side. In
the United States Stratton's statements made him a controversial figure
and generated speculation that he had been brainwashed. Tass, the
Soviet press agency, denied the brainwashing charges and suggested
that Stratton had spoken out of conscience. His wife defended her
husband by saying it was obviously a staged performance. Interviewed
following his return home, Stratton explained that he had acted
drugged to discredit his own statements.

No such excuses could be made in the case of George Smith, whose
memoir *POW: Two Years with the Vietcong*, published by the antiwar
Ramparts Press in 1971, would earn him the title of "the most pro-VC
of all POWs." Smith, who had returned home in 1965, had already
found notoriety when, while still a prisoner, he made statements
critical of "U.S. imperialist aggression." Marine Corps officials at
the time stated their belief that Smith had been brainwashed, and
Newsweek had queried, "If it wasn't brainwashing then what was it?"
Smith's memoir confronted the brainwashing charge in the following
fashion: "I recalled the stories I'd heard about Korea—the Manchurian Candidate scene where they hypnotize you, or drop water on your
head, or . . . something that will drive you out of your mind." The
reality had been far more benign: "Sitting in the shade, listening to a
guy talk while drinking tea—was this brainwashing?" What had been
communicated to Smith in the course of these sessions was a history
lesson on Vietnam, a kind of deprogramming aimed at the version of

the story that had been drummed into him in Special Forces training at the army's Fort Bragg, which turned out to be a "hate program" designed to make him despise the Vietcong. Smith felt compelled to reexamine the narrative that he had entered the war with and to recognize that the Vietcong (unlike the American allies in South Vietnam) really did believe in what they were fighting for. "They weren't," he said, "just being forced."

A still more extreme case was that of Robert Garwood, the one documented instance of a POW who was not repatriated in Operation Homecoming. Garwood had gone native, becoming a notorious figure in the jungle camps, where the Vietcong had employed him as a guard. He did not return to the States until 1979, when he faced trial on charges of treason. His lawyer defended him as having been brainwashed while the prosecution scapegoated him for the U.S. defeat. The Garwood case raised more sharply than any other the questions posed by Guy's charges: could antiwar feelings and sympathy with Communist ideology be sincerely held convictions, or were they merely a self-serving means of gaining preferential treatment? Or were they the product of brainwashing?

As Smith's memoir implied, adherence to the code functioned to keep at bay a fundamental anxiety that any contact with the enemy—whom American soldiers were conditioned in basic training to see in stereotyped terms as Asiatic Communists—might result in ideological contamination. One of the hard-liners expressed this characteristically in saying that he feared for his mind: "Would it be so twisted that I would become a Communist . . . or a vegetable?" The senior officers described the resistance methods they practiced as a form of "reverse brainwashing." In a camp system in which status was determined both by one's rank and by the degree of punishment one had endured, everything hinged on the degree to which one resisted before breaking. The hard-liners took pride in holding out, indeed—some speculated—in provoking their captors to greater acts of brutality. They seemed to welcome the test of wills. Among the ground troops, on the other hand, adherence to the code came to be seen as a pointless form of heroism, rooted in blind obedience to military hierarchy and to rigid ideals of masculinity.

This secondary anxiety concerning masculinity can be detected in the tendency among many of the POWs to label their prison guards homosexuals. The sadism of the camp guards, they believed, was tinged with sexual perversion. Among the POWs it was an article of faith that "90% of [the North Vietnamese] are perverts, 5% are homosexuals, and the rest are no-good bastards." A few of the POWs made allegations that they had suffered homosexual attacks in the camps. If being broken was a test of wills, it was also a test of masculinity; charges of homosexuality represented a defense against the experience of emasculation associated with torture and imprisonment. Given the well-documented extent to which many servicemen in Vietnam were under the sway of the "John Wayne thing"—defined by Yale psychiatrist Robert Jay Lifton as a "constellation of masculine attitudes founded on being tough and tight-lipped"—being "broken," or spilling secrets, was an experience fraught with psycho-sexual consequences.

In reality, there was little evidence that the North Vietnamese were interested in *Manchurian Candidate*–style mind control. They were far more interested in shaping public opinion back in the States through that quintessentially American form of mind control, television. The North Vietnamese recognized the supreme value of propaganda to their effort. As one prison official told Stockdale: "Our country has not the capability to defeat you on the battlefield. But war is decided not by weapons so much as by national will. Once the American people understand this war, they will have no interest in pursuing it. They will be made to understand this. We will win this war on the streets of New York." For the most part they were indifferent to what the prisoners themselves actually thought as long as they could extract taped confessions from them for propaganda purposes. When they tortured POWs, it was not to seize control of their minds but to force them to appear on television.

The Americans, on the other hand, remained haunted by the specter of the Manchurian Candidate. Between the two camps in the POW community, charges of brainwashing were flung back and forth: the hard-liners accused the Peace Committee of succumbing to Communist mind-control techniques, while the Peace Committee members replied that the officers had been brainwashed by the military mentality. To put an end to the finger pointing, the Pentagon decided against pressing charges.

The Cult of the POWs

To Americans at home, the returning POWs—especially those shot down before the traumatic events of 1968—seemed like men stuck in a time warp, whose attitudes reflected those of a consensus that had been shattered by the virtual civil war at home. Yet precisely those values that they had clung to in prison but that had been discredited at home made them attractive to those who saw them as exemplary figures around whom to reconstruct the old myths of American virtue.

That the POWs had long before their homecoming become, in the words of journalist Jonathan Schell, "the objects of a virtual cult" was no spontaneous phenomenon. It was part of an orchestrated campaign set in motion several years previously that came to fruition with the negotiated settlement of 1973. Yet the terms accepted by Nixon in 1973 were virtually identical to those he'd rejected in 1969. What had changed? In the interim the POW issue had moved to center stage, becoming so decisive in American attitudes toward the war that it provided Nixon and Kissinger with the cover they needed to turn defeat into the symbolic victory couched in the phrase "peace with honor."

The roots of the POW issue went back to 1968 and the North Vietnamese Tet offensive of that year, which shattered the U.S. military's optimistic projections of success and the public image of American invincibility. This offensive utterly transformed the political landscape: in its wake, Johnson bowed out of the presidential race, and—following Bobby Kennedy's assassination that summer—the door was opened to the election of Richard Nixon, whose political career had been written off following his defeat to Kennedy's brother in 1960. But Nixon came to power amid very difficult circumstances: the Tet offensive had exposed the hollowness of General William Westmoreland's promises of imminent victory, while the revelations of the My Lai massacre had exposed the breakdown of troop morale and driven increasing numbers of Americans into the antiwar camp. Despite having campaigned as a candidate who would bring peace, Nixon had no wish to go down in history as the first American president to lose a war.

It was amid these circumstances that the POW issue was born as a way of redefining the war and driving a wedge between the liberal and radical wings of the antiwar movement. Almost as soon as he came to power Nixon had his representatives at the Paris peace talks, which Johnson had initiated in the spring of 1968, introduce the POW issue into the negotiations, with the stipulation that no further progress could be made until the POWs were handed over. When the North Vietnamese responded by tying negotiations over the status of the POWs to an American timetable for withdrawal, the administration cried foul, claiming that their opponents were holding the POWs as "hostages." While there was no precedent for this in the annals of military history, the stratagem was highly successful, allowing Nixon to infuse a deeply unpopular conflict with a new sense of moral purpose and, not incidentally, to stalemate the peace talks for four more years. In the end, despite the opening up of new fronts in Laos and Cambodia and the deaths of twenty thousand more American servicemen as well as hundreds of thousands of Indochinese, nothing changed militarily, but the transformation of the war into a symbolic battle allowed Nixon to camouflage America's virtual capitulation behind the smokescreen of a settlement that brought "peace with honor."

So successful was this strategy that by 1972, according to Jonathan Schell, "many people were persuaded that the U.S. was fighting in Vietnam to get its prisoners back." "Following the President's lead," wrote Schell, "people began to speak as though the North Vietnamese had kidnapped 400 Americans and the U.S. had gone to war to retrieve them." This collective delusion would be fueled by events such as the Son Tay rescue attempt of 1970, in which American Green Berets staged a helicopter raid on a prison camp in North Vietnam. The raid was a failure; the camp turned out to have been empty for four months, sparking criticism that military intelligence was inadequate or, more conspiratorially, that it had known the camp was empty and the raid had been a pseudo-event staged to make Nixon look tough. Legitimate or not, the raid fired Americans' imagination and later inspired a genre of POW rescue films, typified by *Rambo: First Blood II,* that became hugely popular during the Reaganite revisionism of the 1980s.

By 1970 the transformation of the POWs into heroes was well under way. The cult of remembrance, mourning, and celebration that developed around them and, later, their still missing comrades-in-arms the MIAs, was promoted by various interest groups, most of them unabashedly prowar. One such group was VIVA, based in southern California, formed to oppose campus antiwar movements. In 1969 the founders of VIVA, acting on a suggestion made by Robert Dornan, a colorful local TV personality, gave birth to the POW bracelets that became ubiquitous in the early 1970s. Each was inscribed with the name of a prisoner; by the end of the war an estimated 10 million Americans were wearing them. The cause of the POWs was championed by many public figures, among them Texas multimillionaire Ross Perot and California governor Ronald Reagan, who had been active in POW causes since playing one in the 1954 Korean War film *P.O.W.* Meanwhile, a group of POW wives formed the National League of Families to rally support for their husbands.

It was against this backdrop that Operation Homecoming, which turned what in previous wars had simply been a footnote to the cessation of hostilities into the peace accords' central achievement, acquired its value as an event of high drama. The POW issue, in effect, put a human face on a conflict whose original rationale had long since been lost. The fact that men had still been fighting and dying on the front was almost obscured by the furor surrounding the POWs; upon their final return, as *Newsweek* put it in a statement that perhaps unwittingly echoed the administration's goal, it was almost possible "amid the cheers and tears of joy . . . for a moment to forget the 45,943 other Americans who had lost their lives in Vietnam and 1,334 more who are still listed as missing and unaccounted for"—to say nothing of the more than two hundred thousand soldiers in VA hospitals.

For Nixon himself the returning men were a godsend—the most effective possible response to the "treachery" on the home front exemplified by the likes of Hanoi Jane and by Daniel Ellsberg's leaking to the press of the Pentagon Papers, which exposed the elaborate deceptions that three administrations had woven around the war. With an outlook still firmly rooted in a time when the "credibility gap" had not yet become a national institution, the overwhelming majority of the POWs were solidly in his camp, supporting him personally and his policies in Indochina unconditionally. To critics like columnist Garry Wills, who following the 1972 election had written that "Vietnam is the shared crime that has turned our country into . . . a pact of blood," the POWs held up the war as a noble cause and refused to express any qualms about the use of tactics questionable from either a military or a moral standpoint; many of them, for instance, reported cheering during the Christmas bombing. Moreover, they agreed with Nixon that the antiwar movement was a symptom of moral decay on the home front.

Anxious to deflect attention from the real meaning of the peace settlement as from the Watergate scandal that was enveloping the White House, Nixon seized every opportunity to associate himself with the POWs. He basked in public statements of gratitude from the men and repeatedly praised their selfless heroism and loyalty. Striking a note of benevolent paternalism, he told a reporter: "I was happy to bring the boys home." This culminated in an event hosted at the White House on May 24, 1973, with more than six hundred former POWs and their wives and dates in attendance. Described in the media as the largest and most spectacular White House gala ever, the event turned into an orgy of patriotism: the guests cheered wildly at Nixon's every word, and Nixon lashed out at critics of his policies. Things got under way at the State Department that afternoon, where the president addressed the POWs on the theme of national security. While the wives had tea with Pat elsewhere, the atmosphere "quickly settled into one of camaraderie between the servicemen and the president who had negotiated their release." In a reference to the Ellsberg trial that two weeks earlier had ended in acquittal, Nixon said it was time to stop "making national heroes out of those who steal secrets and publish them in newspapers"; the guests rewarded him with a fifteen-minute standing ovation. The implication was clear: true heroes trusted unwaveringly in the word of their commander-in-chief and the government he ran. Later that evening at the White House, with Sammy Davis Jr. and John Wayne in attendance, Nixon toasted the men and led a chorus of "The POW Hymn."

Still, given the bombshell revelations enveloping Nixon's presidency, the camaraderie had a somewhat forced quality. Against the backdrop created by the administration's efforts to contain the fallout from these revelations, the president's behavior seemed increasingly at odds with reality; news accounts described Nixon as strangely giddy, noting that he insisted on shaking the hand of every man, in some cases holding the handshake for several minutes. Rallying the men around the national security flag, he turned the event into an occasion to reconstitute the sacred bonds uniting a commander-in-chief with his soldiers; the exclusion of women, together with condemnation of those who could not keep secrets, was highly symbolic. .

It was not by chance that Nixon's efforts to enlist the POWs in his project of recasting the Vietnam War stressed the heroism of men in captivity. The cult of the POWs was rooted deep in one of the foundational myths of American culture: the captivity narrative of the frontier. Originating in the early history of the colonies, this narrative, as Richard Slotkin has written in *Gunfighter Nation*, was a central feature of the conflict enacted between settlers and Indians. Recorded in memoirs and novels, it told of the kidnapping of white settlers, usually women, by Indians. These accounts were always exemplary and deeply moral, speaking of redemption through faith and, foreshadowing the nineteenth-century doctrine of manifest destiny, the regenerative value of violence and the role of the frontier in helping American society periodically purge itself of moral decay. With its tale of righteous suffering, the captivity narrative confirmed the Puritans' sense of themselves as members of a spiritual elect.

The extent to which the war in Vietnam was already experienced and framed in terms of the mythic past was made clear, as Frances Fitzgerald wrote, by the tendency of American soldiers to refer to

Vietnam as "Indian country," thus "putting the war into a definite historical and mythological perspective," in which "the Americans were once again embarked upon a heroic (and for themselves) almost painless conquest of an inferior race." Casting the Vietnamese as Indians and themselves as warriors in the John Wayne mold, American soldiers saw Indochina as a new version of the frontier. Yet when this latest version of America's manifest destiny was transformed into a quagmire, it became necessary to reframe the war around the captivity narrative. The pilot fraternity was especially well cast for this role, insofar as it embodied a characteristically American obsession with technology that was invested with a conviction of moral and cultural superiority.

The ideological function served by the cult of the POWs could be seen in the contrast between Nixon's embrace of them and his distaste for the antiwar veterans. For all their suffering, the POWs seemed, according to most observers, surprisingly unscarred by the war relative to most veterans—their psyches and their faith in institutions, most especially the office of the president, remained relatively intact, their politics unradicalized. Shorn of the long hair and beards that had become trademarks of the antiwar vet, they looked eminently the part of the soldier. As such they served as a welcome antidote to the endless dispiriting images of demonstrations, jobless veterans, drug abuse, divorce or spousal betrayal, and mental illness that had come to define the home front. No account of the actions of antiwar vets failed to include an obligatory description of the beards, long hair, field jackets, and blue jeans worn by these men, even if it then went on to cover the very real problems faced by vets or to castigate the administration's insensitivity to their hardships. By the end of March 1973 over 15 percent of the 250,000 vets in the New York City area were unemployed and 7,500 were on public assistance. Many returning soldiers also faced problems of drug addiction and post-traumatic stress-related disorders.

Despite the Nixon administration's efforts to depict antiwar veterans as a disgruntled minority, their movement was by no means marginal. By the war's end, more than one million men were listed

as deserters, and individual and collective acts of resistance and mutiny
were seriously compromising the American war effort. Surveys found
that anywhere from 60 to 75 percent of enlisted men were opposed to
the war. Amid such circumstances it was hardly surprising that vets
resented the celebrations accorded the POWs and questioned the way
the prisoners' ordeals were being exploited for the purpose of falsifying
history. What to some Americans looked like heroic resistance under
extreme conditions looked to many vets like simply another expression
of the by-the-book militaristic creed that had gotten the nation into the
Vietnam War in the first place. Where one stood on this question
depended on one's view of the war itself: was it justifiable intervention
in a part of the world threatened by the domino principle? an
unjustifiable intervention in a civil war? an imperialist adventure?

On this fundamental question, the simple realities of the U.S. war
effort had begun to play a decisive role. As America's military
commitment in Vietnam grew, increasing reliance on draftees had
replicated within the military itself the cultural divide that the war had
opened up in American society—a divide that had led, in New York
City, to pitched battles between antiwar and prowar demonstrators
and, at Kent State University, the shooting deaths of four students at
the hands of the National Guard. Antiwar sentiment permeated the
armed forces both in Vietnam and back home. Troop opposition took
many forms: peace symbols, letters, petitions, or drug abuse. More
overt acts of rebellion ranged from going AWOL to sabotage to
injuring and even killing officers ("fragging"). During the last year
of the war such resistance culminated in open mutinies on board
several of the aircraft carriers from which the air war was conducted.
Several pilots refused to participate in the Christmas bombings.

In the face of this opposition, Nixon took consolation from the
loyalty of the released prisoners, using their stories to marginalize
opposition voices and particularly outspoken dissenters as unbalanced,
under the sway of alien forces, or brainwashed. Once it was established
in the media, the iconic image of the POW would come to play an
important role in the emergence of a revisionist history of the war as a
just cause fought by warriors who had been "stabbed in the back" by

treachery on the home front: the media, antiwar activists, bureaucrats, unfaithful wives. Indeed, in its attempt to assign blame for the war's outcome, the administration routinely invoked the "breakdown" of the home front. In addition to re-ennobling the war, Operation Homecoming was thus also about resanctifying the home front: "The ceremonies of greeting which attended the return of the POWs in 1973 constituted the *only* large-scale public celebration for troops returning from the war, the closest thing to a postwar victory parade that Vietnam veterans would enjoy—an irony that other veterans noted with some bitterness." Their repatriation, claimed as a symbolic victory, represented a pseudo-event of the highest order, a manifestation of what Slotkin calls the war's "lunatic semiology," in which "sign and referent have scarcely any proportionate relation at all."

To be sure, many dissented from the cult of the POWs, as they had from the war itself. One important voice in challenging the administration's version of the POW story was that of noted Yale psychiatrist and antiwar activist Robert Jay Lifton. In a *Times* opinion piece published on March 28, Lifton analyzed the public interest lavished on the POWs as symptomatic of Americans' desperation for heroes. But he warned that

> the carefully manipulated spectacle through which the Administration, the military and the media (especially television) are synthesizing a hero myth falsifies not only the relationship of the returning prisoner to the war but, above all, the war itself. All but swept away is the role we assigned these men: saturation bombings of civilian areas with minimal military targets.

The extraordinary reception accorded the returning POWs, in Lifton's view, had to be understood in the context of the trauma inflicted on the national psyche by Vietnam. He spelled this out in his book *Home from the War* (1973), which examined the war's psychological effects on soldiers: "In matters of war and destiny, Americans have always felt themselves to be a blessed or chosen people." This was especially true in the decades after 1945, when an era of "extraordinary American technological and military superiority" had fostered fantasies of omnipotence. Among the vets he worked with, Lifton found that such fantasies were deeply ingrained; many seemed to be in the grip of popular versions of warrior myths associated with the figures of John Wayne or Second World War hero Audie Murphy. Lifton, who had earlier worked with Korean War POWs and written on Chinese methods of "thought reform," now argued that American soldiers were essentially programmed for violence. In making this argument he was able to draw on reportage from Vietnam suggesting that many soldiers seemed to be reenacting filmic scenarios. Lieutenant William Calley, who would be court-martialed for his part in the My Lai massacre, recalled his desire to enlist in the following terms: "We thought, we will go to Vietnam and be Audie Murphy. Kick in the door, run in the hooch, give it a big burst-kill, and get a big kill ratio in Vietnam." War correspondent Michael Herr would note the prevalence of similar fantasies among what he called "media freak grunts" who made war movies in their heads and performed for the television cameras they knew were nearby.

These fantasies, according to Lifton, had been shattered in Indochina, leaving the nation to confront some difficult questions. Who or what would fill the "psychohistorical void left by the demise of the traditional cult of the warrior?" "Is there still room for the gung-ho pilot who, in defying death and gravity, recreates the image of the WWII style immortal pilot-hero?" The cult of the POWs, Lifton felt, represented an effort to salvage something of that lost sense of heroism and omnipotence. More than that, it represented a desire to find amid the war's aftermath some remnants of an older image of Americans as a chosen people—to transform the POWs and their captivity narratives into the central figures of a new spiritual elect, reborn, phoenix-like, from the ashes of the war.

The Vietnam Syndrome

Speaking of the ceremonies surrounding Operation Homecoming, one vet observed: "There is no sense of an ending. Usually a war—or anything—is supposed to have a beginning, a middle, and an end . . . This is a false ending." The concern voiced here was not misplaced, for this war, which had already gone on longer than any other war in American history, from 1965 to 1973—or, by some accounts, 1954 to 1973—simply refused to end. Unable to come to terms with what had happened in Vietnam, Americans clung to Nixon's strategy for snatching victory from the jaws of defeat: the reframing of the war around the dramatic captivity ordeal of the POWs, who put a heroic face on a conflict that had become stripped of all higher moral purpose, had obscenely fetishized "body counts" and "kill ratios," and had bombarded the home audience with stark images of body bags and antiwar protests.

Defying the usual narrative conventions governing war, the Vietnam War would continue to be refought on symbolic terrain for years. One indication of things to come occurred in a brief ceremony held in New York's City Hall Park in February 1973, in which members of VIVA planted a crabapple tree as a tribute to the POWs but also to men still missing in action (MIAs). The group promised that they would continue publicizing their cause until all thirteen hundred men still missing in Indochina had been accounted for. VIVA also ran ads in national papers, exhorting Americans to keep the faith: "Don't take off your bracelet! There is more you must do!"

Operation Homecoming, it turned out, was not the end of engagement in Indochina. Far from it: the conviction that hundreds, if not thousands, of Americans were still being held prisoner in Laos became an article of faith in American politics and culture well into the 1990s. Large sectors of the American public clung to this belief, actively encouraged by leading politicians such as Ronald Reagan and Ross Perot, who ritually invoked the suffering and heroism of the POWs and MIAs in their speeches. Around a core of genuine tragedy, an elaborate collective fantasy was constructed, a "fantasy so potent," in the words of one scholar, that it became "virtually a national religion." Indeed, in 1989 POW activist-turned-congressman Robert Dornan would claim of the POW/MIA bracelet that its recognizability as a symbol was "second only to religious symbols such as the cross or Star of David." And a poll conducted by the *Wall Street Journal* in 1991 found that 69 percent of Americans believed POWs were still being held in Indochina.

This belief gained a tremendous purchase in post-Vietnam films. Though Hollywood treated Vietnam gingerly at first, the war's refusal to end would spawn both a new genre of war movies and a new iconography of the veteran as a ticking time bomb. While in Martin Scorcese's *Mean Streets* (1973) a troubled vet makes only a brief appearance at a party, in his *Taxi Driver* (1976) the figure of the war-haunted vet moved to center stage. Travis Bickle, the movie's protagonist, is introduced in the first scene as a former marine who received an honorable discharge in May 1973. Unable to sleep at night, Travis takes a job driving taxis, charting a course through the hallucinatory nighttime cityscape of New York. Following his perceived betrayal by a female campaign worker—"Women," he laments, "are like a union"—he begins to arm himself. Then, following an aborted assassination attempt on a presidential candidate, the movie switches gears and turns into a captivity narrative, with Travis finally rescuing a twelve-year-old prostitute from her pimp in a blaze of gunfire.

John Frankenheimer's *Black Sunday* directly updates the paranoid scenario of his own *The Manchurian Candidate* to the post-Vietnam world. The movie is a thriller about an attempt by Arab terrorists to smash a bomb-laden Goodyear blimp into a Super Bowl crowd that includes the president. The pilot who has been recruited for this plot is an embittered American who spent six years as a POW in North Vietnam. Upon his release he was court-martialed on charges of collaboration and then divorced by his wife, who'd been warned by a navy officer about the high rate of homosexuality and impotence among the POWs. Like *The Manchurian Candidate*'s antihero, this POW is depicted as a man utterly dependent on a female controller—in this case, the terrorist in charge of the operation, who, we are told, joined Black September in 1973, and who is probably modeled on Palestinian hijacker Leila Khaled. The plan calls for them to become suicide bombers. "When we set off the big one," he tells her, "we're both going with it." The plan is only foiled at the last minute by agents of Israel's Mossad, who have taken over the operation from their ineffectual American counterparts.

Not until the 1978 Oscar-winning *The Deer Hunter* was the war itself depicted onscreen in a major Hollywood motion picture—and in that film, not coincidentally, the central focus is POWs. The film concerns three boyhood friends who wind up in one of the South Vietnamese jungle camps, administered by sadistic Vietcong who force them to play Russian roulette, a highly dramatic device that, however, lacks any basis in historical reality. While two manage to make it home, the third disappears into the chaos of postwar Vietnam. When his closest friend returns to Saigon, he eventually locates him playing Russian roulette in a gambling den, a zombie programmed for self-destruction. Though the assassin's gun here is directed against the self, the film shares certain themes with *The Manchurian Candidate*, among them that of virtuous American youth controlled by sadistic Asiatics to destructive purposes. *The Deer Hunter*, as historian Bruce Franklin has written, marks a key moment in the revisionist account of the war: by transforming Americans from perpetrators into victims, the film played a crucial role in rewriting it as a story of trauma inflicted on America.

The POW/MIA myth would continue working its way through the nation's cultural bloodstream during the 1980s, reaching its apotheosis in a new genre of payback movies typified by the Rambo series. These films offered a cinematic corollary to POW James Stockdale's damning judgment, directed not so much at the war itself but at the way it had been conducted, that it represented a "misguided experiment in rational game theory." In them a warrior ethos unencumbered by technocratic fantasies or liberal guilt is pitted against the enemy who must be defeated in order to track down and bring home POWs. The paranoia in these turgid, superheated movies has become global: in addition to fighting the Vietcong, the hero must combat treacherous Washington bureaucrats and women, all of whom conspire to undermine the mission. The hero inhabits a world from which softness, doubt, and dissent must be purged, a world in which women are not allowed to intrude; those who do, to advance the plot in some minor fashion, must be swiftly dispatched. Prison camp commanders are usually depicted as dandified or strangely foppish figures whose extreme pleasure in inflicting pain is linked to a suspect masculinity.

The Rambo series, as one commentator has observed, is about taking back all the symbolic territory that had been lost in the late 1960s and 1970s. It distills the intense pathos surrounding the theme of homecoming in so many of the Vietnam War films into its purest form. Yet while the films offered the consolation of a victory over all enemies, that victory came at a high price: the homecoming that is their ostensible purpose can never be shown; "homecoming" as such has been stripped of its transcendent value by the treachery on the domestic front as well as by the impossibility of relations between men and women. For Rambo himself, there is no longer even any question of going home; publicity for *Rambo: First Blood II* used the line: "What you call hell, he calls home."

In more ways than one, the POW myth that became such a central preoccupation of post-Vietnam culture and politics turned out to be an unstable one. If defeat in Vietnam had, according to Lifton, cast this "chosen people" out of its homeland, the central conceit of the POW films was the promise of a homecoming. Yet these films, which are populated by men condemned to a traumatic or perpetually deferred return, to exile and homelessness, suggest that the homecoming experience ultimately failed to follow the script written for it (whether by the Pentagon, by the senior officers, or by Hollywood). In the end, the rhetorical claim of "peace with honor" and the elaborate machinery of Operation Homecoming could only partially compensate for the deep psychic shock waves sent through America by the spectacle of defeat in the world's first televised war. The resentment at defeat nourished itself in a variety of ways: in the false memories of Hollywood films, in the collective fantasy of unredeemed MIAs, and in the pseudo-histories of revisionist scholars.

It also became a defining feature of American politics. When in the early 1980s Ronald Reagan invoked for the first time the "Vietnam syndrome," he meant the sense of neurotic, and quite un-American, self-doubt that defeat had inflicted on the nation's sense of collective purpose, the reluctance to project its military power abroad. Coming to office at the close of a decade that had begun with American POWs languishing in prisons in Vietnam and that ended with the Iranian hostage crisis, Reagan interpreted his election as a mandate to restore American power. This meant both keeping faith with the POWs, who he celebrated for giving "America back its soul," and invoking Rambo as a symbol of a newly muscular foreign policy. Yet subsequent American military undertakings up to and including the two Gulf Wars continue to be shadowed by the Vietnam syndrome, notwithstanding the claims of various presidents (including the first Bush) that this syndrome had finally been exorcised. As late as November 2003, amid fears that the war in Iraq had enmired America in a new quagmire, Senator John McCain stated in a speech that the first Gulf War had not ended "the hold of the Vietnam syndrome over our national consciousness."

Former POW McCain was in a position to speak with some authority on this subject. As he had discovered in trying to bring some closure to the revenge fantasies acted out in the Rambo films, those who went against the grain of these fantasies found themselves excoriated by MIA activists. After the Senate commission headed by John McCain and John Kerry found in 1992 that there was no credible evidence of any POWs still being held—a decision that paved the way for normalization of relations between the United States and Vietnam—McCain was smeared by far-right activist Ted Sampley as a "Manchurian Candidate" who had fabricated his account of being tortured while a Hanoi POW. This charge resurfaced following McCain's surprise victory over George W. Bush in the 2000 New Hampshire primary.

In the buildup to the 2004 elections, Sampley raised similar questions about John Kerry's war record, referring to him as a phony war hero, calling him "Hanoi John" and raising questions as to his whereabouts at a Vietnam Veterans Against the War meeting at which the assassination of U.S. congressmen was discussed. Such charges attest to the inflationary value of the Manchurian Candidate label, a label that can be attached to anyone, like Kerry, whose service in

Vietnam brought about a fundamental questioning of the ends and means of American power. They also attest to the persistence of a profound cultural anxiety about the psychological legacy of the war in Indochina.

The Vietnam syndrome is in this sense both a cultural and a clinical condition, one whose origins may be traced to the "huge collective nervous breakdown" that, according to Michael Herr, the United States suffered during the Tet offensive in 1968. The legacy of this breakdown was a profound anxiety about the fragility of the American body politic, one that played itself out symbolically in the panic about brainwashing as well as in the flashbacks, traumatic memories, and other symptoms that became the hallmarks of the popular image of the Vietnam vet. These symptoms would in turn become features of the many distortions to which the historical record was subjected. Sampley would go so far as to allege that Kerry's campaign had been endorsed by North Korea, and he was also implicated in a rather crude attempt to implant cultural memories by doctoring a photograph purporting to show Kerry alongside Jane Fonda—whose notorious visit to the Hanoi Hilton in 1972 made her for many in the POW/MIA camp the symbol of treachery on the home front.

Charges that a candidate might be a fifth columnist, however, also ran in the other direction. The Jonathan Demme remake of *The Manchurian Candidate*, released in the summer of 2004 at the height of the presidential contest, updated the original scenario by making its protagonist a POW of the first Gulf War, thus inviting parallels to the current conflict. According to one account, the parallels were deliberate: Sherry Lansing, head of Paramount and a major Kerry fundraiser, evidently saw the film, which includes a portrait of a fearmongering right-wing politician in thrall to a global conglomerate reminiscent of Halliburton, as a way to inflict damage on Bush.

With the 2004 election playing itself out as a referendum on the ends and means of American military engagement abroad, both past and present, Kerry's record of service followed by antiwar activism proved no match for a president elevated by the *New York Daily News* to Rambo-like status. This despite the fact that Bush avoided active duty and despite the many questions that surfaced during the campaign about his so-called "lost year" during 1972 and 1973, when he mysteriously left the National Guard to work on the political campaign of a family friend. Ironically, Bush's record of avoiding active service in Vietnam may have served him well in this regard; having had no firsthand experience of combat, his traditional cold war views on the conflict in Indochina were never subjected to reexamination. Kerry, plagued by his own "Vietnam syndrome," was reduced to a series of verbal gaffes on Iraq that left him open to charges of indecisiveness, while at the same time he had to fend off charges made by the group Swift Boat Veterans for Truth about his own record of service in Indochina. Bush, on the other hand, unscarred by the effects of Herr's "collective nervous breakdown," continued to project an air of serene conviction about the rightness of American involvement in Iraq even in the face of growing public doubts.

The continuing prevalence of myth, false memory, and fantasy in representations of the Vietnam War finally suggests the extent to which Americans experienced the war as a fundamental rupture in their history, indeed as a kind of crisis in the very fabric of history itself. Perhaps for this reason the post-Vietnam period has often been taken as marking the onset of a new era or sensibility. One of its hallmarks is a crisis of the ability to think historically; another, the sense that the era of Western domination is over. As Edward Said, writing about Joseph Conrad's *Heart of Darkness*—the novel that provided the template for the most ambitious of all Vietnam war films, Francis Ford Coppola's *Apocalypse Now*—has said, "There is nothing to look forward to: we are stuck within our circle." This sense of history as cyclical is, as Frances Fitzgerald notes, a particularly apt image for the historical sensibility of the civilization America encountered in Indochina. The Vietnamese vision of history, she writes, is one that, unlike its American counterpart, which is linear and progressive, sees history in cyclical terms, as part of a pattern of growth and decay. Perhaps the lingering trauma of the Vietnam syndrome lies precisely in America's confrontation with this other image of history.

Personality Crisis

You're a prima ballerina on a spring afternoon
Change into a wolf-man howling at the moon

—New York Dolls, "Personality Crisis"

I wanted to see what everyone was throwing up about.

—Ticket-buyer to *The Exorcist*

MARCH 5, 1973: *A New York Times article relates the story of Daniel Voll, a young member of a religious sect based in New York, whose parents had tried to abduct him in order to get him away from the sect. The abduction had gone wrong and Voll had filed assault charges. A key actor in the story is Ted Patrick, self-described "father of deprogramming," who claimed to have personally helped deprogram 112 young people.*

One of the main storylines that emerged from the sixties held that America was engaged in a struggle for the soul of its youth. During that decade American youth had emerged as a new historical force, virtually a nation unto itself, with its own political and cultural agenda. Democratic presidential candidate George McGovern's 1972 defeat, however, left much of this agenda in tatters and marked the definitive end of the sixties. Now, with possibilities for political change seemingly blocked, many young people were turning to increasingly esoteric forms of personal change; the results are amusingly chronicled in Tom Wolfe's essay on the Me Decade.

But the Me Decade had its dark side as well. By 1973 a new paranoia was taking hold of the national mind, which imagined itself beset on all sides by drugs, cults, conspiracies, and other forces that threatened the moral and psychological well-being of the citizens of the republic. The old paradigms of youthful rebellion were taking an increasingly extreme form. In stories such as Daniel Voll's, an earlier phase of generational conflict was overlaid by a new, more sinister element: America's youth were not deliberately choosing to rebel; rather, they were innocents brainwashed into hating their parents, youths in the grip of some bizarre new demonology or personality affliction. From the best-selling novel *Sybil*, a real-life drama about a girl with sixteen personalities, to the blockbuster film *The Exorcist*, with its portrait of a vomit-spewing, demon-possessed prepubescent girl, to heiress Patty Hearst's conversion into gun-toting radical, American youth was perceived as under assault, alarmingly fragile, in need of increasingly extreme forms of intervention. A host of experts emerged to do battle with the inner demons that had been unleashed in the American psyche, armed with an array of new medications such as lithium and Ritalin, with new therapies, with strict brands of religious fundamentalism, and with methods such as those employed by deprogrammer Ted Patrick.

Me and Them

For better or worse, Tom Wolfe has arguably stamped the memory of the seventies more than any other single figure with his definition of that period as the Me Decade, an era marked, in contrast to the previous decade, by the advent of a new concern with personal rather than political transformation. Wolfe's essay on the Me Decade begins with a description of a quintessentially seventies scene: an est encounter group, led by a trainer who urges his audience to "let go" of the inarticulate tensions, frustrations, and resentments bottled up inside themselves. The participants are prodded on to their cathartic moment, to let it all out: "They even provided vomit bags, like the ones on a 747, in case you literally let it *gush out*!" The backstory to such moments was the affluence of the postwar years. "The saga of the Me Decade," Wolfe wrote, "begins with the thirty-year boom. Wartime spending in the United States in the 1940s touched off a boom that has continued for more than thirty years. It has pumped money into every class level of the population on a scale without parallel in any country in history." The crash-landing of the seventies, however, left Americans "shell-shocked and disillusioned" and turning inward, in search of the purely personal "alchemical dream" of changing one's personality. The survivors of this crash landing became easy prey for cults and sects of all kinds that sprang up all over the country: the Jesus freaks, the Moonies, the flying saucer cults, the sex cults, est—all of which, in attempting to satisfy the inchoate yearnings created by the sixties—also (and significantly, in Wolfe's mind) gratified people's need to talk about themselves. In the seventies everyone aspired to become the star of his own movie.

What Wolfe failed to note, however, were the paranoiac undertones of this new narcissism. The Me Decade was also the Them Decade. Most of the new cults defined themselves in opposition to the belief-systems and norms of American society at large. In the most extreme cases, membership in them entailed the rejection of the external world and the severing of all ties—familial, financial, professional—with that world. This was the precondition to what authors Flo Conway and Jim Siegelman have called "America's epidemic of sudden personality change" that took off in the early seventies. While the appeal of the new sects varied widely, membership in many of them was marked by a common experience that Conway and Siegelman define as *snapping*: the sudden and complete transformation of the self under the pressure of the teachings, techniques, and charismatic leaders associated with these new groups. Controversy swirled around these groups: to defenders, the demands of membership were simply the price of loyalty to the "higher truth" common to all religions; to critics, these pseudo-religions practiced brainwashing and "on-the-spot hypnosis" to destroy their followers' personalities and make them blindly obedient to the cult. To Conway and Siegelman, the results were an unequivocal disaster that pointed straight to the violent dead ends of the Manson family, the Symbionese Liberation Army, and the Jonestown massacre. In this gallery of madness, ur–cult leader Charles Manson was Exhibit A, a man who strove to undo the conditioning that parents, schools, and society had instilled in his followers (most of them young women) and reprogram them for the purpose of igniting the race war that he had dubbed "Helter Skelter."

To Siegelman and Conway, the continuing allure of cults and religious sects throughout the 1970s was a symptom of a deeper crisis in the mental health of postsixties America. In the final analysis, they sought to connect the phenomenon of snapping to underlying shifts in the organization of American capitalism. It was a response to the dislocations of the new society that emerged as "a burst of technical innovation and economic competition sent American businesses and industries scrambling for their lives, retrenching, retooling . . . For workers the change was shocking, often traumatic . . . people with steady incomes and stable lives were abruptly stripped of livelihoods and identities." Snapping, in other words, was a characteristic malady of postindustrial society, a malady that made many Americans highly vulnerable to the purveyors of new belief-systems promising certainty amid conditions of tremendous disorientation.

Black Lightning

Among the most successful of the new belief-systems were the fundamentalist Christian sects. They had emerged in the late sixties, at a time when enrollment in more mainstream churches was declining. Typical among them was the group Children of God, founded by David Berg in the late 1960s. Children of God preached a highly doctrinaire brand of prophetic Christianity that demanded around-the-clock study and memorization of the Bible. The group found many converts among the youth who populated the beaches of southern California. There, one day in 1971, Ted Patrick's son had a brief encounter with members of

Children of God, who tried to convince him to join the group. Patrick, a black community relations consultant to the State of California, was so disturbed by what he heard from his son that he began to investigate the sect. His inquiries soon brought him into contact with a group of parents whose children had disappeared into the group's growing ranks. Patrick eventually managed to infiltrate the Children of God and spent several days undergoing indoctrination. What he experienced during these few days convinced him that the group posed a profound threat to American society. In the memoir that he published in 1976, *Let Our Children Go!*, Patrick described the organization's method as a form of "mass kidnapping" whose ultimate purpose was to turn new members systematically against their families and to sever all previous ties. Once inside, they were "starved, exhausted, and harangued into a brain-washed state, taught to hate their parents and to obey the cult leaders blindly." The ultimate purpose, in Patrick's eyes, was quite transparent: Children of God was a racket whose indoctrination techniques combined pious religious training with constant exhortation to sign over all material possessions and assets.

By the time of his encounter with the sect, Patrick had a long career behind him as a civil rights activist and community organizer. His personal trajectory through the sixties, however, had converted him from a police critic to a police supporter and a Republican. Now his close brush with the sect convinced him of the need to take action against its methods of "psychological incarceration." His contacts in the California state government, however, proved reluctant to move against the Children of God out of concerns over religious freedom. At the urging of like-minded parents, Patrick decided to take matters into his own hands. The technique he invented to counter cult indoctrination was called "deprogramming." It involved spiriting the cult member away to a secluded location, a motel room or home, and keeping him there for as long as it took—usually two or three days but sometimes as much as a week—to "break" him. As Patrick described it, deprogramming someone—despite its coercive, extralegal element—was an emotional but nonviolent process that involved confronting him or her with the contradictions between the sect's teachings and what the Bible actually said, and by this means restoring freedom of thought. At least one critic likened Patrick's method to the technique administered to Alex the droog in Kubrick's *Clockwork Orange* to cure him of his antisocial tendencies.

Patrick's initial successes brought him to the attention of parents desperate to recover children who had fallen into the sects' clutches. By early 1973, he claimed in an interview with *Newsweek* that he had intervened in more than six hundred cases across the country, and his notoriety in cult circles had earned him the name "Black Lightning." Backing him was a growing national network of parents and former Jesus freaks who carried out "rescue missions" and offered their home to Patrick's team of deprogrammers. Hailed by parents of cult members as a folk hero, Patrick was denounced by the sects as a fascist leading a vigilante operation. The police by and large tended to look the other way even though most of the youth involved were not minors and their parents therefore had no legal authority over them.

The controversy swirling around Patrick and his "defreaking" methods burst into national consciousness in 1973, when a series of legal actions and lawsuits were filed against him by sect members and civil libertarians. Convinced that any jury would tend to sympathize with the plight of parents whose children had been mysteriously turned against them, Patrick welcomed the opportunity to hold a referendum on the sects and their threat to society. He framed the issue in the starkest terms. "I have reason to believe," he stated in an interview, "that some of these groups are subversive. They are worse than the Manson sect because he had only a small number of followers. If authorities don't do something about this, our nation is going to be controlled by a handful of people." His opponents, the ACLU among them, argued that Patrick was guilty of violating the constitutional right of religious freedom and of committing criminal acts.

It was under these circumstances that the botched abduction of Daniel Voll took place. Voll was a Yale student whose membership in the New York–based New Testament Missionary Fellowship had led to estrangement from his parents and increasing social isolation. When he refused to come home for Christmas, they turned in desperation to Patrick, who flew to New York to assist them in their efforts to recover their son. Two weeks shy of Voll's twenty-first birthday, on the night of January 29, 1973, as he was walking home to his apartment on West 119th Street, his parents and Patrick forced him into a car. The abduction attempt was foiled, however, when Voll managed to attract the attention of a policeman. Patrick was charged with assault and unlawful imprisonment.

The trial began on July 23. In his opening statement, Patrick's attorney argued that Voll's parents were justified in their concern for their son, citing the "dramatic change in personality" he had under-gone since joining the New Testament Missionary Fellowship. The jury was given numerous examples of the extremism of Voll's new belief-system: he had, for instance, dropped out of a psychology course at Yale because, he claimed, it was being "taught by the devil"; former friends, meanwhile, testified that he had become a "zombie." One of the most dramatic courtroom appearances was that of Voll's closest friend at Yale, Wes Lockwood, who had himself been a member of the sect until he was abducted and successfully deprogrammed by Patrick. According to Lockwood, the sect's leader, a woman named Hannah Lowe, told members that their parents were possessed by the devil, and she referred to the Roman Catholic Church as "Babylon, mother of harlots." The members of the sect considered themselves an elite, chosen body of Christianity, a spiritual elect—a description confirmed by a statement by one of the group's members, who, describing countermeasures taken by the group following Patrick's abductions, stated: "We know how members of the Puritans used to feel when they went out with their Bibles in one hand and their muskets in the other." Lockwood further testified that in the initial phase of his deprogram-ming he had spoken to Patrick "in tongues," emitting very loud "nonsense syllables" that Patrick had ridiculed by responding with a "loud purring noise."

Witnesses for the prosecution tried to show that, while technically a minor at the time of the abduction, Voll was to all intents and purposes emancipated from his parents and that they had no legal authority over

him. Voll himself described his own disenchantment with his parents'
Lutheranism and his turn to the more demanding doctrines of Lowe's
sect not as a process of brainwashing but simply as a matter of
personal choice. Voll's lawyer, meanwhile, tried to turn the brainwashing charge against Patrick. In comments to the press, the president of Columbia University, which counted several members of the
sect among its student body, denounced Patrick's actions, while a
representative of the National Council of Churches defended Lowe's
sect as one that helped young people who might otherwise turn to
drugs and argued that Patrick's methods represented a grave violation
of religious freedom.

In the end the jury was swayed by the defense's argument that Voll's
parents' concern for his well-being had a prior claim over his own civil
liberties. Patrick was acquitted of all charges. Though he did not testify
in his own defense, Patrick gave an interview shortly before the trial
ended in which he welcomed the opportunity to expose what he called
a "movement of mind control" and asserted that such groups brainwash members by looking into their eyes. "There's an energy from the
brain waves that comes down through the eyes," Patrick claimed.
"This is what E.S.P. is. They're teaching this in all the universities."

"The Deprogrammer"

Many of Patrick's accounts of his "snatches" had the ring of a spy
thriller; as one anxious parent who had enlisted his services told the
press, "I feel like I'm in an espionage movie. The next one they're going
to have to deprogram is me." Later that summer of 1973, Patrick
would have the opportunity to star in his own televised drama.
Patrick's trial had brought him to the attention of CBS reporter Steve
Young, who contacted him about making a documentary of one of his
cases from the moment of the snatch through the deprogramming.
Patrick was ambivalent, recognizing that getting his side of the story on
camera would be valuable, but worrying that the camera's presence
might affect the deprogramming itself in unpredictable ways. In the

end he agreed to Young's proposition and, shortly after his acquittal, flew to Seattle to meet Young and his film crew. There he met with the parents of one Kathy Crampton and obtained their consent to the film crew's presence at their daughter's deprogramming. This agreement led to an unprecedented moment in reality television—what Patrick called "probably the first and only time in history that a kidnapping was televised nationwide in front of millions of people."

The Cramptons' daughter had joined a cult known as Church of Armageddon, or Love Israel, which practiced what Patrick described as a particularly unsavory form of apocalyptic Christianity that included intense Bible study, eating psychedelic mushrooms, rejection of all medical care, censorship of mail, and physical abuse of children. According to Patrick, one of their pastimes was to give themselves electrical shocks in an effort to determine how much current they could stand passing through their bodies. After becoming a member in January 1973 Kathy Crampton had cut herself off from her family. Her parents had initially considered having her committed but were advised by a lawyer of the difficulties of proving the difference between religious behavior and insanity. They then turned to Patrick.

The snatch took place early one morning with the cameras rolling in a cemetery near the house where the cult lived in Seattle. All went smoothly until Kathy made a break for freedom at a gas station en route to San Diego, where the deprogramming was to be performed. In the confusion that followed, Ted Patrick was first taken into custody for kidnapping, and then, after the local sheriff recognized him and recalled his acquittal in the Voll case, released. In the meantime the camera crew had recorded a conversation between Kathy and a state trooper in which, in response to his questions, she gave her name as Corinth Israel and her age as eighty-five (cult members added sixty-six years to "earth age"). Police brought in a psychiatrist who examined Kathy and pronounced her not a threat to herself or others, after which her mother and Patrick immediately took her into their custody again. With the charges dropped, they proceeded on their way to San Diego, with the film crew "hanging on to every turn of events and photo-graphing everything." Once they had arrived at their destination, the crew set up its equipment, and the deprogramming got under way. But the lights, mikes, and cameras proved to be a major distraction, as Patrick recounted: "Kathy kept performing for the cameras, which only complicated my task." She also made several escape attempts.

Patrick's fears were being realized: the presence of the cameras affected the session to such a degree that "they were really running the deprogramming." Even when he switched venues and moved the deprogramming to his own home, the crew refused to stop, forcing its way into the house and leaving only when Patrick threatened to destroy the equipment. By this time the process had already been fatally contaminated. Crampton was never fully deprogrammed, remaining in a "floating" state in which she drifted in and out of reality. She finally managed to escape again, returning to Seattle, where she gave a press conference and presented her version of events. Patrick would be forced to stand trial again later in this case. As for the documentary, it proved to be a bitter disappointment for those involved. "All of us," he recalled, "emerged looking like villains, kidnappers, violators of Kathy's civil rights." Speaking to the press, the head of the cult made fun of the brainwashing charge, saying that the group's members simply studied the Bible, "and that as far as cleaning up your mind, you know, I think we're all cleaning up our minds. If that's called brainwashing, I don't know. I just think we all need it . . . I think we could all use a lot of it."

The Dark Side of the Moonies

Patrick's account of what transpired in the initial encounter between cultists and new members rested on his son's description of being accosted on the beach, which Patrick related in his memoir. "Every time we tried to leave," his son reported, "they grabbed us by the arms, made us look into their eyes. I never saw eyes like that before. It made me dizzy to look at them." Essentially, Patrick believed that cult members performed a kind of "on-the-spot hypnosis" on unsuspecting youth. This was the preliminary to the much more grueling process that came later. "Once they get them, they brainwash them. The technique," he went on, "is the same as the one the North Koreans used on the POWs." Deprivation, exhaustion, and constant haranguing were all employed to bring about what he called, citing Yale psychiatrist Robert Jay Lifton's account of the methods of Communist "thought reformers," "ego destruction." This process was augmented by various props; Children of God, for instance, "programmed its members to the Bible, turning it into a device for self-hypnosis."

It is the presence of this Korean War template that probably explains why, of all the new sects, Patrick saw the Moonies as the most sinister. Nineteen seventy-three marked the arrival of the Reverend Sun Myung Moon and his overwrought blend of Christianity and staunch anti-Communism in the United States. In the fall of that year Moon embarked on a twenty-one-city lecture tour throughout the country, kicking off the tour with an appearance at New York City's Carnegie Hall, where Moon introduced himself as a divine being sent to earth to lead people out of a world he described as a "secret hell" controlled by Satan. Moon was a Korean industrialist turned evangelist who sought to breed an ideal race, a new spiritual elect. In order to realize this vision, his followers, Moonies, were required to participate in mass marriage ceremonies in which total strangers were paired off with each other. Moon, who was originally from what is now North Korea and claimed to have been held in Communist prisons, also proved adept at ingratiating himself with political authorities, becoming staunchly pro-Nixon and ordering his followers to attend anti-Nixon rallies as counterdemonstrators.

Moon's Unification Church, which quickly became one of the largest and richest cults in America, was known to its devotees as The Family. Moon, the church's "Father," used the full panoply of conversion techniques to win his followers' hearts and minds and reduce them to a state of near-infantile dependency. Church leaders preached that America was "going to hell" because of crime, suicide, drugs, abortion, divorce, and college radicals. Members were told to suppress all sexual impulses. Telling followers repeatedly that the last days were upon them and that the Messiah would come from Korea,

Moon offered the ultimate relief from oedipal conflict for those who experienced the crises of the seventies as punishment for the rebellion and excess of the sixties.

Moon's success, however, soon invited scrutiny. Almost as soon as he arrived, his church became embroiled in controversies over his alleged brainwashing and financial exploitation of members. Patrick soon found himself on the front lines of the movement to expose Moon's Unification Church as a fraudulent menace. Voicing concerns similar to those that were playing themselves out in the Vietnam POW-brainwashing scare, Patrick saw the Moonies as the advance guard of an attempt on the part of sinister Korean agencies to establish influence over American society and government. In his memoir Patrick painted a particularly vivid image of Moonie fanaticism. Moon, he wrote, told his followers, "I am your brain," and demanded single-minded loyalty to the cause. His followers in turn engaged in chants such as: "We're going to smash Satan today! Mansei! Victory for the father of ten thousand years! Mansei!" According to Patrick, this was what Moonies shouted to each other as they went off on missions, "in the manner of Kamikaze pilots shouting Banzai!"

In Patrick's eyes, Moon's smiling visage, appearing on thousands of posters all over Manhattan prior to one of his appearances at Madison Square Garden or Yankee Stadium, made him the poster boy for those techniques of reeducation or thought-reform pioneered by the Chinese Communists in the fifties that had entered the vernacular as "brain-washing." He alluded to Moon's close ties to the South Korean dictator Park Chung Hee and the presence within his inner circle of former members of the Korean CIA, and he suggested that Moon was trying to turn the United States into another South Korea. For Patrick, there could be no doubt that Moon's cult was a "theological-political instrument"; he regarded Moon as "public enemy number one as far as the cults are concerned." "I don't have to tell you," he wrote, "that the term 'brainwashing' came from Korea during the Korean War when many of our POWs were subjected to intensive political indoctrina-tion." The experiences of the cult members, like those of the POWs, thus constituted another variation on the Puritan captivity narrative. If

Patrick's pronouncements seemed alarmist and hyperbolic, Moon's church returned the compliment. Patrick was described to church members in lurid terms; one reported being told that he "strapped you to a bed, beat you, tortured you, raped you," and was surprised on first meeting him that Patrick, a rather unimpressive-looking figure in person, was not "a big black gorilla in tight leather pants."

Operation Mop-Up

By 1973 Ted Patrick had become a minor celebrity, recognized in towns across the nation. The Voll trial and its surprising outcome became a topic of conversation around the country, and the CBS documentary made him a household name. Stories of Patrick and his network of followers orchestrating their snatches, and descending on cult members for rapid-fire deprogramming sessions before heading off to yet another encounter, as well as periodic standoffs with cults and the law, gripped the public imagination.

One notable feature of Patrick's exploits was the virtually complete absence of any encounters with radical political groups. With only two exceptions, Patrick's efforts were confined to religious cults. One of these exceptions was heiress Patty Hearst. Hearst, who following her kidnapping by the Symbionese Liberation Army in February 1974 was kept blindfolded in a closet for several weeks, emerged from this ordeal having undergone a total personality makeover. In her new persona as "Tania," she would assist in a bank robbery and be embraced by the radical left. At her later trial the prosecution depicted Hearst as a willing accomplice, a "rebel looking for a cause," while the defense portrayed her as a POW. Psychiatrist Robert Jay Lifton, testifying in her defense, drew parallels between the SLA's tactics and those of Chinese thought-reformers. Patrick became involved when he met with Hearst's parents, accompanied by the parent of an ex-Moonie who compared the mind-control techniques of the Unification Church with those of the SLA. Patrick warned that until she was deprogrammed, Patty would remain under SLA control and cited the case of Squeaky

Fromme, former member of the Manson family who had recently attempted to assassinate President Ford. Without deprogramming, Patty would remain, according to Patrick, a menace, a potential Manchurian Candidate: "Manson went to jail and those girls were not deprogrammed. They're still programmed to what he told them."

While the SLA saga has become the iconic tale of the New Left's implosion in the early seventies, Patrick also became peripherally involved in what was in some ways an even more bizarre chapter in the history of American radicalism. This was the series of events surrounding so-called Operation Mop-Up, launched in 1973 by the members of the National Caucus on Labor Committees (NCLC). This group had originated as an SDS splinter organization led by a man known as Lyn Marcus in the aftermath of the Columbia University student strike in 1968. Formed as a nonviolent alternative to the SDS group the Weather Underground, under Marcus's direction the NCLC had taken an increasingly extremist role in the sectarian power struggles that consumed the Left in the early 1970s. By the spring of 1973 the NCLC's break with the rest of the radical Left was complete and Marcus had initiated the violence of Operation Mop-Up. From May to September of that year NCLC members engaged in a systematic campaign of terror against its rivals the Communist Party USA and the Socialist Workers' Party, using bats, chains, and other weapons to intimidate members, many of whom had to be hospitalized.

At the same time Marcus's political views were taking an increasingly strange turn, becoming marked by a grotesque combination of megalomania, conspiratorialism, and psychosexual theorizing. The flavor of the latter is conveyed in an August 1973 memo in which Marcus blamed sexual impotence on the figure of the Mother and claimed to his followers, "To the extent that my physical powers do not prevent me, I am now confident of ending your political—and sexual—impotence; the two are interconnected aspects of the same problem." Even more bizarre were his pronouncements concerning the vast conspiracy that, he claimed, the FBI, the CIA, and various foreign agencies, including the KGB, were orchestrating against him personally. In what has been dubbed by one author as "The Great Manchurian Candidate Scare," Marcus became convinced that a former NCLC member who'd left the group and moved to East Germany, where he'd become romantically involved with a psychiatrist, had been brainwashed and programmed by the KGB to assassinate Marcus. The crisis in the group only intensified when suspicion fell on yet another group member, Christopher White, who'd married Marcus's former wife in 1972. In late December 1973, accusing White of having been brainwashed as part of the assassination plot, Marcus held him prisoner in his apartment and subjected him to his own deprogramming techniques, including food and sleep deprivation, hypnosis, and the administering of drugs. Marcus provided a *New York Times* reporter with a tape recording he'd made of the deprogramming, on which could be heard sounds of weeping and vomiting and an ominous voice saying, "Raise the voltage."

Marcus's charges against the CIA bore an uncanny resemblance to what he himself was subjecting his followers to. So busy denouncing what it called the "fascist" actions of American intelligence agencies that it ignored at first the parallels between its own tactics and those of Hitler's Brownshirts, the NCLC would eventually explicitly align itself with the shock troops of the populist Right. Following a trajectory that ultimately led him from the far Left to the farthest fringes of the Right, Lyn Marcus—whose real name was Lyndon LaRouche—directed the organization's energies to battling the forces of finance capitalism and the Jewish conspiracy that allegedly lay behind it. This strange convergence of the ideologies of Left and Right was commented on by Ted Patrick, who became involved later that year when he was contacted by the parents of nineteen-year-old Gail Roeshman, who had become briefly entangled with the NCLC. Roeshman was abducted and held in a Philadelphia motel for several days while Patrick went to work on her. After later releasing her into her parents' custody, Patrick described the subject of his first political conversion in the following way: "She was psychologically kidnapped by that Labor group. They use this on-the-spot hypnosis and brainwashing and mass psychology, the same as Hitler and Red

China. You know the whole nation of Red China is under ESP mind control."

The Micro-Politics of the Family

What was causing this seeming epidemic of snapping? Why had American youth become so vulnerable to strange belief-systems? To some, the phenomenon seemed a predictable reaction to the shattering of the hopes awakened by the sixties; to others, the by-product of changes in the chemistry of American society, particularly its economic system. One of the most prevalent theories held that the phenomenon could be traced to underlying pathologies in the American family. In her account of the Patty Hearst trial, journalist Shana Alexander suggested that the breakdown of the nuclear family in the sixties had ushered in a new era of experimentation in communal living. Substitutes were sought in the form of communes, countercultural families, intense brotherhoods like the Moonies, the Children of God, and the Manson family. Alexander also suggested that this phenomenon reflected bad parenting, of the authoritarian kind as well as, less predictably, its opposite: the well-intentioned, yet fundamentally misguided, kind of parenting that strove to place parents and children on the same footing. This inevitably sowed confusion in the mind of the child, who secretly longed for strong authority figures, if only to rebel against: "To kids like Patty, revolutionaries and others who take firm, dogmatic positions look like saviors. That accounts for the success of the Moonies."

In a similar vein were columnist Anne Roiphe's comments in a *Times* magazine piece in which she discussed the case of two sisters who had become members of Hannah Lowe's New Testament Missionary Fellowship and whose parents had enlisted Ted Patrick's help. Roiphe quoted one of the sisters calling her mother Satan and accusing her of wearing miniskirts although, as Roiphe pointed out, the woman dressed quite decorously. Despite clear evidence that the girls' perceptions of their parents were deeply disturbed, Roiphe did not let the parents off the hook and indeed came close to laying the blame for their daughters' religious fanaticism at their feet. In this respect she was partly echoing a style of argument that had gained great cultural currency in the early 1970s. In his book *The Politics of the Family*, published in 1971, noted British psychoanalyst R. D. Laing had argued that instead of looking inside a patient's head for clues to the origins of mental illness, doctors would be better off exploring the family structure that had produced the patient. Out of this kind of inquiry arose the idea, which rapidly took hold in early seventies culture, that the family itself represented the single biggest factor in producing psychopathology. As Roiphe concluded, citing Laing, "We [parents] may in fact have driven them into madness."

The notion that mad families, and in particular mad mothers, produced mad children was borne out in one of the most sensational accounts of personality crisis that appeared in 1973. This was the book *Sybil*, a true story of a woman with sixteen personalities that shone a light into the darkest corners of the American psyche and forced upon its reader the conclusion that its subject's fragmented personality was a logical response to a pathological family milieu: a mother who suffered from schizophrenia and subjected her daughter to sadistic abuse verging on torture; a weak, distant father who turned a blind eye to his wife's insanity and his daughter's suffering; and a grandfather in whose fevered mind Christian fundamentalism mixed with apocalyptic cold war scenarios.

Sybil was first and foremost a mystery story—a "whodunit of the unconscious," as author Flora Rheta Schreiber termed it—structured around two central questions: what happened to the patient during her mysterious blackouts, episodes of lost time that could last days; and what had caused her to suffer these blackouts? The answer to the first question came with the discovery, under prodding by her psychoanalyst Dr. Cornelia Wilbur, that the patient "was not alone in her own body." Analysis disclosed that Sybil harbored within herself sixteen selves, two of them boys, each with a distinct personality, voice, and manner of dressing. The answer to the second question entailed a journey back into Sybil's intensely fundamentalist small-town upbringing.

The single biggest impediment to the treatment was the patient's loyalty to the mother who had been her tormenter. The analysis unfolded as a hostage drama, with Sybil feeling imprisoned by the paralyzing love she still felt for her mother, and each of the selves feeling in turn hostages of Sybil. The traumatic memories uncovered during the course of the eleven-year analysis revealed a shocking tale of child abuse at the hands of a mother who suffered from symptoms of schizophrenia. It was in response to these traumatic experiences that the other selves had emerged, ready to take over at times of over-whelming stress that Sybil could not cope with. Mapped onto those early memories—which made one of the selves, Nancy, feel as though her mother was "exploding in [her] mind"—were more contemporary scenarios of the world itself blowing up: "Why . . . have they built civil defense shelters? Why do we see signs of the end everywhere? Satan will destroy the world and God will make it perfect, so there will be no more sin." Gender war also raged within: the boys described them-selves as prisoners of the women, proclaiming that "the time for our freedom is at hand" and that "this is still a man's world." Schreiber left little doubt that the seeds of Sybil's illness lay in the bad family dynamic: weak father, domineering, crazy mother.

The best-selling success of *Sybil* attested to its resonance throughout a nation that was itself in the midst of a shattering collective identity crisis. As critic D. W. Harding, writing in the *New York Review of Books*, suggested, the multiple personality thriller was on its way to becoming a standard genre. Reviewing her case along with a new book about the famous nineteenth-century paranoid Daniel Paul Schreber, Harding suggested that both were victims of a classic double bind: the power of the bad parent "to discredit in advance their children's criticisms." With regard to her mother, Sybil suffered from a version of Stockholm syndrome, a debilitating love of her tormentor. A similar fate was shared by Schreber, the subject of Morton Schatzman's *Soul Murder: Persecution in the Family*, a study of the "micro-politics" of the family rooted in the theories of R. D. Laing. The book examined the case of Schreber, the subject of a famous essay by Freud in which he described paranoia as a defense against homosexuality, through the lens of the authoritarian child-rearing methods of late nineteenth-century Germany. The leading theoretician of these methods was none other than Schreber's own father, who used his children as experimental subjects to test his theory that the child's will must be systematically broken. Recommending the extensive use of mechanical apparatus (for correcting posture, handwriting, etc.), the elder Schreber's writings were so popular that they made him, in Harding's words, the Dr. Spock of the day. To the "feeling of the law," he wrote in one typical formulation, must be joined "a feeling of the impossibility of struggling against the law"—a classic double bind that virtually programmed his son for madness.

To survivors of the sixties, here was one answer for the seeming failures of that decade's utopian aspirations: the schizoid awareness that institutions were toppling and yet remained more firmly in place than ever, was rooted in the discovery that secretly, people love what oppresses them. Before it could take place in the arena of politics, change would have to take hold at another level, that of the family. Failing that, revolutionaries would be condemned to a seemingly inescapable cycle rooted in the "micro-politics" of the family: blaming the mother for their own "impotence" (both political and sexual) and erecting in her place wild travesties of patriarchal authority such as Marcus/LaRouche, Moon, or Charles Manson. Like Schreber's, Sybil's story bore out the view that families—of whatever kind—could be maddening, indeed "schizogenic." Indeed, the notion of the "schizogenic family" was, according to critic Harding, "rapidly passing into contemporary folklore."

The Exorcist

Nothing in the contemporary folklore, however, could have prepared the American public for what awaited it at the end of 1973. If the media accounts of Ted Patrick's exploits, with their stakeouts, getaways, and battles over mind control, sometimes read like a script for a film called *The Deprogrammer*, Hollywood supplied its own lurid version of such a story with the year-end release of *The Exorcist*. Directed by William Friedkin from the best-selling novel by William Peter Blatty, *The Exorcist* told the story of Regan O'Neill, a sweet, horse-loving twelve-year-old who becomes possessed by the devil and transformed into a vomit-spewing, head-spinning monster who masturbates herself with a crucifix. The film sketches its context lightly but tellingly: Regan has recently moved to Washington, D.C., with her film-actress mother Chris, who is making a movie about campus turmoil that she describes as the "Walt Disney version of the Ho Chi Minh story." This symptom of social breakdown is underlined when Chris at one point receives an invitation to the White House. The unspoken presence of the Watergate scandal provides the backdrop to the crisis of patriarchal authority dramatized in the film. Regan is the product of a broken family; her father's absence—symbolized by his failure to call her on her birthday—clearly leaves the door open to the mayhem that follows. Yet while there are antecedents to Regan's troubles, the film, as film critic Vincent Canby pointed out, insists on the literalness of its story, refusing—in a way that is antiscience and deeply reactionary—any reading that would attempt to reduce Regan's problems to psychology. Regan is initially subjected to a battery of tests by a team of experts, who first diagnose hyperactivity and prescribe Ritalin before raising the more serious possibility of a seizure disorder. To Chris, it seems obvious her daughter is "psychotic, a split personality." CAT scans, however, reveal nothing, and the doctors' utter lack of comprehension forces Chris to turn in desperation to Father Damien Karras, a psychiatric counselor at the local archdiocese.

Father Karras has his own troubles: he is wracked by guilt over the recent death of his mother as well as by his own lack of faith. As author Peter Biskind has noted, Friedkin and Blatty were both men with serious mother fixations; during filming Blatty, who had read a book called *Breakthrough: Electronic Communication with the Dead*, tried to record his late mother's voice on tape. Karras adopts a similar technique in trying to plumb the mystery surrounding Regan, who begins speaking in tongues and then becomes a suspect in the police investigation into the death of Burke, the director of the film-within-the-film. Friedkin employed state-of-the-art special effects to heighten his film's supernaturalism and deny all efforts to read Regan's condition in secular terms: she levitates, her head spins around 180 degrees, and writing appears on her skin ("Help me!"), suggesting she has become a hostage in her own body. While the story of Sybil remains within the postwar liberal therapeutic framework, *The Exorcist*'s demonic special effects bury that framework beneath its supernatural conceits. Faced with such graphic evidence, Karras regains his faith and arranges for a more experienced demonologist, Father Merrin, recently returned from an archaeological dig in Iraq, to perform the exorcism. The two men eventually liberate Regan from the demon's power, though only at the cost of their own lives.

Released the day after Christmas, the film was an instant smash hit, eventually becoming what was at the time the third top-grossing film in Hollywood history. While critics panned it, audiences could not get enough of what was essentially, according to Canby, a movie about a girl being tortured. New York theaters reported that filmgoers were waiting in lines, in subzero temperatures, for up to four hours to get tickets, and that many viewers were coming back for second, third, or fourth showings. The strong public response translated not only into box office success but also into incidents of fainting, hysteria, and vomiting that closely mimicked Regan's convulsions. The spectacle of Regan's possession seemed to induce episodes of snapping among audience members. One theater manager said, "It's like a cult. People must see it." Others reported heart attacks and miscarriages among filmgoers; a Chicago newspaper reported that six people who'd seen the movie had wound up in psychiatric hospitals. The film provoked a violent debate over its special effects and the fact that it had mysteriously escaped an X rating. Although the Church had consulted on the film and two church members were given small roles in it, clergymen were divided over its merits as a "religious experience." Fundamentalists would later blame the film for spawning a minor epidemic of claims of demonic possession, and an exposé of the Unification Church that NBC aired in 1975 claimed that ex-Moonies were showing up at psychiatric clinics in droves, freaking out and having visions of the devil "just like in *The Exorcist*."

The phenomenon of *The Exorcist* was partly about the spectacle of cinema's power to evoke violent reactions in its audience. Audiences swooned over the special effects, which Friedkin had fought for even as the film went far over budget. He grandiosely attributed the film's "documentary quality" to the graphic nature of the images provided by these special effects. Friedkin emerged as a demonic master of the cinema, his aura heightened by stories that circulated in the trade papers concerning his sadism toward the actors and toward his own girlfriend. The fact that he had forced her to have two abortions during the production suggests one of the many possible subtexts to the palpable anxiety about female sexuality expressed in the film. At times Friedkin seemed willingly to invite parallels between himself and the demon possessing Regan. To its depiction of a crisis of male authority—with multiple figures laying claim to the title of "bad dad"—the film adds, in its portrait of the hypersexualized Regan, a "male nightmare of female puberty" that, as Biskind puts it, is "drenched in a kind of menstrual panic." In the year of *Roe v. Wade*, having a teenage girl jam a crucifix into her vagina conjured up a ghastly image of "self-inflicted abortion." As Pauline Kael recognized, the film's medieval atmospherics made it a highly effective recruiting poster for the Church—seemingly the only institution whose authority had survived the sixties.

In this reading of the film, the devil becomes a special effects master. According to author Blatty, "the object of demonic possession is not necessarily to possess an individual but to sow doubt, confusion and horror among onlookers." This the film accomplished: for their money, reported one reviewer in the *Times*, "filmgoers get not only the events on the screen, but also—according to all reports—the spectacle of the less hardy among them succumbing to fainting spells and bouts of vomiting." As one female moviegoer was quoted saying in *Variety*, "I wanted to see what everyone was throwing up about." These comments suggest that the demonology portrayed in the film is partly about the power of the medium. The film-within-the-film sows its own seeds: its director, who Regan hopes will become her new father, is killed (his head twisted 180 degrees), and the suggestion of some impropriety in his presence in her bedroom exposes him as a false father; meanwhile, the detective investigating the director's death is depicted as an obsessive movie fan, asking Chris for her autograph and telling Karras that he resembles Sal Mineo. How, wondered Kael, does one possibly exorcise the effects of a movie like this? She closed her review with an anecdote about the movie's casting; according to publicity, Friedkin had looked at five hundred girls before settling on Linda Blair for the part of Regan. Kael found herself wondering about the mothers of those girls: "When they see *The Exorcist* and watch Linda Blair urinating on the fancy carpet and screaming and jabbing at herself with the crucifix, are they envious? Do they feel, 'That might have been my little Susie—famous forever'?"

The Great UFO Wave of 1973

If what was at stake in the hijacker crisis of the early 1970s was America's imperiled sovereignty in the skies, late in 1973 new questions would arise concerning the nation's control of its own airspace. Well before Patty Hearst became the poster child for Stockholm syndrome, hundreds of ordinary Americans were already experiencing their own version of this syndrome in connection with visitations from outer space. In what came to be known as the Great UFO Wave of 1973, a series of sightings began in late summer and climaxed in October, ushering in a new era of official and public interest in UFOs, later commemorated by Steven Spielberg's 1977 film *Close Encounters of the Third Kind*. According to one account this wave of sightings originated in Texas, after the *Dallas Times Herald* ran a story about an old UFO crash that sparked renewed interest in the topic. This was quickly followed by a series of reported sightings at locations throughout the South and Southwest. Soon similar reports began popping up across the country, and aerial objects were reported flying across the United States at supersonic speeds, although both the FAA and NORAD denied detecting any such movements.

These sightings soon introduced yet another variant on the captivity narrative into the national consciousness: the UFO abduction. After two men in Pascagoula, Mississippi, reported they had been taken aboard a UFO by creatures with clawlike hands, abduction stories began to circulate. Rather than an American-led colonization of space, the reverse seemed to be occurring. Although some abduction stories included accounts of disturbing medical experiments, others recounted their experiences in quite different terms, describing their captors as beings possessing a "higher consciousness." And while the authorities tried to downplay these stories to minimize panic, some communities, as the *Times* reported, laid out the welcome mat. The town of Palacios, Texas, issued a welcoming proclamation, and the mayor of the town was quoted as saying, "No one has ever made those fellas welcome." By late November a Gallup poll was reporting that 15 million Americans had seen UFOs, and that 51 percent accepted them as being real. In December 1973 J. Allen Hynek, a respected astronomer at Northwestern University, opened the Center for UFO Studies in Chicago. Hynek was, among other things, the man responsible for coining the term "close encounters" in his book *The UFO Experience: A Scientific Inquiry* (1972).

Debunkers were quick to point out that October, when this wave of sightings peaked, was a very bad month for Americans. War broke out in the Middle East, and in response to a Soviet threat to send troops to the region Kissinger, acting on behalf of an increasingly strung-out president, put the nation on nuclear alert. This decision was greeted by many in the media as a sign that the president had gone mad. Later, following OPEC's declaration of an oil embargo, gas prices began to soar, with oil shortages expected by winter. Meanwhile the rot at the center of the American government became ever more malodorous. Spiro Agnew resigned amid tax evasion charges, and there was renewed talk of Nixon's impeachment. Arguing that people "see things" as a reaction to social stress, several prominent psychologists suggested that the UFO wave was a predictable response to a month of particularly bad news.

Kohoutek

Amid more bad news, the year ended on a note of anxious speculation concerning the meaning of another kind of celestial visitation. The stock market closed at 850, down 200 points from the beginning of the year. The full effects of the oil embargo were now being felt across the nation, including at the White House, where the annual Christmas tree could only be lit at 20 percent of its customary brilliance. Yet Christmas cheer was the least of the worries facing the administration, whose support was now hemorrhaging in the wake of the revelations concerning a missing eighteen-and-a-half-minute segment of tape from the Oval Office's secret recording system, on which Nixon and Haldeman had discussed responses to the Watergate break-in. Nixon's few remaining supporters, meanwhile, were growing increasingly concerned about the beleaguered president's psychological condition. His close confidant the evangelist Billy Graham would later blame Nixon's downfall on the drugs, including sleeping pills and amphetamines, that the president habitually used: "I think it was sleeping pills. Sleeping pills and demons. I think there was definitely demon power involved . . . My conclusion is that it was all those sleeping pills, they just let a demon's power come in and play over him."

Amid this darkening constellation of circumstances, the scheduled passage of the comet Kohoutek across the skies in the week between Christmas and New Year's was greeted in fundamentalist Christian circles as a sign either of imminent doom or of Christ's Second Coming. Such signs had become increasingly commonplace in the months since the outbreak of the Yom Kippur War in the Middle East, an event that, to readers of Hal Lindsey's *The Late Great Planet Earth*, the best-selling book of biblical prophecy, heralded the Armageddon foretold in the Book of Revelation. Some religious leaders likened Kohoutek to the star that, according to Christian legend, led the wise men to the newborn Christ in Bethlehem. One author writing in *Christianity Today* suggested that Kohoutek "may well be like a cosmic performance of 'You are there: Christmas 5 B.C.'" In preparation for Kohoutek, members of the Children of God maintained a silent vigil outside the United Nations in Manhattan. Dressed in sackcloth and wearing wooden yokes around their necks, they held up banners and passed out pamphlets with messages like the following: "Will the Kohoutek Comet make you think about God and His destiny for you and the world? You cannot escape it. Are you ready for it?" The Children of God's leader, Dave Berg, interpreted the comet as a warning to Americans to leave the country by December 31, because "some kind of disaster judgment of God is to fall because of man's wickedness." In the event, Kohoutek's passage was somewhat anti-climactic; touted as the Comet of the Century, it turned out to be nearly invisible to the naked eye.

Warholism

The art form of the future is celebrity-hood.

—Richard Hell

Will someone want to do a 1970s remake of shooting me?

—Andy Warhol

JUNE 13, 1973: *The nightclub Le Jardin opens on 43rd Street and Broadway, billing itself as a "discotheque pour monsieur." Opening night culminates with a special midnight performance by Candy Darling singing "Give Me a Man." Spotted in the crowd by* Interview *magazine's "Small Talk" reporter Bob Colacello were lightweight boxing champion Chu Chu Malave; happy hooker Xaviera Hollander; Gerri Miller, the stripper in Warhol's* Trash, *dancing topless; Sal Mineo with a large entourage; and several other minor celebrities.*

An underground movie magazine for the first few years of its existence, Andy Warhol's *Interview* would become transformed in the early 1970s into a glossy homage to the cult of celebrity. With his tape recorder and Polaroid camera ever present, Warhol positioned himself as the presiding figure of this cult, its pope. The pages of *Interview* were filled with question-and-answer sessions with figures from the worlds of film, fashion, music, and politics, whose opinions on everything from Watergate and abortion to vitamins and the Atkins diet were faithfully recorded. *Interview* became an essential guide to the new social topography fashioned by Americans' growing obsession with fame and stardom. The collapse of older certitudes in the wake of the sixties left a vacuum into which Warholism opportunistically rushed. What replaced those certitudes was nostalgia, camp, and irony, the claustrophobic minutiae of life inside the media echo chamber, the compulsive sharing and unburdening of the soul that Tom Wolfe identified as the signature of the Me Decade.

The cult of celebrity inevitably had its casualties. By the early 1970s several of Warhol's Superstars, including perhaps the greatest of all— Edie Sedgwick—were dead. Lance Loud explained his family's implosion on national television by saying, "The Andy Warhol prophecy of fifteen minutes of fame for any and everyone blew up on our doorstep." The success of *Interview* reflected a larger cultural assault on the boundary between private and public that, acted out at the highest political level, would scandalize the nation. After learning that phone conversations of an intimate nature had been monitored, the Democrats filed suit against the Watergate burglars for invasion of privacy. Pat Nixon, appalled at the revelation that her husband had been secretly taping all White House conversations, nevertheless defended him against demands to turn the tapes over with the argument that "they were like private love letters, for one person only." Such abuses were satirized in *Interview*, whose pages included a regular gossip column titled "Invasion of Privacy."

For those—especially figures from the world of rock music—on whom the glare of stardom shone most brightly, it became intoxicating to act out one's life in public. Rock stars enjoyed perhaps more fully than anyone else the promise of radical individualism that was one of the legacies of the sixties. Yet the rock star lifestyle also gave the destructive side of this promise unmatched opportunity for expression, as the meteoric trajectory of several key bands of this period, including the New York Dolls, suggests. The possibility that stardom might be a pathological condition forms the premise of Don DeLillo's 1973 novel, *Great Jones Street*, the story of a Dylan-like rock musician who tries to "step out of his legend," to disappear from the public eye, in the belief that privacy has become the most revolutionary wish of all.

The Warhol 1970s

By the end of the 1960s, wrote Warhol in *Popism*, his account of that decade, "everyone, absolutely everyone was tape-recording everyone else." Tape recorders and Polaroids were "taking over people's social lives." Inevitably, writes Warhol, "I began to think about starting a magazine of nothing but taped interviews." This was the genesis of the publication that would become *Interview*, an underground magazine with a tiny distribution in its early years that was reinvented by 1973 as a leading chronicle of celebrity culture.

As a sickly and rather solitary child, Warhol had found refuge in the fantasy world conjured up by Hollywood fan magazines. Once he moved to New York, he frequently wrote fan letters to figures such as Tab Hunter and Truman Capote. Visitors to the Upper East Side town house that Warhol eventually made his home were astonished by the knee-deep collection of fan magazines that testified to his continuing fascination with the world of movie stars. By the sixties he was no longer simply a fan but an active participant, painting the likes of Marilyn Monroe and Jackie Kennedy and mingling with figures such as Dennis Hopper and Bob Dylan. His emergence as a leading representative of Pop Art coincided with the advent of what Daniel Boorstin, in 1961, called the culture of "the image," whose inaugural event, as we have seen, was the televised debates between Nixon and Kennedy. These debates represented, in Boorstin's eyes, a clinical example of the "pseudo-event." The pseudo-event, wrote Boorstin, was not spontaneous but was planned or incited for the purpose of being reported or reproduced. It satisfied a thirst for such manufac-tured happenings whose recent increase was a product of the expo-nential expansion of the mass media.

So pervasive had the influence of the techniques of mechanical reproduction become that, according to Boorstin, "we begin to be puzzled about what is really the 'original' of an event." Yet where

Boorstin lamented this development, Warhol celebrated it, fashioning an entire oeuvre out of serialized reproductions of simple, iconic images that were radically severed from any original. And where Boorstin deplored the breaking of the "old heroic mold" and its replacement by the cult of the celebrity ("the human pseudo-event"), Warhol transformed his own youthful fascination with stars into a highly influential artistic practice.

Warhol's emergence as the biggest fan in a world made up of celebrities and their audience represented the culmination of his move-ment away from art and his increasing absorption into the worlds of music, film, and fashion. If his Factory had been an incubator for many of the experimental tendencies of the New York underground of the 1960s, by the early 1970s it had been transformed into an increasingly professionalized operation dedicated to chronicling the lives of celeb-rities. This change reflected many developments: the exhaustion of the sixties; the sputtering of Warhol's dream of breaking into Hollywood; and the departure or death of many of the free spirits of the old Factory. At the same time it reflected Warhol's own withdrawal from the manic scene that had surrounded him in the sixties, and his intense paranoia in response to the assassination attempt at the hands of disgruntled Factory hanger-on Valerie Solanas that left him nearly dead in 1968. Solanas, author of a revolutionary feminist tract called the SCUM (Society for Cutting Up Men) Manifesto, had simply walked into the Factory one day and shot Warhol. At the new offices at Union Square to which the Andy Warhol Enterprises had relocated to accommodate Warhol's expanding empire, closed-circuit television monitors and bulletproof glass were installed and access to the inner sanctum was tightly controlled.

Interview magazine represented a key part of the mainstreaming of the Warhol sensibility. At the same time its transformation reflected a larger cultural reaction against the turbulence of the sixties. Nos-talgia, as new managing editor Bob Colacello later wrote, "was all over New York in 1973 and 1974." Warhol's talent for tapping into larger social currents was reflected in the magazine's overt celebra-tion of the glamour of a former era. The May 1972 issue dropped

Andy Warhol's Film Magazine for *Andy Warhol's Interview* and printed its cover in color for the first time. Among the first issues of the newly redesigned magazine were special issues devoted to Marilyn Monroe and James Dean; later issues celebrated screen icons like Gloria Swanson. Ultimately, writes Colacello, this "reactionary nostalgia" for the glamour of the old Hollywood "would swamp the revolutionary spirit of the sixties and make it all right to be stylish and irresponsible again."

Nevertheless the nostalgia that permeated *Interview* was far from simple, insofar as it was refracted through a camp aesthetic that reflected the continuing influence of the sixties, particularly the experimentation with gender that marked that decade. *Interview* provided readers with unrivaled access to the world of celebrities that coalesced around Warhol in the seventies, and in this sense the magazine was akin to Warhol's "home movies" of the previous decade: "We were," wrote Colacello, "letting [our readers] into the party." What distinguished this party was its inclusion of drag queens like Candy Darling, Jackie Curtis, and Holly Woodlawn, who imparted a uniquely histrionic quality to their clonings of the Hollywood glamour-ideal.

Boorstin had fretted over the potential for mass deception in a society based on images; in doing so, however, he may have underestimated Americans' skill at seeing through the tricks of image culture. Part of the success of *Interview* can be traced to the fact that it used its unparalleled access to allow the reader to glimpse not merely the image but the work that went into the construction of the image. Here the influence of the drag queen sensibility became paramount. The extreme care that Candy Darling took in creating her impersonation of Kim Novak was an essential part of her aura. "It is very hard work" to be a drag queen, as Warhol wrote in *The Philosophy of Andy Warhol*. "It's hard work to look like the complete opposite of what nature made you and then to be an imitation woman of what was only a fantasy woman in the first place." With its endless details concerning makeup and other intimate aspects of its subjects' lives, *Interview* took the reader behind the scenes, as it were, both involving them in and at the same time distancing them from the image.

Typically, wrote Boorstin, the pseudo-event "is not a train wreck or earthquake, but an interview." Warhol's magazine was in this sense the ultimate homage to the society of the pseudo-event. In the same way that the camera in Warhol's films had recorded everything to the point of utter boredom, so the tape recorder that was the essential tool of *Interview* magazine registered absolutely everything no matter how trivial. The question-and-answer sessions that filled its pages were both hilariously banal and sociologically fascinating. The July 1973 issue included an interview with Malcolm McDowell, the English star of *A Clockwork Orange*, just released in the United States, as well as the recently released *Oh Lucky Man!* Mingled with comments about his fear of flying, hijackings, the Atkins diet, abortion, and Watergate, McDowell was also asked by interviewer June Jade to share with the reader whether he wore underwear in bed and what kind of vitamins he took. A typical exchange was the following:

J.: **Do you wear underwear?**
M.: Not in the summer and certainly not in bed.
J.: **Not in bed?**
M.: Well, I sleep with my socks on in bed.
J.: **Why, do you get cold feet in bed?**
M.: Yes and when my feet are cold I wear socks.
J.: **Where else do you get cold feet then?**
M.: Well, there are my feet.
J.: **Yes, but what other frightening experiences give you cold feet?**
M.: Oh, now we are getting down to the serious part of the interview, we're getting metaphorical now are we? I can see this is the serious part. I get cold feet when I get on an airplane.
J.: **Really?**
M.: I hate flying. I really loathe it. Especially the landings, I find that very hard to take.
J.: **I hate when you take off and the back of the plane goes . . . uuunnnggg. Like the bottom of the plane dropped off.**
M.: And the wheels go . . . kerfboong.

J.: Have you ever worried about being hijacked to Cuba?

M.: No, I would love that.

J.: Me too. Havana cigars, tropical drinks on the veranda. Havana la la la la la Havana.

Or the following exchange, prompted by a question about the 1972 satire *Richard*, on the pre-Watergate life of Richard Nixon:

J.: You know that movie RICHARD with Richard M. Dixon? Well you know Nixon went through a big change over after he lost in California.

M.: A sex change?

J.: Well, whatever. And he went to psychiatrists and all that. Well in RICHARD they portrayed that with a Clockwork Orange thing with him sitting in the theatre with his eyes clamped open watching his "Checkers" speech and him barfing.

M.: I didn't see it actually but I was told it was good. Any other good movies that you've seen?

J.: I like old movies on TV.

M.: All old movies are good, simply because they are old.

J.: That is because in the old days there were such fabulous stars, with beautiful dresses and everyone was so glamorous.

M.: Do you think the movie star is a dying race?

J.: I'm afraid so. There just isn't anyone great anymore. I like Raquel Welch but there isn't anyone like Garbo or Hepburn or Carole Lombard. Or even the smaller ones, well not small but women like Myrna Loy and . . .

M.: Olivia De Havilland. Well it is sad.

J.: I don't want to go to the movies and watch someone have a nervous breakdown or fucking or whatever. People need glamour and frivolity for their fantasies.

For Tom Wolfe, the "primary gain" of the various cults that emerged in the wake of the sixties—leaving aside their particular belief-systems and rituals of renunciation—was narcissistic. What they offered was the endless gratification of talking about one's self, of sharing intimate details with large groups of strangers. Making what was private public elevated the ordinary individual to the level of dramatic personage. It was precisely this line between ordinary private person and dramatic public personage that Warhol and his followers played with, first in their films and then in *Interview*. Warhol's statement concerning the strange effect that speaking on tape had on the speaker, particularly on his or her "problems," is revealing: "An interesting problem was an interesting tape. Everybody knew that and performed for the tape. You couldn't tell which problems were real and which problems were performed for the tape. Better yet, the people telling you the problems couldn't decide any more if they were really having the problems or just performing." The interviews, wrote one critic, "read just like conversations, sometimes boring and trivial, but with the fascination of eavesdropping." Indeed, once the tape recorder was turned on, as Richard Nixon had discovered, it did not discriminate but picked up absolutely everything.

The new Warhol Factory resembled the Nixon White House in more ways than one—a resemblance that became a source of amusement to its members. Pat Hackett, the woman who transcribed Warhol's tapes (and coauthored *Popism*), was known as Rose Mary Woods and was teased about the "missing eighteen minutes" on one of his tapes for *Interview*. As Watergate unfolded, this little joke evolved: Paul Morrissey and Brigid Berlin became the Factory's versions of John and Martha Mitchell, and Bob Colacello became Bebe Rebozo. Asked his reaction to the discovery that Nixon had secretly been taping all his conversations, Warhol blandly stated: "Everyone should be bugged all the time." Brigid Berlin joked with Warhol that he should be president and that the White House's Blue Room would look much better if wallpapered with his Campbell's Soup Cans.

But beyond the fact that both Nixon and Warhol taped, Colacello detected a further parallel: "What the Nixon White House and the second Factory really had in common was a sense of being under siege. Nixon was paranoid; so was Andy Warhol, especially after Valerie Solanas was let out of prison in 1971." It was the shadow of his attempted assassination that ultimately led Warhol to turn his back on the sixties, in the person of the revolutionary feminist Valerie Solanas, whose cause had been taken up by NOW and who would become a perverse antihero for punk musicians. Lance Loud, who as a teenager had sent Warhol fan letters and talked with him by phone, found that all contact was broken off after the shooting: "I tried to write him but the letters came back. He suddenly became very, very private. He got very scared after that for a long time." The sense of mingled terror and deadpan commentary that inflects much of Warhol's work is nowhere better conveyed than in his question: "Will someone want to do a 1970s remake of shooting me?"

Warhol became even more paranoid when Nixon's "enemies list" was leaked to the press, and his name was included as McGovern's biggest financial supporter during the 1972 campaign. This was the result of a fluky bit of accounting that valued his donation of 350 posters to the candidate—depicting a repellent, silk-screened image of Nixon with the words "Vote McGovern" scrawled across them—at a wildly inflated $350,000. The IRS promptly responded by investigating Warhol's 1972 tax returns. Warhol subsequently went to great lengths to steer clear of political endorsements.

The truth was that for Warhol, politics represented simply another facet of celebrity culture. When in late 1972, after a five-year hiatus from painting, he began work on his Mao series, one dealer expressed concern that rich clients might object to the subject matter. But Warhol responded by pointing out that "Nixon had just been to see Mao, and if he was okay with Nixon, he would probably be okay with people like [wealthy collectors Gunther] Sachs and Stavros [Niarchos] too." In this respect Warhol's instincts were proved right. The Mao portraits proved a huge success, a demonstration that the power of superstardom might ultimately surpass that of political ideology. Even Jesus Christ was a Superstar, as the hit movie released in the summer of 1973 proclaimed.

Warhol's paintings of the 1970s largely eschewed the controversial subject matter of his earlier work. Whereas his early works had been permeated by deathly imagery (car crashes, electric chairs, disasters), now his subject matter took on a more conventional quality. Yet insofar as his earliest portraits—those of Marilyn and Jackie—had dealt with tragic subjects, his portrait work of the 1970s was also shadowed by a sense of tragedy. In the hands of Warhol, who now gave off an air of one who had come back from the grave, celebrity was invested with the trappings of a death-cult sensibility.

It is this sensibility that J. G. Ballard explored in his novel *Crash*, whose publication in 1973 represents one response to this aspect of Warholism. Norman Mailer, in his 1973 book on Marilyn Monroe, wrote that "as the deaths and spiritual disasters of the decade of the sixties came one by one to American Kings and Queens, as Jack Kennedy was killed, and Bobby, and Martin Luther King . . . so the decade that began with Hemingway as the monarch of American arts ended with Andy Warhol as its regent." That this was felt at the time as a disaster in its own right is demonstrated by the rather apocalyptic comments of Philip Leider, former editor of *Artforum*, about the 1973 death of Earthworks artist Robert Smithson. Crediting Smithson with a stature akin to that of Pollock in an earlier generation, Leider proclaimed that Smithson's death left a void in the art world. "The void," he observed, "got filled with Warholism." On the other hand, for those who did not easily fit the rather heroic mold cast by minimalism or its successor the Earthworks movement, Warholism represented a source of liberation and inspiration.

"The 60s," Warhol proclaimed, "were clutter. The 70s are very empty." At the center of this sense of emptiness stood Warhol himself, his image by this time a virtual signifier of absence and passivity. In a passage in his *Philosophy*, Warhol reads aloud from scrapbook clippings describing his enigmatic public persona: "The affectless gaze . . . the bored languor, the wasted pallor . . . the perfected otherness, the wispiness, the shadowy, voyeuristic, vaguely sinister aura, the pale, soft-spoken magical presence, the skin and bones." The ambiguous sense of presence-in-absence that was already the trademark of Warhol's persona of the 1960s had by the 1970s been perfected; he gave a spectral face to the void that was his own diagnosis for the condition of that decade. If revolutionary feminist Valerie Solanas and her SCUM

Manifesto represented the threat of castration, then Warhol presided over the ambiguously counterrevolutionary society of the seventies as a kind of castrated father figure—albeit one in whom castration was paradoxically a sign not of weakness but of mysterious vigor.

Ciao! Manhattan

By the early 1970s Warhol's world was littered with the carcasses of dead and burned-out former Superstars. Among them was Andrea Feldman, who starred in such Warhol films as *Heat* (1972) and who committed a very public suicide on August 8, 1972 (the tenth anniversary of the death of Marilyn Monroe, with whom Feldman identified herself). Like Solanas, who told the police that Warhol had had too much control over her, Feldman seems to have attributed malevolent powers to Warhol. This power evidently extended even to the arrangements she made for her suicide, which was witnessed by several friends whom she had taken care, without revealing her intentions, to invite to her building. Among them was the poet Jim Carroll, who described the incident in his memoir *Forced Entries*. Feldman was acting out the logic of a sensibility according to which everything can be converted into a spectacle, an image. As Warhol had said of his own attempted assassination: "It was just as if I was watching another movie."

No clearer testament to the end of the Warhol sixties could be found than the movie *Ciao! Manhattan*. Released in 1973, John Palmer and David Weisman's art-house film chronicled the rise and fall of former Superstar Edie Sedgwick, who died a few weeks after filming was completed in 1971. The movie is actually two films in one: the first, in color, shows Edie living in a pharmacological and alcoholic haze in the drained swimming pool of her mother's estate in Santa Barbara. It is structured around an extensive series of flashbacks taken from the black and white footage of a never-completed underground film shot in New York 1967 by Factory scenesters Genevieve Charbin and Chuck Wein. Edie relates her life story, via these flashbacks, to a dim-witted, flying saucer–loving Texan who has stumbled into her life. Meanwhile, her mother periodically ships her off to a clinic run by the lecherous psychiatrist Dr. Roberts, where she is groped, administered jolts of electricity, and injected with a powerful sedative. The contrast between Edie's degraded state and her former glamorous days as Superstar and fashion model serves as a comment on the wreckage to which the sixties reduced its greatest icons.

For a brief moment in the mid-1960s, Edie had been the brightest of the Stars in the Factory's firmament, starring in several of Warhol's films in addition to gracing the cover of fashion magazines like *Vogue* and, according to Patti Smith, inspiring Dylan's album *Blonde on Blonde*. In a manner that to some extent mirrors the SLA's later conversion of Patty Hearst, Edie's exchanging of her socialite life for the freaky glamour of an underground cult made her perhaps Warhol's greatest conquest. At the same time the relation between the two contained elements that directly anticipate *An American Family*; Warhol wrote that "I always wanted to do a movie of a whole day in Edie's life . . . What I liked was chunks of time all together, every real moment." Edie had served as Factory muse and as a kind of double of Warhol's; after she dyed her hair silver, they became virtually indistinguishable, a weird pair of doppelgängers, both equally androgynous: as Patti Smith said, describing the first time she saw Edie's stick figure in *Vogue*: "She was like a thin man in black leotards." By 1967, however, Edie had dropped out of the Factory scene and had begun her descent into the spiral of drug abuse and hospitalization that marked her last years.

Ciao! Manhattan portrays its subject as still helplessly in thrall to the cult of celebrity. Though her fifteen minutes of fame are long since up, Edie obsessively ruminates on her glory days, and makes repeated attempts to reach *Cosmopolitan* editor Helen Gurley Brown by phone. Her bedroom in a tent in the swimming pool is adorned with life-sized images of herself and other members of the Warhol Factory, some of whom—including Paul America, Viva, Brigid Berlin, and Baby Jane Holzer—make cameo appearances. Called "The 'Citizen Kane' of the Drug Generation" by the *Village Voice*, the film explores the dark underside of a celebrity-obsessed culture. On her way down Edie briefly crossed paths with Lance Loud, who was on his way up; she appeared in a few frames of the final segment of *An American Family* at a fashion show held in Santa Barbara that Loud also attended. Loud, who had first become aware of Edie through a 1966 *Time* magazine article about the lifestyle she shared with Warhol, met her at the party following the show, as he later recounted: "Edie came up, drawn like a moth to flames by those cameras. I was frightened. I thought suddenly it would appear that I was standing there with a ghost of myself in the future."

Reviewing the film in the *New York Review of Books*, critic Robert Mazzocco saw it as a parable for the end of the sixties. Within the drugged-out world its characters inhabit, there were "no idols left to fall": Edie, in his eyes, was a fitting metaphor, along the lines of Marilyn, "of beautiful blighted youth at the edge of the precipice." He credited it with a sci-fi dimension as well, reminiscent of the writings of William Burroughs, noting "the aura of some sort of white coat futuristic fascism bubbling around its edges, not the fascism of the jackboot but the fascism of shrinks and sanatoria, drugs and doctors." *Ciao! Manhattan* foreshadows the chemical version of the Me Decade, but it also prefigures that narcissistic version of the Me Decade lived out in the high-wattage glare of the cult of celebrity, when the Factory became part of mainstream America. When Jean Stein and George Plimpton published their *Edie* in 1982, its underlying message confirmed what, according to Bob Colacello, people had long known: that Warhol liked to watch people self-destruct.

Pop Art/Pop Music

The Warholian sensibility gained an exceptionally strong purchase in the world of rock music. The seminal art-rock group the Velvet Underground virtually became the Factory's house band in the mid-1960s, and after the band's breakup in 1970 its leader, Lou Reed, remained close to Warhol. According to Lenny Kaye, the guitarist in the Patti Smith Group, Reed's solo album *Transformer*, released in December 1972, is a tribute to the Warhol scene, insofar as transformation was what that scene offered people. Many of the songs contain character portraits of Factory figures—particularly the drag queens, to whom "Walk on the Wild Side" was a tribute—and the song "Andy's Chest" references Solanas's assassination attempt. Reed's next album, *Berlin* (1973), was purportedly an homage to the German-born Factory goddess Nico, who replaced Edie in Warhol's entourage. Music critic Lester Bangs characterized Warhol's influence on Reed as follows: "Lou learned a lot from Andy, mainly about being a successful public personality by selling your own private quirks to an audience greedy for more and more geeks." On the other hand, Bangs indirectly held Warhol responsible for what he called "the virus" of superstardom that had infected American culture, from pop music to politics.

Warhol's influence was not confined to the Velvet Underground but, as music critic and film director Mary Harron has written, extended to bands like the Ramones and the Talking Heads, which adopted his deadpan approach toward the ephemera of the American popular landscape. Warhol's greatest contribution, she continued, lay in his unsurpassed understanding of the importance of using the media "before they used you, by *consciously* developing an image." His success, she wrote, "also made it more important to have an image. He probably created David Bowie, and it seems right that Bowie, whose talent for celebrity rivals Warhol's own, should be the only rock star to write a song about him." Bowie's freaky glamour attests to the strange effects that entry into the Warholian universe had on its members' identities. Becoming part of this universe meant abandoning any simple or naïve form of identity, particularly those having to do with gender or sexuality.

Bowie's career during this, his Ziggy Stardust period, certainly represents the most calculated effort to seize control of the machinery of stardom. A conceptual album about a mythical pop star, Bowie's Ziggy Stardust has been called the first postmodern record for the way it deliberately blurs the distinction between performer and creation. In a piece written in 1974, *Beat International* editor Steve Turner described the steps involved in Bowie's reinvention as a self-consciously manufactured superstar. To be a cult figure, began Turner, you had to recognize the public need and then set out to fill it. Required reading for this process would include biographies of Dylan and Monroe as well as works like Joe McGinniss's *The Selling of the President* and Boorstin's *The Image*. In attempting to make sense of the Bowie phenomenon, Turner quoted liberally from these works, particularly McGinniss's, citing one key memo written by Nixon handler Ray Price: "The response is to the image, not to the man . . . It's not what's there that counts, it's what's projected." Image control was everything for Bowie and his managers, who fashioned artfully composed images to whet the public's appetite without ever fully satisfying it. In the weekly diary he wrote for *Mirabelle* magazine in 1973, Bowie devoted a month's worth of entries to revealing his secrets about hair and makeup to his fans.

Yet a crucial part of building an aura, according to Turner, was knowing when to stop: "Every good student of cult figures knows that it's important to either die or disappear from public view before interest dies away." The famous man, as the first page of Don DeLillo's novel *Great Jones Street* announced, "is compelled to commit suicide." Hence the significance of the much-publicized event at London's Hammersmith Auditorium, July 3, 1973, at which Bowie ended his Ziggy Stardust tour and simultaneously "retired" from the music world. This exemplary pseudo-event was recorded in D. A. Pennebaker's documentary *Ziggy Stardust and the Spiders from Mars*, which was shown on ABC the following year. The point of this maneuver seems to have been to rescue Bowie from the image fatigue that inevitably devalues the currency of a star's public persona. Turner implied, however, that it may already have been too late; how, he wondered, "does a cult figure feel at the end of the first two years as he sees carbon copies of his Ziggy idea walking the streets and living out the fantasy?"

Beyond the Valley of the Dolls

By the early 1970s, courting stardom meant entering a cultural space within which it became possible, even necessary, to try out new personae, to stage a kind of perpetual crisis of the self. Indeed this had become part of a larger cultural imperative, one that Betty Friedan, for instance, had urged on her readers as a way of escaping the clutches of the "feminine mystique." Warhol's put-down of the aggressively macho posturing of his art-world predecessors the abstract expressionists, and the Factory's rejection of the hetero ethos of hippie culture, ensured that gender in particular became an unstable, mutable signifier. The multiple permutations of the Bowie persona, for instance, invariably involved experiments in cross-dressing.

It was in 1973 that gender-bending crossed over, if only briefly, from the underground to the mainstream. The November issue of rock magazine *Creem* anointed 1973 as the "year of the transsexual tramp." Major stars such as Bowie, Iggy Pop, and Brian Eno as well as a host of lesser figures all deliberately incorporated sexual indeterminacy into their public personae. But in a year in which seemingly everyone wanted to be a queen, no group took this desire more to heart than the New York Dolls. The Dolls explicitly adopted as their model the drag queens in Warhol's orbit. Several of their early performances were organized in conjunction with the Warhol crowd and fronted by Jackie Curtis, the transvestite famous for her rejection of all gender labels—"I'm not a boy, not a girl. I'm me, Jackie"—whose impersonation of James Dean was memorialized in the last verse of Reed's hit "Walk on the Wild Side." Lead singer David Johansen cultivated particularly close connections with the Warhol crowd; one of his girlfriends, Diane Pulaski, had played a bit role in *Trash* and first introduced him to the Warhol retinue at Max's Kansas City, where he soaked up the art/drag scene. Later Johansen became romantically involved with Cyrinda Foxe, who was proclaimed "Warhol's newest superstar" in the December 1972 issue of *Interview*.

The Dolls had formed in 1972, first introducing their distinctive brand of trash rock to audiences at the Mercer Club on New York's

Lower East Side. They soon developed a cult following among audiences who loved their outlandish blend of the camp-glam sensibility with a deliberately primitive musical ethos that hearkened back to the earliest days of rock and roll. Stylistically and thematically decadent, the structure of their songs was simple in the extreme. It rejected the virtuosic excess of early-1970s rock anthems and brought back the three-minute format of 1950s rock music and of girl bands like the Shangri-Las. Within this format the band sang about utterly ordinary themes: loneliness, heartbreak, and riding the subway train. The opening track of their first album, "Personality Crisis," introduces the schizoid sensibility that marks their work with Johansen's wailing "Yeah, yeah, yeah!" followed immediately by a "No, no, no!" The most eloquent of their songs, like "Human Being," contain pleas that the freaks and monsters of the world be treated with tolerance. In "Frankenstein," the singer's entreaty to his girlfriend ends with the plaintive question:

> Is it a crime, is it a crime
> For you to fall in love with Frankenstein?
> I've got to ask you one question:
> Do you think that you could make it with Frankenstein?

By the summer of 1973, when their first album, *New York Dolls*, was released, the Dolls were the toast of New York. The cover of this album showed the band members—singer David Johansen, guitarist Johnny Thunders, rhythm guitarist Sylvain Sylvain, bassist Arthur Kane, and drummer Jerry Nolan—in full regalia, wearing heavy makeup, platform shoes, and elaborately teased hairdos, looking like "Stones doppelgängers in drag." Claiming that he was a "tri-sexual" (he'd try anything), Johansen had by this time made gender-bending a part of his ongoing repartee with the music press. While this was clearly a pose, it was not only that. Even if they were not gay, the Dolls seemed to be willing to go much further than other new bands of this period such as KISS and Aerosmith in erasing the distinction between their real selves and their stage personae.

The Dolls' answer to the bloated music of the early 1970s was a form of "enlightened amateurism," a deliberate unlearning of musical reflexes that represented a radical departure from bands like the Stones, to whom they were often otherwise compared. The wild popularity enjoyed by the Dolls attests to the pent-up desire for a new form of music. The musical landscape of the early 1970s was awash in sixties standards and bands still wedded to the now-tired formulas of that decade. Meanwhile the music industry as a whole was moving toward rationalization and concentration; as Greil Marcus would write in *Lipstick Traces*, songs like James Taylor's "Fire and Rain," Led Zeppelin's "Stairway to Heaven," and The Who's "Behind Blue Eyes" were being played ad nauseam on the radio, contributing to the rapid homogenization of musical tastes that would usher in the later era of corporate rock.

It was onto this enervated music scene that the Dolls burst in 1973, with a style that combined provocation with a sensibility that was pure camp. This sensibility, as Susan Sontag had written in her "Notes on Camp," is depoliticized, essentially emptied of critique, and in this sense the Dolls, as Morrissey of the later band the Smiths would note, represented "the first real sign that the Sixties were over." The glam-rock that musicians from Reed to Bowie to the Dolls embraced in the early 1970s represented a reaction to the authenticity and sincerity of the 1960s. Or to put this another way, if the sixties emphasized *being*, the seventies were about *becoming*—a distinction Reed captured on *Transformer* in his homage to drag queen Holly Woodlawn, who "plucked her eyebrows" and "shaved her legs" and turned from a "he" into a "she."

The highly self-referential nature of this music scene extended to its deliberate foregrounding of excess and madness. Its decadence was a response to what music critic Greil Marcus describes as the realization that society's promises were no longer being kept. Primarily interested in the roots of punk music, in *Lipstick Traces* Marcus constructs a genealogy of mid-1970s youthful nihilism that goes back to the 1950s: "The world promised in the 1950s"—a world of material abundance and leisure—"a world apparently on the verge of realization in the

1960s, seemed like a cruel joke by 1975." It was the realization of this joke that spawned the music scene of the early and mid-1970s. As Reed's album *Berlin* made clear, a central stylistic reference point for these musicians was the former German capital, a city long synonymous with preapocalyptic decadence. In a New York on the verge of social and financial breakdown, "like a used car held together by K-Y and clothes hangers," evocations of Weimar Berlin at the moment of the Nazi seizure of power were common currency. Bob Fosse's film *Cabaret*, which was based on Christopher Isherwood's Berlin stories and which scooped up several Oscars at the 1973 Academy Awards, established a historical antecedent for the glam scene. According to journalist and author Legs McNeil: "Glitter was about decadence . . . rock stars living their lives from Isherwood's Berlin stories. You know, Sally Bowles hanging out with drag queens, drinking champagne for breakfast and having *ménages à trois* while the Nazis grab power."

Defining their sensibility as antithetical to the utopianism of the 1960s, the Dolls made self-conscious decadence a specialty. In place of authenticity, they offered pure artifice, the split persona of "Personality Crisis":

> You're a prima ballerina on a spring afternoon
> Change into a wolf-man howling at the moon

While for Daniel Boorstin the star system represented "a generalized process for transforming hero into celebrity," fans of the Dolls found their message liberating. As Richard Hell of the band Television, one of the successors to the Dolls, would say, "One thing I wanted to bring back to rock & roll was the knowledge that you invent yourself. That's why I changed my name, why I did all the clothing style things, haircut, everything . . . If you just amass the courage that is necessary, you can completely invent yourself. You can be your own hero."

What was the relation between image and reality? Was this mock depravity, madness as a kind of pseudo-event—as it seemed to be for bands such as Alice Cooper and KISS—or the real thing? For Hell, precisely the patent artifice and vulgarity of the Dolls' image endowed them with a weird new kind of authenticity, one that trampled on the pieties then prevailing in the music world. According to Hell: "The Dolls were the real thing—on stage and off they were real life rock & roll stars because they wanted to feel that way, the way they imagined it would be like, and so they did it." Like other figures such as Bowie, the Dolls' act was for Hell the product of a quite specific form of self-consciousness: "Their stage acts are studied, they have carefully designed the image of themselves that they mean to project . . . I think this is great. The art-form of the future is celebrity-hood."

For others, even those sympathetically inclined, the band's act could be more confusing. Profiling the band in *Interview*, Ed McCormack made a point of telling his readers, "The New York Dolls have mothers too," while pointedly leaving aside any mention of their fathers. No sooner was the natural gender order invoked, however, than it was immediately placed in question. Lead guitarist Johnny Thunders's mother was quoted as being in shock over a picture of her son in drag, complaining to his girlfriend: "What are you doing to my son? What's this with the hands on the hips and the bellybutton sticking out and the little polka-dot bikini pulled over his pants?" The girlfriend explained that it was an act, driven by "the importance of a rock group having a distinctive image." The makeup and the pantyhose, she reassured her, were just part of the act; they did not mean that her son had changed. But in McCormack's mind at least this point remained somewhat unclear; later in the article he seemed to contradict his earlier reassurances when he commented that the Dolls gave voice to New York's underground, to the "fantastic creatures" that "some people in the New York underground who hang out in the back room of Max's Kansas City have made of themselves—as though to give birth in some weird onanistic fashion to some wholly different creatures from the ones their parents birthed!"

The schizoid contrast between form and content that marked the band's live performances could generate confusion in the audience. A *Creem* profile of the Dolls described them as "movers and shakers of identity crises" and listed one of their hobbies as straight-baiting. After a fight broke out at one Long Island concert, Johansen observed: "It must have been some primordial reaction to sexual confusion because the guys started beating the shit out of each other . . . meanwhile, the girls were looking at us in a trance." In their natural Manhattan milieu, on the other hand, the Dolls' performances were likely to be greeted by a crowd that, as one critic for a British underground paper wrote, wore "day-glo, lurex, tinsel, glitter dust on flesh, and clothes, studs, satin, silk and leather, lurid reds, pink angora tops, green boas and totally transparent blouses." The entire thing, he went on, "is almost an outrageous parody of the 1930s American glamour concept." He concluded: "No, all this is real, as a nation coming out from under 10 years of unpopular war, a history of Puritanism and genocide, greets four more years of Nixon with its most potent weapon, Faggot Rock, the music of total drop out!"

In the end, things became confusing for the band members as well. For sheer spectacle, nothing could compete with the all-too-brief trajectory of the New York Dolls' passage through the music scene. From the outset opinion on the band was wildly polarized: *Creem* readers voted them both the best and the worst new band of 1973. Musically, the Dolls' sound would go on to have a major influence on the genesis of punk music. Their combination of amateurism and sophistication heralded the birth of the music scene that crystallized around a new venue that opened in December 1973, the bar CBGB, located on the Bowery in New York's East Village. Yet despite their tremendous local following and the strong sales of their first album, the Dolls did not travel well outside of New York, failing to translate their cult status into the national stardom expected of them. This was later blamed on the conservatism of the music industry, which took their public image as "a bunch of degenerate queers" at face value. In truth, the Dolls represented a phenomenon that could not easily be assimilated into a music industry growing increasingly conservative. At the same time, however, their own growing confusion concerning their public image was a contributing factor to their eventual demise. The pleasure they took at living the rock star fantasy, which constituted a large part of their appeal, also certainly contributed to their undoing. According to Harron, Warhol inspired the parody of decadence as a subject for rock music; the question with the Dolls was, when did it stop being parody?

Legendary for his drunken public appearances, Johansen became increasingly unruly on stage and was arrested after one concert in Memphis for impersonating a woman and allegedly inciting a riot. Meanwhile drug-taking blurred the line between real and put-on insanity for some of the other band members. It was no longer possible, as Warhol had noted, to tell which problems were performed for the tape and which problems were real. As Thunders's speed habit spiraled out of control, he became increasingly paranoid, at one point accusing Johansen of working for the CIA and Nixon. According to rhythm guitarist Sylvain, "It was like he got instant schizophrenia," while another member of their retinue chalked up Thunders's drug-taking to his inability to escape the image he had embraced: Thunders "put his image as a guitar player above his playing, and unfortunately, his image became self-destructive."

Premonitions of this outcome had been there from the band's earliest beginnings. Its first drummer, Billy Murcia, had died by drug overdose, an event, as Sylvain observed, that had given the band a lot of publicity: "We were living this movie: everyone wants to see it and we were giving it to them." Already by the end of 1973 the Dolls were learning the cost of their celebrity. The band, in the words of author Jon Savage, had "begun with a script and now—in the confusion between person and persona that always occurs in pop—they were living the movie for real." One of the band's more poignant songs is "Private World," which records the singer's desire to get away and barricade himself in a room in response to a breakdown. Given the insanity of the band members' lives, it was a natural response; as Arthur Kane described it: "We were Dolls 24 hours a day . . . When the fans located us it became crazy. They knew where we lived and where we hung out. There were always people around us, we were never protected," he lamented, while at the same time conceding that "it's something that we did to ourselves." Despite the efforts of Malcolm McLaren, British fashion impresario and future manager of the Sex Pistols, to refashion the Dolls' image and put them back on the course to stardom, the band was broken beyond fixing by early 1974. McLaren's attempt to stage a Warholian coup by outfitting them with red vinyl and copies of Mao's Little Red Book, and making them perform in front of a Communist flag, proved a dismal failure. Revolutionary camp was not an idea destined for success. After their aptly titled second album *Too Much Too Soon* generated only modest sales, the band split up.

An Image Is an Image

If the cult of celebrity had its casualties—those incapable of resisting either its allure or the fate that awaited them once their fifteen minutes were over—it also had its conscientious objectors: figures such as novelist Thomas Pynchon and filmmaker Terrence Malick, who, by refusing all interviews and shunning the public eye, jealously guarded their privacy as well as their aura as artists existing apart from society. Another such figure is the novelist Don DeLillo, whose mania for privacy was reportedly such that he once responded to someone who approached him for an interview by handing him a scrap of paper on which were written the words "I don't want to talk about it." The example of David Bowie, like the disappearance from the public eye of Bob Dylan several years earlier, hangs over DeLillo's 1973 novel, *Great Jones Street*, the story of a rock star who tries to "step out of his legend." The novel's antihero, Bucky Wunderlick, quickly learns that his attempt to escape his own celebrity has made him, if anything, even more of a celebrity—the object of obsessive media speculation and rumors concerning his whereabouts. At the same time he earns the admiration of a secretive, cultlike group called the Happy Valley Farm Commune, for whose members "privacy has become the most revolutionary wish of all." They are stockpiling weapons and manufacturing a new drug in preparation for a violent campaign to "return the idea of privacy to American life." When Wunderlick begins to talk about going back on tour, the cult members try to convince him that it would be better for his musical legacy to commit suicide by drug overdose.

While the Edie Sedgwick story as related in *Ciao! Manhattan* suggested that a person could be literally unhinged by fame, that too much exposure was fatal, it also suggested there was something pathological about investing too heavily in images. Speaking of her first time seeing a picture of Edie, Patti Smith noted: "She was such a strong image that I thought, that's it, it represented everything to me . . . radiating intelligence, speed, being connected with the moment." Smith wrote a eulogy for Edie after her death and, in a piece in *Interview* magazine in the summer of 1973, spoke at length of *Ciao! Manhattan* and her infatuation with Edie: "I've always been hero-oriented. Art . . . was a way to ally myself with heroes, 'cause I couldn't make contact with god. The closest, most accessible god was a hero-god"—one such as Edie. Smith was also deeply invested in aura, or as she put it, "I was very image-oriented." Seeing Edie "bloated and wasted" in the film reminded Smith that "heroes die, images fade"; she attributed her transition to a new and more complicated relation to images to having overcome her earlier infatuations, when "I was still very much into image . . . I always felt I was in a black and white 16 mm film."

Growing up, she said, she had been a huge fan of Bob Dylan and Arthur Rimbaud but had also read *Vogue* and *Bazaar*, because "an image is an image." She then recounted a recent experience in which she had had the opportunity to pay homage to her hero Edie by appearing in a Saks fashion show. Wearing a velvet coat and fur boa, she then dropped them to the floor, revealing a long, ratty T-shirt underneath and eliciting gasps from the women in the audience. By 1973 Smith was on the threshold of becoming herself a bigger star than Edie. After hanging around Max's Kansas City hoping to be noticed by Warhol and his entourage, she began performing there and at other venues in New York, on one occasion reading her poetry as an opening act for the Dolls. In the fall of 1973 she performed at a Rimbaud festival at the gay discotheque Le Jardin, which had opened in June, reading her poems with the accompaniment of Lenny Kaye on guitar. The seeds for her later superstardom were sown, and it was not long before she herself was caught up in the machinery of celebrity culture.

Her friend Penny Arcade noticed the change in her interaction with her fans: the person Patti Smith had been, "she was now using that in this public way—it was now for everyone."

Patti Smith's onetime lover, the poet and memoirist Jim Carroll, also fell into Warhol's orbit during this period. His published diaries, *Forced Entries*, which cover the period 1971–73, relate the life of a person who exists in the reflected glow cast by Warhol's high-wattage Superstars while trying to overcome his own drug addiction and establish himself as a poet. Andrea Feldman's public suicide, to which he had been issued an invitation, was one of the events that shocked Carroll into consideration of the hazards of falling under the Warholian spell. For Carroll, poetry and other forms of creation originated in an essentially private struggle that was violated by Warhol's habit of taping phone conversations and then replaying them for others. Ultimately, the line separating Warhol's ubiquitous tape recorder from the secret recording system discovered to be operating in the Oval Office became thin indeed for Carroll; he referred to Warhol's phone taping as "FBI-CIA art."

In one entry in his book, Carroll describes a chance meeting with Earthworks artist Robert Smithson. It is evening, and Carroll finds himself trying to follow a strange, nighttime apparition: a labyrinth fashioned by a laser that crisscrosses the streets of lower Manhattan, finally ending up at Max's Kansas City. The labyrinth bears a resemblance to Smithson's recently finished masterwork, the Spiral Jetty. Smithson suggests that the labyrinth is a way of concealing secret knowledge as well as the artist who made it, who harbors both secrets and fears, including a fear of fame. "The point is," he tells Carroll, "we don't all of us want fame."

Carroll's diaries end with him recovering from drug addiction and withdrawing from his formerly hectic life as nonstop scene-maker into a more reclusive existence. The final entries concern his struggles to cure himself of a hideous abscess that has disfigured his right arm for months and has proved resistant to all efforts at treatment. It becomes for Carroll the emblem of his addiction: "a memorial tattoo that I myself inscribed, as if for an old lover, in homage to that sickness I took years to perfect." It finally bursts in a grotesque sequence that is like something out of *The Exorcist*—"This was the toxic residue of all my past sins . . . the petty demons marching out"—and that leaves the author to finally realize what, according to the members of DeLillo's Happy Valley Farm Commune, represents the most revolutionary wish of all: "I feel a comfort in being alone."

Reinventing the Fifties

> The most powerful cultural force
> operating in the 1970s is nostalgia.
>
> —Paul Monaco

AUGUST 1, 1973: *The late summer release of director George Lucas's* American Graffiti *would turn out to be one of the surprise success stories of the year. Made for the modest sum of $750,000 and capitalizing on a wave of fifties nostalgia, Lucas's film became a smash hit, joining a series of recent low-budget films that were changing the face of the industry while at the same time laying the groundwork for the later blockbuster era exemplified by his own* Star Wars.

Both in the opportunities for new directors and in the content of the films, the contours of the oedipal drama acted out nationwide during the late sixties became particularly clear in Hollywood. Between the collapse of the traditional studios in 1969–71 and their later resurrection in the mid-1970s, Hollywood experienced a brief flowering of director-driven filmmaking. Nineteen seventy-three was the annus mirabilis of this New Wave, the year when several older maverick directors and a new generation of younger filmmakers released a series of seminal films. Included among the year's crop were Martin Scorsese's *Mean Streets*, Robert Altman's *The Long Goodbye*, William Friedkin's *The Exorcist*, Woody Allen's *Sleeper*, Nicolas Roeg's *Don't Look Now*, and Sam Peckinpah's *Pat Garrett and Billy the*

Kid. Many of these films, like *The Exorcist*, were conscious exercises in parricide.

Two of the more precocious films released that year were George Lucas's *American Graffiti* and Terrence Malick's *Badlands*. Both films looked back to the 1950s and to the origins of one of the most enduring myths of the 1960s: the teen rebel, personified by screen icon James Dean. While both films were deeply marked by that myth, they handled it in radically different ways. Both constructed a relation to the 1950s mediated by the experience of the decade-long war in Vietnam. In the case of Lucas's film, this experience is, however, all but invisible; he bathed the 1950s in a nostalgic glow, virtually eliminating any trace of real generational conflict and mentioning only in pass-ing—in the postscript that informs us of the subsequent fate of his four characters—the traumatic war that separated 1973 from that more innocent time. In doing so, Lucas lent his talents to the larger cultural project of erasing a decade of bad history. The success of *American Graffiti* helped launch a huge fifties craze, symbolized by the TV show *Happy Days*, which began airing in 1974. It also demonstrated that by 1973 the formula for the later blockbuster era, with its demand for happy endings and easy resolutions of the oedipal drama—out of fashion since Arthur Penn's 1967 *Bonnie and Clyde*—was once again firmly in place. Malick's film, on the other hand, collapsed Vietnam and the fifties into a single, highly charged cinematic space. Weaving its own disenchanted variation on the Bonnie and Clyde story of young outlaw lovers, *Badlands* wraps the rebellious poses and gestures of the sixties in a framework of cool reserve, while at the same time suggesting that Lucas's search for a usable past in the fifties was deeply compromised.

Crisis of the Old Regime

In his account of Hollywood during the 1970s, *Easy Riders, Raging Bulls*, Peter Biskind relates the following anecdote to illustrate the clash between the Old and New Hollywood that occurred in the late

1960s and early 1970s. Fresh off the success of *Easy Rider*, Dennis Hopper accosted George Cukor, director of classics like *The Phila-delphia Story* and *A Star is Born*, at a dinner party. The drunken Hopper jabbed his finger into the courtly Cukor's chest and an-nounced: "We're going to bury you. We're gonna take over. You're finished."

Hopper had good reason to be feeling confident. Nominated for an Oscar for Best Original Screenplay, he was now a hot property, much in demand with the studio heads who were anxious to cash in on the new youth market the film had tapped into. There was every indication of better things to come for him and his generation. By the end of the 1960s, the days of the studios that ran the film industry seemed numbered. Hollywood was an industry in crisis. The sources of its troubles included competition from television, which had made deep inroads into the film industry's audience; and the antitrust legislation of the early 1950s, which had broken the studios' hold over the theater chains that controlled exhibition. The industry's conservatism and risk-aversion left it increasingly out of step with the times. Wedded to formulas that no longer worked, Hollywood continued to churn out bloated, expensive, star-laden pictures that failed to connect with the new generation that had come of age in the 1960s. This younger audience, whose tastes reflected the changes that swept American society during this decade, simply ignored films like *Hello Dolly!*, one of the box office bombs of 1969. By the end of the decade virtually all the major studios were losing money. The period 1969–71 marked the nadir: an industry whose audience had reached a peak of 78 million a week in 1946 saw it bottom out at 15.8 million a week in 1971.

It was out of the crisis of the studio system that the New Hollywood was born. A generation of filmmakers steeped in the auteurist cinema of the French *nouvelle vague*—according to which a film was the product of a distinctive directorial voice rather than the studio sys-tem—as well as in the countercultural politics spawned by the war in Vietnam, suddenly found that the customary obstacles to advancement in the industry were gone and that there was a demand for directors who could tap into the sensibilities of the new youth market. The inaugural film of this cultural revolution was Arthur Penn's 1967 *Bonnie and Clyde*, which starred Warren Beatty and Faye Dunaway. Warner Brothers promoted this story of young outlaw lovers with a tagline that read: "They're young . . . they're in love . . . and they kill people." The film ushered in a new era of stylized realism in American filmmaking; when, at the end of the movie, part of Clyde's head is blown away, Penn intended the shot to evoke the Zapruder film showing Kennedy's assassination. Though in the end they are gunned down, the film endowed its antiheroes with an aura of populist romance, offering, according to film critic J. Hoberman, a justification for violence reminiscent of countercultural heroes like H. Rap Brown and Franz Fanon. In her rave review of the film, Pauline Kael expressed the anxiety it aroused among shocked older viewers in the following terms: "Will we be lured into imitating the violent crimes of Bonnie and Clyde because Warren Beatty and Faye Dunaway are 'glamorous'? Do they confer . . . glamour on violence?" Clyde more than compensates for his inability to perform sexually by his prowess with a gun and even more by his native cunning at publicity, his sense of style. The real originality of *Bonnie and Clyde*, writes Hoberman, "lay in the realization that the lust for celebrity in the Global Village might be as potent a drive as sex."

The enormous success of *Bonnie and Clyde* made its stars icons of late-sixties radical chic and opened the door to a wave of youth-oriented films led by *Easy Rider*. In an effort to capitalize on the success of these films, the major studios created new youth divisions headed by younger executives who were charged with funding small, inexpensive productions that would deliver the youth market—those under twenty-nine, who by this time represented 73 percent of the total audience. The premium within these youth divisions was on new talent, and they gave a largely untested generation of writers and directors, many of them fresh out of film school, an unprecedented license to make their own films. Young directors like Francis Ford Coppola, Bob Rafelson, Hal Ashby, William Friedkin, and Peter Bogdanovich, as well as older figures like Penn, Robert Altman, and Sam Peckinpah, took advantage of the studios' crisis to make their own highly personal films, many of them darker and far more violent than traditional Hollywood fare.

The abruptness and suddenness with which these changes took hold in the film industry engendered a perception of change, even revolution, among the vanguard of the New Hollywood. This was particularly true in the case of Hopper, who since his first appearance alongside James Dean in *Rebel Without a Cause* had cultivated an image of himself as an industry rebel. By the end of the 1960s this image, fueled by the success of *Easy Rider* and by large quantities of drugs, had assumed grandiose proportions. Hopper began to style himself a cultural revolutionary lobbing Molotov cocktails at a corrupt old order symbolized by the studio system, which he saw (particularly in its treatment of Indians) as complicit with the whole history of American expansionism. His provocatively titled film *The Last Movie* (1971) was intended as an exercise in genre deconstruction that, by exploding the myths of the Western, would set the record straight about the American past and about its current involvement in Indochina. During the making of this film Hopper reportedly wore a ring that had once belonged to his friend Dean and that had passed into his possession after Dean's death. Evidently both Hopper and his crew members believed that it allowed him to channel Dean's spirit.

That the Western—the most myth-laden of all Hollywood genres— would become the ground on which the conflict between the Old Hollywood and the New was fought out was hardly surprising. To critics of the war in Vietnam, of whom there were many in the younger Hollywood generation, the connections between the mindset that had involved the United States in that war and the old myths of the frontier were all too obvious. The imagery of the Wild West cast a long shadow across the imagination of what war correspondent Michael Herr called the war's "media freaks." While archgunslinger and ardent anti-Communist John Wayne propagandized the war effort with his "crypto-Western" *The Green Berets*, among the members of the Hollywood counterculture the ideology of the Western was commonly implicated in the war crimes that had been exposed at My Lai.

The conflict between the Old and the New Hollywood would be made explicit at the 1973 Academy Awards. One month after two hundred armed supporters of the American Indian Movement (AIM) had seized control of Wounded Knee in South Dakota, on February 27, 1973—an event that led to a two-month-long siege with many Vietnam-like features—Marlon Brando, named Best Actor for his role in *The Godfather*, sent Indian activist Sacheen Littlefeather in his place to protest the film industry's treatment of Native Americans. Hollywood, in the person of Clint Eastwood, responded by suggesting that someone should say a word on behalf of all the cowboys killed in Westerns. But the days of the Western were numbered. The crisis in Hollywood mirrored the crisis of this most basic of its genres. As Richard Slotkin observes, the end of the war in Vietnam in 1973 marked the end of "the preeminence of the Western among the genres of mythic discourse." The frontier violence that Slotkin identified as an essential feature of American narrative had failed its mythic, regenerative function. No longer serviceable as a genre, the Western entered a steep decline; from a high of twenty-nine in 1971, the number of Westerns released by Hollywood studios fell off to seven in 1974 and continued to decline thereafter.

Brando was hardly alone in his flirtation with radical causes. Warren Beatty, whose role as Clyde Barrow had inaugurated Hollywood radical chic, hobnobbed with members of the Black Panther Party. Jane Fonda traveled to Indochina, met with North Vietnamese officals and American POWs, and posed atop one of the antiaircraft guns used to shoot down U.S. pilots. The producer of *Easy Rider*, Bert Schneider, who also oversaw the creation of several other seminal New Hollywood films, including *The Last Picture Show*, the Oscar-winning Vietnam documentary *Hearts and Minds*, and later Terrence Malick's *Days of Heaven*, embraced political radicalism in the figure of charismatic Black Panther leader Huey Newton. Schneider helped fund Newton's political activities and later, in 1973, after Newton jumped bail on numerous charges, helped spirit the fugitive out of the country.

No cause energized the film community more in 1973 than the standoff at Wounded Knee, South Dakota. At the time South Dakota was widely perceived by AIM as "John Wayne country"—as far as Native Americans were concerned, the most racist state in the nation. Wounded Knee was located on the Pine Ridge reservation, home to the poorest county in America, and was controlled by tribal leader Richard Wilson, who was treated by the U.S. government as a "friendly" and ran the reservation as his personal fiefdom. Among the offenses for which he had earned the enmity of many of the Indians who inhabited the reservation, none loomed larger than his giveaway of eighty thousand acres to the United States for the creation of the Badlands National Monument.

Coming one month after the Paris peace accords signaled the end of what Slotkin calls "America's latest Indian war," the siege at Wounded Knee was inevitably overlaid by elements of the conflict in Indochina. The site itself was highly symbolic: in 1890, in a massacre of My Lai dimensions, U.S. Army troops had killed 350 Lakota Sioux men, women, and children there. The three hundred or so members of AIM and other militant Indians who "retook" the site in 1973 included many veterans of the Vietnam War, who now used their experience of Vietcong guerrilla tactics to improvise a system of defenses capable of withstanding the enormous firepower arrayed against them. Local and federal law enforcement as well as, illegally, U.S. Army troops subjected the occupiers to scorched-earth tactics resembling those used in Vietnam. One of the doctors brought in to tend to the injured Indians compared the scene to Vietnam: "It's like a flashback to Danang." Wilson painted AIM as a Communist organization.

Heavily outnumbered and outgunned, the Indians relied on the expert orchestration of the media to shape the battle of public opinion. As one AIM member told the press, "If it were not for you people, the government would have slaughtered us as it did in 1890." Letters, telegrams, and phone calls of support poured in from around the world, and AIM used its connections in the film industry, including figures like Brando and Harry Belafonte, to garner more support. These maneuvers earned the siege at Wounded Knee the label "guerrilla theater" from some members of the press. What had begun as a protest against local conditions eventually turned into a referendum on the history of U.S.–Indian relations. Yet although the presence of the media certainly hamstrung U.S. efforts to resolve the situation by force and brought publicity to AIM's cause, in the end it was not enough. South Dakota senator and former presidential candidate George McGovern was brought in to mediate but left without obtaining any results. Ultimately, after two of their members were killed, the Indians were forced to lay down their weapons with virtually nothing to show for their two-month-long occupation of Wounded Knee. This denouement, in the estimation of one scholar, "demonstrated the powerlessness of radical protest."

Brando's role in this cause célèbre was not without its own element of farcical guerrilla theater. The statement read by Sacheen Little-feather included Brando's claim that "I thought perhaps I could have been of better use if I went to Wounded Knee." Instead of leaving for Wounded Knee with Littlefeather that night, as he had promised her, Brando left for his retreat in Tahiti—abandoning Littlefeather, an Indian activist who would go on to have a modest career in Holly-wood. Brando would later be mocked for the stunt he had pulled with his "fake Indian princess." Yet Brando did help harbor AIM leader Dennis Banks, a fugitive from justice for his role at Wounded Knee, whose efforts to evade capture with the help of a network of associates were worthy of a Hollywood treatment. Banks's adventures in the radical underground brought him into contact with the likes of Patty Hearst and Jim Jones.

Coppola Under Siege

With the war winding down and the Black Panther Party in steep decline, radical causes were on the wane. This was increasingly true as well of the internal politics of the film community. Power relations in Hollywood had been a burning issue for the younger generation, especially the new directors, many of whom harbored a righteous anger at the old order: "The studio system is dead," declared George

Lucas, "It died . . . when the corporations took over and the studio heads suddenly became agents and lawyers and accountants. The power is with the people now. The workers have the means of production." Such inflammatory rhetoric bore the unmistakable stamp of Lucas's mentor Francis Ford Coppola, who more than any other member of the New Hollywood nurtured the dream of tearing down the old studios and creating an alternative studio system. Coppola placed his faith in the new technology that he believed was about to revolutionize the industry. The cheap, lightweight, portable cameras and other equipment that had become available in the late 1960s, he believed, would enable filmmakers to emancipate themselves from the control of the studios, move off the studio lots and film on location, and ultimately render the old studio system completely obsolete. Coppola's first effort to escape from the powerful orbit of the studio system resulted in the creation of his Zoetrope Studios in San Francisco, which he and his coterie of younger directors, including Lucas, envisioned as a countercultural version of MGM.

Yet Coppola's empire building ran into trouble from the outset, due as much to his own excesses, waste, and megalomania and to his inability to find commercially viable projects as to the entrenched resistance of the studios on which he was still dependent for financing. Already by 1970 Zoetrope was flirting with financial disaster, and Coppola was forced to work on studio projects in order to dig his way out from under a mountain of debt. The eventual failure of this undertaking was reproduced by that of Coppola's later venture for achieving artistic independence: the so-called Director's Company consisting of three New Hollywood wunderkinder—Coppola, Friedkin, and Bogdanovich—that was formed in 1972. This experiment in fusing the new auteurist cinema with the financial muscle of the studio system foundered and was shut down by its parent company, Paramount.

But these ill-fated attempts to achieve the independence that Coppola believed necessary to artistic creation did nothing to diminish his own talent for making landmark films. His two biggest hits—the first two *Godfather* films, released in 1972 and 1974—were both studio

projects, which he took on only reluctantly but managed nevertheless
to infuse with his own intensely personal vision. Along with Friedkin's
The French Connection (1971) and *The Exorcist* (1973) and Bogdanovich's *The Last Picture Show* (1971), the *Godfather* series helped
drive Hollywood's recovery in the early 1970s. After years of stagna-
tion at the box office, the 1974 grosses were the biggest since 1946.
The audiences who began returning to the theaters were, it is true, also
lured by more traditional fare such as the big-budget disaster films that
became a staple of this period, led by *The Poseidon Adventure*, the top-
grossing film of 1973. Yet the New Hollywood directors played a vital
role in restoring Hollywood's connection with its audience and thus
eliminating the very crisis that was the precondition for their own all-
too-brief ascendancy.

Not coincidentally, many of these films were marked by a parricide
theme. Their plots were set in motion, as Biskind writes, by the "moral
and emotional vacuum at the center of the home" caused by the
absence, death, or killing of the father. This was explicitly the case in
The Exorcist, as we have already seen in Chapter 4, as well as in
Badlands, as we shall see later in this chapter. But the killing of the
father, or—to put it another way—the critique of the values of the
fathers' generation, could also be accompanied by an idealization or
lament for a lost patriarchy. This was exemplified by a wave of
"immigrant" films led by *The Godfather*.

Not incidentally, the attempted assassination of Don Corleone in
The Godfather is motivated by his refusal to countenance his rival
Sollozzo's plan to muscle in on the drug trade. Don Corleone's
opposition to drug trafficking is that of an old-fashioned patriarch
who deplores the corrosive effects of narcotics on the traditional values
of his generation. The don's stand commented on the drug culture that
was becoming a staple not just of films from *Easy Rider* to *The French
Connection* but also of the countercultural lifestyles of many New
Hollywood figures. If we are to believe the accounts of producer Julia
Phillips (who won the 1973 Best Film Oscar for *The Sting*) and others,
Hollywood was completely awash in drugs during this period. According to Jack Nicholson, cocaine became wildly popular in Holly-

wood in 1972, a development for which Dennis Hopper, with characteristic immodesty, claimed credit. Drugs, and in particular cocaine,
certainly influenced Hopper's spectacular rise and no less spectacular
fall—as a result of the failure of the drug- and paranoia-drenched *The
Last Movie*—from the pinnacle of auteurism. But cocaine was just one
of the highs available to the members of the New Hollywood. At a
party one night at the house of Joan Didion and John Gregory Dunne,
Julia Phillips found herself in the bathroom, where she took careful
note of the contents of her hosts' medicine cabinet: "Outside of my
mother's, it was the most thrilling medicine cabinet I had ever seen.
Ritalin, Librium, Miltown, Fioranol, Percodan . . . every upper, down-
er, and in-betweener of interest in the PDR, circa 1973."

Survival of the Old Regime

Already at its moment of triumph, the New Hollywood was crumbling
as quickly as it had been built. The survival of the values of the father
in Michael Corleone, who started out by rejecting them, serves as a
metaphor for the fate of the directors' cinema and the limited nature of
the revolt staged by the new generation. Joan Didion was one of those
less impressed by the story of oedipal conflict that was so much a part
of the ethos of the new auteurism. In a piece titled "In Hollywood,"
published in 1973, she trained her gaze on the film industry. While
getting her hair cut one day, she reported, she had read in the trade
papers that *The Poseidon Adventure* was grossing $4 million a week
and that Adolph Zukor, legendary head of Paramount Pictures, was
celebrating his hundredth birthday that year. Both facts suggested to
her that beyond any surface appearance of crisis in the film industry,
the underlying reality remained more or less the same: the studios still
put up almost all the money, still controlled distribution, and still
earned most of the profit. Auteurist pretensions notwithstanding, the
"Monroe Stahrs [the name of the whiz-kid producer in F. Scott
Fitzgerald's Hollywood novel *The Last Tycoon*] come and go," their
careers and the films on which they are based as ephemeral as the

"truly beautiful story" her hairdresser tried to interest her in, a story that aspired to be turned Cinderella-like into a film. The name of the game in Hollywood, she took pleasure in reminding outsiders overly credulous of the story of collapsing studios, was not any individual "property" but rather survival in the Darwinian business of making the deal that led to the film. Zukor represented for her the ultimate Hollywood survivor in a town in which "the players change but the game will stay the same." The Zukor story had a pointed lesson: Didion related it as a cautionary tale to the film critics and industry outsiders (usually New Yorkers) who celebrated the demise of the old studios. Against those who asserted this as a moment of rupture with the past, Hollywood emerged in Didion's ironic telling as "the last extant stable society," the final bastion of capitalism, able to put down, or coopt, all revolutions.

If for Didion, the perception of revolutionary change concealed underlying continuity, Pauline Kael—an unabashed outsider and partisan of the new directors' cinema—was more inclined to give credence to this perception. Yet she could not ignore the signs of growing malaise in the New Hollywood. These she diagnosed as a symptom of the exhaustion of the counterculture. What Kael, writing in *The New Yorker* in the fall of 1973, called "the Vietnamization of American movies" had galvanized a moribund industry. Though Hollywood steered clear of directly addressing the war—and would continue to do so until the late 1970s—its films were nevertheless indelibly marked by it. By finishing off "the American hero as righter-of-wrongs," Vietnam had introduced a new moral ambiguity that, in Kael's estimation, had energized filmmaking, creating a new realism in place of the "old mock innocence." The realism that had entered pictures in the 1960s had had a salutary effect: breathing new life into stale genres and formulas and demolishing others altogether. The myths of the Old West that had played themselves out in Vietnam were turned upside down in the genre deconstruction of films like Samuel Peckinpah's *The Wild Bunch* and Robert Altman's *McCabe and Mrs. Miller*.

The vogue enjoyed by the new cinema was rooted in the tastes of the "film generation"—the nearly three-quarters of the audience now under twenty-nine—who created a demand for something reflecting the "fertile chaos" of the decade of Vietnam. Yet this period of fertile chaos now seemed to Kael to have almost run its course. Its violence, which had once shocked complacent audiences, now left them merely desensitized; movie after movie now produced only "numbness and exhaustion" in their viewers: "In this climate," concluded Kael, "Watergate seems the most natural thing that could happen. If one were to believe recent movies, it was never any different in this country: Vietnam and Watergate are not only where we have got to but where we always were."

In an article the following year, Kael offered an even darker prognosis of the state of American cinema. Movies, which had helped form the counterculture, were now presiding over its demise: the "young anti-draft, anti-Vietnam audiences that were the 'film genera-tion'" had succumbed to a facile cynicism. The edge had been taken off the cultural critique; it had begun pandering to a new nihilism in the filmgoing audience, a "celebration of rot," and a masochistic desire to see the disasters of recent years staged as entertainment. It was also a harbinger of the studios' recovery; they had begun to thrive again in this demoralized atmosphere, which created a kind of demand that they were uniquely equipped to meet. "The movie executives were shaken for a few years," wrote Kael. "They didn't understand what made a film a countercultural hit. They're happy to be back on firm ground with *The Sting*."

Kael saw the studios' renewed ascendance as a symptom of the increasing sophistication with which, by means of extensive advertis-ing campaigns, they turned movies like *The Poseidon Adventure* and *The Towering Inferno* into "media-created events." In terms reflecting the liberal intelligentsia's shock at Nixon's reelection the preceding year, she wrote: "Film advertising dictates audiences' choices, just as campaign advertising dictates election outcomes." The hollowing out of the democratic process was mirrored in Hollywood's return to oligarchical control and its use of advertising as "a form of psycho-logical warfare." While Paramount marketed big hits like *The Great*

Gatsby, it neglected Coppola's paranoid *The Conversation* out of what Kael suggested was a desire for revenge against the director who had styled himself the New Hollywood's Fidel Castro. In the end it had been the studios who survived the oedipal strife, and they were now vindictively bent on "infantilizing" both their artists and their audience.

If one of the principal, if often vaguely formulated, themes of the counterculture had been the inevitability of capitalism's overthrow, by the mid-1970s it was becoming all too apparent that capitalism Hollywood style was perfectly capable of swallowing all revolutions. The space of confusion, opportunity, and experimentation that had briefly been opened up by the temporary crisis of the studios was closing by 1975, when Steven Spielberg's *Jaws* announced the advent of a new age of blockbuster films and profits that put the studios firmly back in the driver's seat. What the auteurs took to be the historically foreordained collapse of the studio system turned out to be merely an interregnum that would last only until Hollywood discovered the new formula for success and the marketing techniques that would guarantee it.

Nostalgia

One symptom of what Kael called the Vietnamization of movies was a new sense of psychic rootlessness and dislocation in the American public. "There is no way," she wrote, "to estimate the full effect of Vietnam and Watergate on popular culture, but earlier films were predicated on an implied system of values which is gone now, except in the corrupt, vigilante form of a *Dirty Harry*." Kael's diagnosis indicated the larger sense of exhaustion that had overtaken the film generation as the sixties fizzled out with the end of the war and Nixon's reelection. Even the candidate of the counterculture, George McGovern, invoked this sense of exhaustion with his campaign slogan—"Come Home, America"—which summoned the nation to a "joyful homecoming" to the "ideals that nourished us in the beginning."

The demise of the counterculture and the end of the war fueled a wave of nostalgia that could be seen in the popularity of films like *The Sting* and *The Great Gatsby*. Perhaps most symptomatic was the rediscovery of the 1950s, the last time when, according to Didion, the American national narrative still functioned. For Didion, the principal legacy of the 1960s had been that she "began to doubt the premises of all the stories I had ever told myself" growing up in the 1950s. This loss of a narrative paradigm mirrored the loss of home as a fixed social coordinate, a stable part of Americans' mental geography, and it fueled a look back to a time when such coordinates could be taken for granted. After 1973 nostalgia would become both a dominant aesthetic force in American film and a pervasive influence in American culture more generally, from *Happy Days* to the proliferation of theme parks and historical preservation projects. In *Home from the War* psychiatrist Robert Jay Lifton analyzed the new nostalgia as part of a project of psychohistorical restoration, which used technology to recover "an imagined past of total harmony." Eventually, as Richard Slotkin suggests, the crisis of political culture that overtook the nation in 1973, and that was reflected in its mass cultural genres, would result in the elevation of nostalgia to a potent political force, manifested in the election of an old movie star, Ronald Reagan, as president at the end of the decade.

Scribblings of a Lost Civilization

George Lucas was a charter member of the "film generation," a graduate of the University of Southern California's film school who fell under the spell of Francis Ford Coppola and became a disciple of Coppola's gospel of independence from the studios. "The future is going to be with independent filmmakers," Lucas proclaimed in a 1973 speech to the Rotary Club of his hometown Modesto. "It's a whole new kind of business. We're all forging ahead on the rubble of the old industry." Yet of all the new directors, it was, somewhat surprisingly, only Lucas who achieved the independence that Coppola preached.

Lucas was very much the product of the 1950s culture depicted in *American Graffiti*. Growing up in California's Central Valley, his early influences were TV, comics, and Disneyland. Later he developed an obsession with cars and cruising, an obsession that Modesto—a town known for attracting cruisers from all over the Valley—offered ample opportunity to indulge. This fixation persisted even after he saw several friends killed in crashes. Only when Lucas himself suffered a near-fatal car accident in 1962 did he switch from cars to filmmaking.

Once at USC he quickly established himself as one of the stars in the new film school world. There he met, among others, John Milius, who wrote the screenplay for a film that Lucas himself was originally meant to direct but that was eventually helmed by Coppola: *Apocalypse Now*. He also directed a student short, *THX 1138*, that became the basis for his first feature. The unhappy experience of working on *THX 1138* cemented Lucas's lifelong antipathy toward the studio system. The film, a chilly, abstract look at a society of the future whose citizens are controlled by pharmaceuticals, was originally intended to be part of the slate of films that Coppola hoped, with the help of financing from Warners, to make the basis for Zoetrope's bid for independence. Warners, however, felt that it, along with several other projects Coppola tried to interest them in (including *Apocalypse Now* and *The Conversation*), lacked commercial potential and pulled the plug on their deal. Lucas took this setback extremely personally and thereafter devoted himself to winning independence from the studios. Success eventually came, on a scale that Coppola himself could only dream about, with *Star Wars*. It came, however, at a price: Lucas's apparent renunciation of his countercultural impulses, at least in aesthetic terms. As Kael would note caustically, the sellout is the "hero-survivor of our times."

The results became apparent for the first time with *American Graffiti*. Prior to this film, Lucas had worked on what he described as "very angry" movies: *THX 1138* and *Apocalypse Now*. He later explained: "We all know, as every movie in the last ten years has pointed out, how terrible we are, how wrong we were in Vietnam, how we have ruined the world, what schmucks we are and how rotten everything is. It had become depressing to go to the movies. I decided it was time to make a movie where people felt better coming out of the theater than when they went in. I became really aware of the fact that the kids were really lost, the sort of heritage we built up since the war had been wiped out by the '60s, and it wasn't so groovy to act that way anymore, now you just sort of sat there and got stoned. I wanted to preserve what a certain generation of Americans thought being a teenager was really about—from about 1945 to 1962."

American Graffiti was picked up by Universal, which had created a youth division in 1969 headed by Ned Tanen. By the time Tanen signed Lucas, the bloom was off the rose and Universal was getting ready to shut down this division. *American Graffiti* was to be its last project. In it, Lucas paid homage to the culture of his youth and in particular to the initiation rites of car-obsessed boys on the cusp of adulthood. The film centers on four characters: clean-cut class president Steve Bolander; brainy Curt Henderson; nerdy Terry Fields; and hot-rod artist John Milner. Set in a town modeled on Modesto, it relates the events of one night in their lives as Steve and Curt try to decide whether to head east on the following day to start college.

The movie follows its four characters as they and assorted female characters trace and retrace the circuit that defines life in the town: from the all-night diner Mel's to the main drag, where the cruising happens, and back to Mel's—with stops along the way at the school dance, the make-out spot on the outskirts of town, and assorted other locales. Its episodic structure weaves together several major and a few minor narratives. Most have to do with the male characters' efforts to "score" romantically and/or sexually, although the basic trope of sexual desire for women is often trumped by the male characters' highly eroticized relation to their automobiles. The attention paid to period details—from the décor of Mel's to the choreography and music of the school dance—is lavished with particular care on the vintage cars and the rituals of cruising that dominate the action. The film's primary sensation is one of movement: cruising becomes an end in itself, an often aimless and circular activity, yet nevertheless one that leads with a certain inevitability toward a denouement that involves the ritual of vehicular flirting with death known as drag racing.

This sense of movement is reinforced by the film's soundtrack, which plays a key role in driving the narrative forward. Almost before the audience has settled into its seats, the music picks them up and deposits them, Dorothy-like, in its lavishly re-created theme park of a long-ago decade, when pop music first established itself as a powerful force in American culture. The story is strung together by a soundtrack that explicitly stages the power of music to create a community and seamlessly bind disparate characters and narratives together. This community includes the audience, which is quite literally swept along in the film's review of the Fifties Hit Parade that would dominate much of the radio dial in the 1970s.

Yet the richness of the film's period detail and its powerful sense of movement is achieved at the cost of a highly sanitized representation of the fifties as an era. It utterly lacks the sensitivity of its most obvious antecedent, the James Dean film *Rebel Without a Cause*, to the genuine problems faced by American youth in the 1950s. Adults are almost entirely absent from the story. We meet no parents until the final, fleeting departure scene at the airport, and those few adults we do meet are caricatures of authority. Lucas effectively severs the youth culture depicted in the film from any real context, reducing intergenerational conflict to the purely gestural level, typified by Steve's suggestion to one of his teachers at the dance that he "go kiss a duck." When Curt runs afoul of the members of a local gang, the Pharaohs, he manages to win them over and become—for a few hours at least—an honorary member of their community of juvenile delinquents by playing a prank on a couple of bumbling policemen. Rituals of adolescent rebellion are played for laughs, without consequence.

Rather than the scenes of domestic strife that mark *Rebel*, Lucas chooses to keep the action far from any setting that might interfere with his exercise in nostalgia. This choice reveals its significance in the scenes between Steve and his girlfriend, Laurie. Entertaining doubts about his decision to go away, Steve wonders aloud why he should "leave home to find home." Though he ultimately opts to remain with Laurie, the pathos of these scenes is undercut by the way the film places the very idea of "home" in question. For one thing, the film contains no images of domestic interiors. For another, the place occupied by parents and home has already been taken over by music and pop culture, a displacement that has two effects on the film's internal structure. On the one hand, the artifacts of that culture are stripped of any real content or significance by virtue of the fact that the film offers no real system of traditional values against which its songs and filmic references might generate friction and heat. On the other hand, the fact that popular culture has usurped the place of the traditional home, offering in its place a kind of imaginary community, exposes the contradictions in the film's exercise in nostalgia. In a very real sense "home" has been externalized; it is the strip, their cars, and the music that define the "interior" that the film's characters inhabit. The characters experience their lives within the echo chamber of movies and music, which has hollowed out those traditional notions of home to which the film on some level wishes to pay homage.

But if home has been externalized, there is no need to lament its passing. Music, purged of any oppositional impulse, is a deterritorialized force, as Curt discovers in the scene in which he finds his way to the radio station on the town's outskirts and encounters disk jockey Wolfman Jack. The radio personality is both the only person of color in a white community and a representative of the larger world that beckons. He pretends to Curt that he is simply an assistant who plays the Wolfman's prerecorded tapes, and he states enigmatically: "The Wolfman is everywhere." It is Curt who comes closest to realizing the extent to which the traditional idea of "home" has become hollowed out; he becomes the one character who, in the end, escapes this stultifying world.

American Graffiti, dubbed by Fredric Jameson "the inaugural film of postmodern nostalgia," in this sense maps out some of the same cultural terrain analyzed in Robert Venturi and Denise Scott Brown's

Learning from Las Vegas, itself seen as a founding text of postmodernism. Like Venturi and Brown's book, Lucas's film celebrated the
American commercial vernacular, the authentic folk culture preserved
in drive-ins and strips. It depicts from a local perspective the Pop
landscape of "big spaces, high speeds, and complex programs,"
described by Venturi and Brown as the hallmark of the new American
city exemplified by Las Vegas. In suggesting that the Las Vegas Strip
represents the modern-day counterpart to the Roman Forum, Venturi
and Brown's book weirdly resonates with Lucas's intention, signaled
in his title, to unearth the scribblings ("graffiti") of an ancient
civilization now felt to be lost.

The sense of loss that permeates the film is concentrated in the figure of
hot-rod specialist John Milner, the character who is most firmly rooted
in the mythical landscape of the 1950s. In one of the film's central scenes,
Milner takes his companion, twelve-year-old Carol, to a wrecking yard.
As they stroll among the wrecked cars, Milner meditates both on the
inevitability of his death in a pile-up and on the passing of America's
bygone romance with the automobile. Of the film's characters, it is
Milner who most obviously bears a resemblance to the James Dean of
Rebel Without a Cause; Carol drives home the point by remarking
sardonically after Milner has gotten a ticket from a traffic cop: "You're a
regular JD." But though he looks the part, Milner is too much a figure of
pathos to be a genuine juvenile delinquent.

Milner's epitaph for the fifties is: "The whole strip is shrinking."
This sense of loss reflects the nation's distance from that decade, post-
Vietnam America's "privileged lost object of desire." In a more
immediate sense, it signals the onset of a troubled new era in the
American love affair with the automobile. Two months after the
premiere of Lucas's film, Saudi Arabia would halt shipments of oil
to the United States in retaliation for its support of Israel in the Yom
Kippur War that broke out in early October. This was shortly followed
by a total Arab oil embargo that lasted from mid-October to mid-
March and that led to drastic gasoline shortages, sky-high prices, and
long lines at gas stations. Nor was this the only sign of trouble in the
automobile industry. Car manufacturers found themselves increas-

ingly on the defensive, blamed for pollution and smog, traffic jams, and poor safety records. Meanwhile competition from smaller foreign models was making large inroads into American manufacturers' market share; in 1973 sales of American cars dropped by 11 million. These developments led on the one hand to intensifying demands on the part of manufacturers for increases in worker productivity and on the other to mounting labor unrest. The AFL-CIO warned that the United States was becoming "a nation of hamburger stands, a country stripped of industrial capacity and meaningful work . . . a service economy . . . a nation of citizens busily buying and selling cheese-burgers and root-beer floats." Forced to resort to desperate methods to boost sales, one car dealer essentially staged a demolition derby on his lot, airing television commercials that depicted his new cars with smashed fenders, headlights, and windshields. The ruse seemed to work; customers were reportedly eager to buy the cars once they had been "chastened and repaired."

Against such a backdrop, the film's final scene, which restages the drag race in the Dean movie, served as a poignant reminder of the rituals of a bygone era. Milner's challenger is Bob Falfa, a brash young stud eager to claim's Milner's title as fastest hot-rodder in the Valley. A party to this contest is Steve's girlfriend Laurie, who Steve has broken up with after she refused to have sex with him, and who, as Falfa's passenger, barely escapes the wreck that claims Falfa's car. Falfa and Laurie go off the road and are pulled from the car just before it erupts in a fireball—the one moment when genuine danger threatens to break through the film's otherwise placid façade.

In the film's postscript, Lucas uses titles to tell the audience about the subsequent course of its four main characters' lives. Milner, we are informed, is later killed by a drunk driver; Fields goes MIA in Vietnam; Steve becomes an insurance agent in Modesto; while Curt becomes a writer (and presumably draft dodger) living in Canada. The female characters, including Laurie and Carol, remain conspicuously absent from this postscript, an absence that Pauline Kael saw as a cold slap to women, a constituency that now, she noted, constituted over half of the filmgoing audience.

Yet if Lucas's film chose here to ignore the sensibilities of a large part of its audience, in other respects it seems to have answered a tremendous need among American moviegoers for reminders of an earlier, less conflicted era. Made for under $750,000, *American Graffiti* went on to earn $55 million at theaters, making it one of the most successful movies of all time measured in terms of cost of production relative to box office receipts. The success of this film at the box office was a leading indicator of the shift in Hollywood's fortunes and of the formula that would make it possible—a formula that Lucas would later ride to record-shattering success with *Star Wars*. Part of the key to this formula lay in its handling of the theme of generational conflict or revolt. By invoking this theme, then ending on a note of reconciliation and intergenerational harmony, Lucas's films helped assuage the guilt of the younger generation's oedipal impulses. This was further accomplished by effectively sealing off the film from history, including the war in Indochina that had become the ground of the most intense intergenerational conflicts in memory. By contrast with the sixties counterculture, the fifties juvenile delinquents of Lucas's film seemed utterly benign.

Kael viewed the film as a symptom of decay, the passing of something: "The end of the 'film generation' means a sharp break with the past . . . the members tuned in for the last time at *American Graffiti*— that pop comic view of their own adolescence, before they became the counterculture." But the film also encouraged an older generation that had been driven away from theaters by the darkness of the auteurist vision to return for a nostalgic revisitation of a period now safely purged of any generational conflict or social pathology that could not be played for laughs. Writing in the *Times*, Steven Farber observed: "For those of us in Lucas' generation, watching *American Graffiti* is like going home"; the film, he wrote, conveyed "a sense of community—the shared language, music, and humor that contributed to the last authentic national folk culture." Not the least of its virtues, as far as Farber was concerned, was that "its portrait of adolescence transcends all generation gaps." In celebrating an older, indeed obsolete version of youth culture, *American Graffiti* repaired the rift that had formed in the American moviegoing audience. It reconstituted the 1950s as a moment of consensus and mythic harmony, in which even dissonant elements were turned into lovable characters or "scary" moments in a fifties theme park.

The Death of Radical Chic

Lucas's reworking of the material depicted in *Rebel Without a Cause* reflects that film's status as urtext of teen alienation. Beyond its sensitive handling of the theme of juvenile delinquency, this status was due above all to the volatile performance of its star, James Dean. But Dean's talent and charisma were only half the story; his elevation into screen icon was in large part the result of the tragic mirroring of life and art in his short-lived career. By the time *Rebel* reached screens across the country, Dean was dead, victim of a car accident that weirdly mirrored the contest that, in the film, takes the life of gang leader Buzz.

Dean's sudden death at the height of his fame made him the object of a worldwide cult. Within a year of his fatal crash there were, in the United States alone, 4 million dues-paying members of the groups that paid homage to his memory. Similar groups sprang up across the globe. According to one account, the death car was exhibited privately around L.A., and some fans paid for the privilege of sitting behind the bloodstained wheel. The sensitive Dean, a kind of anti-Wayne, had many progeny, both on screen and in the music industry. His imitators, noted his biographer David Dalton, spanned the entire spectrum of gender identities, from Elvis Presley, who liked to be called "the James Dean of rock 'n' roll," to the androgynous figures of Mick Jagger and David Bowie, to Warhol Superstar Jackie Curtis, whose obsession with Dean earned a line in Lou Reed's 1972 hit "Walk on the Wild Side." As the definitive rebel-hero of the fifties, James Dean, writes Dalton, was at "the root of the culture of the Sixties and Seventies."

What ensured Dean's potency as a symbol was his simultaneous incarnation of the star system and its dark side. He remained the first and most totemic in a long line of icons who died young, from Buddy Holly and Marilyn Monroe to Jimi Hendrix and Janis Joplin. As the virtual personification of a culture now felt to be lost, it was perhaps inevitable that Dean would figure so prominently in the public imagination of 1973. Eighteen years after his death, rumors continued to circulate that he was still alive, fomented by stories such as a 1973 article in the *National Examiner* with the headline "JAMES DEAN DID NOT DIE IN 'FATAL' AUTO ACCIDENT. Paralyzed and Mutilated, He's Hidden in a Sanatorium." Pop impresario Malcolm McLaren would change the name of his London clothing store in 1973 to "Too Fast to Live, Too Young to Die"—a slogan American gangs reportedly took up as an anthem after James Dean's death. J. G. Ballard's 1973 novel *Crash* wove elaborate fantasies around the vehicular deaths of Dean, Jayne Mansfield, and John F. Kennedy, making the public fascination with these tragedies an expression of a larger cultural death wish that was the legacy of the sixties. In the mind of his protagonist Vaughn, who is obsessed with celebrity car crashes, Ballard created a vision of "the whole world dying in a simultaneous automobile disaster, millions of vehicles hurled together in a terminal congress of spurting loins and engine coolant." The mythic dimensions of the Dean story would receive their definitive treatment in David Dalton's Warholian biography of 1974, *The Mutant King*.

In looking back at James Dean, these various exhumations were also looking back at the origins of the elaborate star-making machinery that, with the advent of television and the maturation of tabloid journalism, had taken shape in the fifties. As much as it was the product of the sixties counterculture, the new "film generation" was also a product of a vast new audience, the so-called global village, whose genesis lay in the fifteen-year period between Sputnik and Watergate. In revisiting the Dean myth, they were also examining the exponentially greater force that the cult of celebrity had acquired in American society since the fifties.

Nowhere were the pathological effects of this cult on Dean's progeny more vividly demonstrated than in the story of Charles Starkweather, the author of a crime spree in 1958 that left eleven people dead. Starkweather was a semiliterate garbage collector in Lincoln, Nebraska, who became obsessed with Dean after seeing *Rebel*. His fixation eventually led him to copy Dean's style of dress and mannerisms and later to entitle his prison memoir *Rebellion*. Starkweather found his soul mate in fourteen-year old Caril Ann Fugate, who shared his love of movies and cartoons. Together with his jailbait girlfriend, Starkweather embarked upon a killing spree that began with Fugate's parents and ultimately claimed the lives of nine others. He was eventually apprehended by the law and executed in the electric chair. Fugate, meanwhile, was let off, the authorities apparently unable to decide whether she had been a willing accomplice or a terrorized victim. The Starkweather tale was the dark counterpart to the James Dean story: a nihilistic homage to what music critic Jon Savage calls the "impulse to pure destructive speed that had been impacted into youth culture with the death of James Dean."

This was the pulplike material that twenty-nine-year-old Terrence Malick chose as the basis for his first feature film, *Badlands*. Malick, who grew up in Texas as the son of an oil company executive, studied philosophy at Harvard and later went to Oxford as a Rhodes scholar. At one point he traveled to Germany and met Martin Heidegger; later he translated Heidegger's *Essence of Reason*. Subsequently he worked as a journalist, being sent on assignment to Bolivia by *The New Yorker* to cover the trial of Regis Debray, reportedly arriving there the day after the death of Che Guevara, one of the heroes of late-sixties radicals. In 1969 he became part of the first matriculating class at the American Film Institute. He found his first employment in the film industry working as a script doctor on Jack Nicholson's directorial debut, *Drive, He Said*, and on the original draft of *Dirty Harry*. Unlike the celebrity-obsessed protagonist of his first feature, Malick himself cultivated a reclusive style, granting almost no interviews and eventually disappearing from the public eye for twenty years following the release of his second film, *Days of Heaven*, in 1977.

He began writing the script for *Badlands* in 1971 and eventually raised $350,000 to make the film. Shooting took place in the summer of 1972 in Colorado, with Martin Sheen and Sissy Spacek starring in their first major roles and with a nonunion crew on a shoestring budget. After a year of editing, *Badlands* premiered on the closing night of the New York Film Festival, October 15, 1973, to rave reviews. Most critics—Kael being virtually the lone exception—were highly impressed by the film's spare, poetic, lyrical, yet chilling sensibility. Despite the critical acclaim, however, *Badlands* was apparently too dark for most audiences and did not fare well at the box office.

The film relates the story of Dean look-alike Kit Carruthers and fifteen-year old Holly Sargis, young lovers who become criminals when Kit kills Holly's father, who doesn't want his daughter going around with a trash collector. Beginning in the town of Fort Dupree, South Dakota—a few hundred miles north of Wounded Knee—the film follows them as they go on the lam and move ever deeper into a vast, increasingly empty landscape, leaving a trail of corpses behind them until Holly finally becomes disenchanted with her trigger-happy boyfriend and the nomadic lifestyle they have adopted. Deserted by his girlfriend, Kit decides that he too has had enough of being a fugitive and is ready to take the inevitable next step in his transformation into pop outlaw. After a wild, cross-country chase scene he gives himself up to Montana sheriffs. Kit's myth-making impulses are on full display in this scene. As he prepares for his capture, he turns on the car radio to provide the scene with a soundtrack, arranges his hat in the rearview mirror, checks his pulse, then assembles a pile of rocks to memorialize the scene. Once they have taken him into their custody, the sheriffs play along with Kit's scenario, first engaging in a bit of gratuitous gunplay, then asking Kit why he went on his murderous escapade—a question to which Kit obligingly responds by saying that he always wanted to be a criminal. Subsequently one of the sheriffs turns to his partner and remarks, to Kit's evident gratification, "I'll kiss your ass if he don't look like James Dean." Later, at the army base where Kit has been taken to wait for the plane that will return him and Holly to South Dakota, state troopers and national guardsmen engage in friendly banter with him about his favorite singer (Eddie Fisher) and compete with each other to claim the mementos (a lighter, a comb, a ballpoint pen) Kit doles out. He plays the part of celebrity to the hilt, happy in the knowledge that his outlaw status will ensure immortality.

In Kit and Holly, Malick creates two characters whose conscious-ness, like that of the characters in Jean-Luc Godard's *Breathless*, is thoroughly permeated by filmic references. When they leave town after killing Holly's father, the two decide to adopt new names appropriate to their sense of themselves as pop outlaws: Priscilla (Presley) for her, James (Dean) for him. Kit imitates the postures, mannerisms, and facial expressions of his idol. The highly mediated nature of their outlook explains their general desensitization to the mayhem they cause; experiencing life secondhand has stripped them of the capacity to empathize with their victims or comprehend the consequences of their actions, and the film conspires in this self-distancing by adopting a position of studied neutrality toward Kit's violence. Like Herr's "media freaks," Kit's mayhem is the product of a larger society.

At the same time the film gives ample rein to the romantic narratives endlessly looping through its characters' heads. Kit seeks constantly to leave his imprint on the world; the pile of rocks he assembles to mark the spot of his capture is just one of a series of gestures intended to serve notice that, as he tells Holly at their first meeting, "I got some stuff to say. Guess I'm kind of lucky that way. Most people don't have anything on their minds, do they?" Following his murder of Holly's father, Kit records a message on a Voice-a-Graph Dictaphone at the town train station, and similarly, during a later scene at the house of a wealthy man where they have temporarily sought refuge, he records his thoughts on a Dictaphone. Moreover, throughout the course of the film, Kit frequently breaks into gratuitous remarks that seem intended merely to establish some kind of authorial claim over the events depicted on-screen. One of the film's jokes is that the things Kit has to say are either quite banal or else affirmative of the social order.

The counterpoint to Kit's seemingly random remarks is provided by Holly's voice-over, delivered in a flat, affectless tone that nevertheless exhibits a tendency toward ornate turns of phrase lifted out of romance novels and movie magazines. "Little did I realize," she tells us at the film's beginning, "that what began in the alleys and back-ways of this quiet town would end in the Badlands of Montana." Holly's voice-over narration provides us with the first example of a classic American genre—outlaw lovers on the lam—told from the perspective of the female lead, and it functions to ironically undercut Kit's own efforts to establish an authoritative voice. In one of the rare interviews he granted before ceasing contact with the press, Malick observed that Holly was the more important of the two characters: "At least you get a glimpse of what she's like. And I liked women characters better than men; they're more open to things around them, more demonstrative." He defended her tendency to speak in platitudes by noting that this was a common occurrence with many people: "As though in struggling to reach what's most personal about them they could only come up with what's most public."

The absence of any authoritative narrator, and the fracturing of the narrative into multiple voices, is symptomatic of the film's drama of paternal crisis and its attendant moral consequences. This in turn is linked with the loss of the frontier, a motif established in an early scene in which Holly's father is seen painting a billboard advertising a housing subdivision in the middle of an empty plain. The most lyrical scene in the movie occurs when Kit, after killing Holly's father, burns down the Sargis home. Against the strains of Orff's *Musica Poetica*, the midcentury Victorian interior of the house—piano and sheet music, curtains, framed picture, peacock feathers, dollhouse, Mr. Sargis's corpse—is enveloped in voluptuous flames. This destruction of the family home condemns the star-crossed lovers to a series of desperate attempts at creating substitute homes. The first of these occurs when they hide out in a cottonwood grove by a river, creating an elaborate, multistoried treehouse reminiscent of the Swiss Family Robinson (a tale cited by Malick as one of his sources) and furnished with the objects and knickknacks that they rescued from Holly's house. Later they take a wealthy man and his maid hostage and spend several hours playing house in his palatial home: testing the chairs, rearranging objects, trying on clothes, ringing the dinner bell, strolling the grounds. The pathos of this sequence suggests the degree to which the two have become exiled from any stable sense of home or belonging. "The world," Holly tells us wistfully at one point, "was a far-away planet to which I could never return."

This sequence also makes explicit a theme that up to now has remained only implied. On the face of it, *Badlands* is a faithful retelling of the Starkweather-Fugate story, through which it refracts the iconography of fifties teen rebellion. Yet if the Dean myth is one source, it also has an obvious antecedent in the film that ushered in the New Hollywood, *Bonnie and Clyde* (Malick thanks Arthur Penn in the credits). In its treatment of Kit's celebrity fixation, *Badlands* restates a central theme of *Bonnie and Clyde*: the potent allure of celebrity. Penn's film established the template against which *Badlands* measures itself: outlaw lovers whose bond is less sexual in nature than the product of a desire for the freedom and glamour conferred by cars and guns. Yet Malick's reworking of this theme effects several changes in the paradigm established by *Bonnie and Clyde* and, earlier, Godard's *Breathless*. Most significantly, the violence of Malick's film has been deglamorized. To the extent that the romantic elements of its filmic predecessors have been preserved, they exist only in the minds of its central protagonists.

The audience is further distanced from a romantic interpretation of the film's violence by the schizoid character of its protagonist. Kit introduces himself to one character by saying: "Name's Carruthers—I shoot people every now and then," yet he reproaches people on his trash route for not paying their bills and insists that Holly bring her homework along when they go on the lam. Despite his self-consciously outlaw persona, Kit is throughout preoccupied with minor offenses and infractions of the law, observing in one scene in which he and Holly stroll down the street of a town: "Somebody dropped a paper bag on the sidewalk. If everyone did that, the whole town would be a mess."

In this sense *Badlands* serves as a bookend to the film that inaugurated the cultural politics of the New Hollywood. Malick's film both apostatizes and empties out the romanticized fascination with violence and the aura of populist romance that marked Penn's film. Of Kit, Malick would say:

> He thinks of himself as a successor to James Dean—a rebel without a cause—when in reality he's more like an Eisenhower conservative. "Consider the minority opinion," he says into the rich man's tape recorder, "but try to get along with the majority opinion once it's accepted" . . . He wants to be like the rich man he locks in the closet, the only man he doesn't kill, the only man he *sympathizes* with, and the one least in need of sympathy. It's not infrequently the people at the bottom who most vigorously defend the very rules that put and keep them there.

If rebellion had been a hallmark of the 1960s counterculture that *Bonnie and Clyde* had put a glamorous face on, the variant on this story told in *Badlands* suggested that youthful revolt had run its course. In a world unhinged by spasmodic eruptions of violence like the Manson murders, Kit stood schizophrenically both for the glamour of the outlaw and for the conservative values of the "silent majority" claimed by Nixon as his constituency. For Kit, killing Holly's father has a purely limited, domestic significance; in most respects he remains quite deferential to authority figures. Violence has become disconnected from any form of cultural critique. If Penn's film made violence chic, *Badlands* emptied out the rebel's gesture of any conviction or political content.

This severing of the link between violence and cultural critique becomes clear in those scenes in which the film sketches a context for its characters' violence. The nature of this context is at first straightforward. The sequence in which Kit and Holly hide out by the river is replete with visual cues suggesting a link to the war in Indochina: Kit devises a system of warning signals, ambushes, and hiding places reminiscent of the guerrilla warfare being waged by the Vietcong and of the besieged group at Wounded Knee. This link is strengthened by a shot of Holly, in the manner of an Asian peasant, toting firewood by means of a rope supported against her forehead. She further informs us that "we planned a huge network of tunnels under the forest floor." Here at least the principal characters are identified with the symbolic position of the Native American/Vietcong, and this aspect of their plight is further dramatized by mention of the increasingly large forces arrayed against them. "It was like the Russians had invaded," intones Holly in ironic reference to the cold war–like hysteria created by the bloody swath she and Kit are carving across the Badlands. Yet the power of the state remains strangely veiled until the final scenes in which Kit is taken into custody, and here, when it is finally exposed in the form of the troops at the airbase, the tone is not so much one of punishment and retribution as of complicity. Malick repeatedly scrambles the conventional opposition between outlaw violence and state power; in the film's last scene Kit, seated next to a state trooper on board the plane that is taking Holly and himself back to South Dakota to stand trial, admires the lawman's hat and wishes that he could own one himself.

In a key late scene that sets up the final interactions between Kit and the lawmen, Kit and Holly dance in the headlights of the car to the Nat King Cole song "A Blossom Fell," which plays on the car's radio. Kit rhapsodizes: "Boy, if I could write a song like that, a song about the way I feel now, it would be a hit." The scene hints at the secret complicity that exists between the outlaw and the larger culture that sanctions him. The only thing left to Kit at this point is celebrity, the desire to write a hit song, to become a star, and the representatives of law and order seem happy to grant him this status. To paraphrase Hoberman, writing about Peckinpah's *Pat Garrett and Billy the Kid*, it is as though America is killing its outlaw self and then having it come back as a pop-music ghost. One is reminded in this connection of the fact that before Charles Manson became a mass murderer, he was a would-be rock star. As Dalton says of Dean: "He made star status the only acceptable form of success, the only desirable form of adulthood. This method of aging without growing up found its ultimate incarnation in rock stars, a sort of unanointed royalty who rule by divine right."

Malick's autopsy on the corpse of the counterculture takes aim precisely at this aspect of Dean's legacy. In escaping the studio system, the New Hollywood directors also strove to escape the shackles of the star system. Stars were expensive, and they imposed constraints on the directors' auteurist impulses. For this reason many directors chose to work with relatively lesser-known actors, many from New York. But the star system, like the studio system itself, would prove to be far more powerful than the new generation realized, as Pauline Kael observed in her post-mortem on the film generation: "The country has never been more star crazy than it is right now . . . The phenomenon of stardom operates in television, in radio, in literature, in the academic world, in politics, in the women's movement."

No contemporary film comments more explicitly on the pathologies of the star system and the deformities it wrought on the American psyche than *Badlands*, a film made by a director who would eventually become a legendary recluse. Malick's deconstruction of the 1950s operates on two levels: by projecting images of the Vietnam War back onto that decade, he suggests the compromised nature of the nostalgia to which post-Vietnam America was succumbing. At the same time his film is a critique of the youth-obsessed star system whose origins lay in the fifties. Like the characters in Lucas's film, Malick's characters, Kit and Holly, live their lives within the fantasy universe conjured by movies and music. Kit's resemblance to James Dean is what gets him the girl. In the end it also, in a dark twist, earns him the perverse respect of the lawmen. The film's final images on the army base suggest that Kit has been received into the special brotherhood where outlaw violence and official violence become indistinguishable. In concluding on this note, Malick's film offers a dark meditation on the violent roots of American empire.

Power Shift

Maybe New York shouldn't survive.
Maybe it should go through a cycle
of destruction.

—Richard Nixon

AUGUST 29, 1973: *Four months after the dedication ceremony of the world's tallest buildings, architect Minoru Yamasaki's World Trade Center in Lower Manhattan, HUD announces its decision to complete the destruction of Yamasaki's now-notorious Pruitt-Igoe housing project in St. Louis. The demolition, begun the previous year, of these award-winning structures is widely seen as the death knell of architectural modernism. One critic observes that the "high-rise ghetto as bombsite has become a potent media image."*

The regional power realignment that is one of the larger stories of the 1970s is dramatized by the crisis of New York City and the emergence of dynamic new Sunbelt cities like Houston, Anaheim, and Las Vegas. Nineteen seventy-three was a significant year in the downward spiral of the nation's largest city. A series of articles published in the *New York Times* that winter revealed that the South Bronx had become a scarier place than Vietnam and a worldwide symbol of urban despair. As power broker Robert Moses put it in an interview that year, the South Bronx was "beyond tinkering, rebuilding and restoring." In the courts Mayor John Lindsay's administration was trying to shut down *Deep Throat* as part of its campaign to clean up Times Square, while

Governor Nelson Rockefeller was passing draconian sentencing laws in response to a wave of drug-related crime. But the problems confronting the city were becoming increasingly unmanageable. Unemployment and welfare rolls were skyrocketing while the city's budget was imploding. After realizing that his reputation had gone the way of Kennedy's "best and brightest," Mayor Lindsay decided in 1973 against running for reelection. Two years later New York City was bankrupt.

At the same time Nixon's Sunbelt-based silent majority was enjoying new clout in both the political and the cultural arena, despite Nixon's own downfall, which indirectly served his agenda by bringing the big government epitomized by the Lyndon B. Johnson and the Lindsay administrations further into disrepute. In places like Orange County, California, the president's birthplace and place of legal residence, a new movement had coalesced that would lead the way in the reaction against the sixties and the social pathologies that that decade was seen as having unleashed: porn, crime, drugs, abortion, and homosexual rights. It was here also that a backlash against government spending on welfare would crystallize, sowing the seeds for the tax revolts of the late 1970s.

By the 1970s suburbia was emerging as a force to be reckoned with both politically and culturally. The homes, tastes, mores, and political views of the people who inhabited these vast zones of sprawl, hitherto disparaged as cultural wastelands, were now being documented as though a new civilization had been discovered in America's midst. Like anthropologists studying an exotic tribe, architects, filmmakers, photographers, and others descended on Sunbelt communities, intent on uncovering their secrets. The intense interest demonstrated in texts ranging from architects Venturi and Brown's *Learning from Las Vegas* to photojournalist Bill Owens's seminal collection of photographs *Suburbia* to the PBS series *An American Family* mirrored the regional power shift from the traditional manufacturing cities of the Northeast to the new postindustrial suburbs and edge cities of the South and Southwest.

The Crisis of New York

One measure of New York's descent into crisis could be gotten from the contrast between the peace celebrations that greeted the end of war in 1945 and those of 1973. When, shortly after seven P.M. on August 14, 1945, the news that Japan had surrendered flashed across the Times Tower news ribbon, Times Square became the scene of joyous celebration. By ten that evening an estimated 2 million people had flocked there to join in the celebration, among them the sailor and young woman whose spontaneous kiss would be captured in Alfred Eisenstadt's celebrated photograph. Following the announcement of the January 1973 peace accord, however, no such celebrations occurred in Times Square. According to one account, the area now seemed seedy, almost deserted; only a few Vietnam veterans gathered there, "some drinking, others apparently on drugs, most simply enraged, screaming at the camera, at the society, about having been deceived by the war and ignored on coming back, one especially enraged black vet shouting 'You can tell that bastard [Nixon] the war isn't over.'"

By the end of the year, things had gone from bad to worse in Times Square. On the heels of the oil embargo, the *New Yorker*'s "Talk of the Town" ran a gloomy piece describing the consequences for the city of Nixon's energy conservation plan. The Great White Way, it lamented, seemed doomed. Major advertisers like Coca-Cola were pulling the plug on the colossal electric signs that framed Times Square; without commercial lighting, the celebrated crossroads of the world would become "just another bleak traffic intersection." One city official warned that if Times Square were allowed to become "dark and dreary," it would have a terrible effect on morale, and he pleaded that Times Square be allowed to remain as "colorful and tasteless as it has always been."

Yet if, as this official claimed, Times Square was a "symbol for the whole world," it was becoming an increasingly ambivalent symbol, one whose colorfulness and tastelessness were being put in jeopardy not just by the energy crisis but by a new moral crusade on the part of city government. During the 1960s Times Square had become home to a thriving porn industry that catered to a clientele emboldened by the era's new sexual liberties. But by the early 1970s the Lindsay administration had embarked on a campaign to clean up the X-rated theaters and massage parlors that ringed the streets around Times Square. In 1973 this campaign reached a new pitch with the city's efforts to shut down a film, *Deep Throat*, whose enormous popularity served notice of the mainstreaming of porn. Made for $25,000 in a hotel room in Miami and released in 1972, it became the eleventh-highest-grossing domestic film of 1973. It eventually went on to gross $600 million, making it one of the most profitable films of all time. In New York City celebrities like Johnny Carson, Jacqueline Kennedy Onassis, and Truman Capote were seen slipping into the New Mature World Theater on West 49th Street to see the satirical tale of a party girl with a clitoris in her throat. *Deep Throat* showed that X-rated films could be not just profitable but respectable, appealing to audiences beyond the usual clientele of furtive middle-aged men. The *Times* reported that a new "porno chic" had taken hold among the city's cultural elite. The film's title entered popular parlance as a synonym for illicit, secret knowledge when it became the code-name of the source that abetted Woodward and Bernstein's investigation into Watergate (only recently revealed to have been the FBI's number-two man, Mark Felt).

The film's popularity made it the target of groups who saw it as a symptom of a new "permissiveness" threatening the moral fabric of American society. The New Mature World Theater's operators were hit with obscenity charges. The trial, which began in late December 1972 and stretched into January 1973, was closely followed by the media. The experts who were called to testify on both sides turned the trial into a referendum on the sexual revolution. A professor of medical psychology from Johns Hopkins University praised *Deep Throat* as a "cleansing film" and suggested that it could have a healthy effect on people's sex lives, going so far as to speculate that people would be less likely to get divorced if they included the film in their sex education. A second professor welcomed the film for showing that a woman's sexual gratification was as important as a man's. A New York psychiatrist, on the other hand, testified that the film distorted the true nature of female sexuality by propagating the "Women's Lib thesis" that a clitoral was superior to a vaginal orgasm. In a late February decision that strengthened Lindsay's hand in cleaning up Times Square, Judge Joel Tyler—who was apparently unaware even of the concept of clitoral orgasm—finally ruled that *Deep Throat* was "indisputably and irredeemably obscene." He later fined the New Mature World Theater $100,000.

The debate triggered by *Deep Throat* touched a deep nerve in a society still grappling with the consequences of the sexual revolution. Declaring his own war on porn, Nixon unleashed the full power of the federal government against its purveyors. The FBI investigated *Deep Throat*'s distributors, and zealous prosecutors pushed for stiff fines against theater owners. Later that summer the Supreme Court—with Nixon appointee William Rehnquist siding with the majority—issued a landmark ruling on the wider ramifications of porn's new mainstreaming. In the case of *Miller v. California*, the Court dealt a setback to free speech forces, determining that local communities had the right to pass laws banning materials that "appeal to the prurient interest in sex" and were deemed as lacking "serious literary, artistic, political or scientific value." It was, the *Times* editorialized, a victory for Nixon's campaign against "permissiveness" and the product of a "Nixonized Court." That the case had originated in California's ultraconservative Orange Country—Nixon's birthplace and place of legal residence—served eloquent warning of the new power of "community" as moral arbiter.

The irony of the ruling was that it did virtually nothing to stop the hard-core industry, whose modest bottom line allowed it to make profits even by limiting distribution to more tolerant urban centers. Linda Lovelace's exploits in *Deep Throat* turned her into one of the year's biggest celebrities, endowing her with such star power that, to an observer at one gathering, she seemed endowed with an "aura so thick and gold that even the least spiritual of the guests can see it glitter." She remained in demand throughout much of the year, showing up on TV shows nationwide and, despite being forced to field "more hostile questions than anyone except perhaps the head of the American Communist Party," handling all the attention with good grace. It was, as artist-author Jules Feiffer predicted, more serious Hollywood films that tackled sexual topics—such as his own *Carnal Knowledge* (1971) or Bernardo Bertolucci's *Last Tango in Paris* (1973)—that were affected by *Miller v. California*. While filmmakers like William Friedkin, director of *The Exorcist*, worried about the chilling effect that the ruling would have both on their own box office and more generally on the film industry's willingness to take risks, other commentators predicted that violence would become Hollywood's new pornography. Another irony of the case was the odd alliance forged in the backlash against sexploitation. With porn becoming a front in the emerging culture wars, conservatives found their cause joined by feminists protesting the degradation of women in such films. Lovelace herself later claimed she'd been hypnotized by her husband and joined the antiporn crusade.

Blaxploitation

The movie *Shaft* opens with a view out of detective John Shaft's office overlooking Times Square, then shows him dodging traffic as he descends to street level—an opening sequence that immediately establishes his bona-fides as master of the intricate arts of urban survival. If *Deep Throat* became the sexploitation film par excellence, *Shaft* would establish the paradigm for a new type of exploitation film that arose out of the African-American experience. The early 1970s witnessed a remarkable flowering of black filmmaking in the form of a wave of movies that adapted the conventions of the private eye and the gangster picture to the conditions of the black inner city. The best of these films, like *Across 110th Street*, strove to transcend the limitations of the genre by constructing a dark portrait of the effect of drugs and crime on black neighborhoods. Some, like *Coffy* and *Cleopatra Jones*, gave the genre a further twist by centering the story on strong female characters.

Blaxploitation's success reflected a singular convergence of factors: the crisis of the Hollywood studios, coupled with the emergence of a hip urban black audience whose sensibilities had been shaped by the civil rights movement and then by the growing cultural nationalism of the black community. During this period black directors like Gordon Parks and Melvin Van Peebles emerged to take advantage of the general vogue for youth-oriented features and of Hollywood's desperate search for new formulas. Conditioned by the rising expectations created by the civil rights struggle, black audiences demanded images of black life on screen that went beyond the stereotypes of conventional Hollywood fare. The new cultural consciousness forged by the sixties was expressed in growing criticism of the role of the mass media in reinforcing white audiences' prevailing racial stereotypes and, perhaps more damagingly, holding blacks hostage to a false, distorted set of racial images. Black faces were almost completely missing from television and movie screens in the early 1960s; and when they did begin to appear in greater numbers later in that decade, it was generally in roles designed to reassure white audiences. According to self-styled guerrilla filmmaker Van Peebles, "The biggest obstacle to the Black revolution in America is our conditioned susceptibility to the white man's program."

All this changed in the early 1970s with the appearance first of Van Peebles's *Sweet Sweetback's Baadasssss Song* (1971) and then of Parks's *Shaft* (1972), followed shortly by *Superfly*, directed by Parks's son Gordon Jr. These films introduced audiences to a new type of assertive, sexual black film hero who seemed to fill the void left by the collapse of the Black Panther Party. The Panthers, many of whom had been languishing in prison for years, were finally torn apart by an internal civil war in 1972, a war that had been exacerbated by the campaign of harassment and destruction waged against the organization by the FBI's COINTEL program since 1968. With party leader Huey Newton having gone into exile in Cuba, and former SNCC chairman H. Rap Brown—famous for his statement that "Violence is as American as cherry pie"—convicted on robbery and assault charges in the spring of 1973, the heroes of the sixties had now vacated the public stage. Militant black nationalism seemed to have run its course with the symbolic decapitation of an organization that FBI director

J. Edgar Hoover had once deemed "the greatest threat to the internal security of this country."

It was now left to Richard Roundtree and Ron O'Neal to fill movie screens with images of a tough yet tender black masculinity that could more than hold its own against "whitey" (usually portrayed as either an Italian gangster, a corrupt cop, or a homosexual). Immensely popular, their films spawned a wave of imitators, all trafficking in sex, drugs, and violence. Most stuck closely to the basic formula of action-adventure in the ghetto, pitting the heroes against a corrupt white power structure. In some cases, as in 1973's *Black Caesar*— which strove to emulate the success of *The Godfather*—it was to erect a new, black gangster-based power structure. In others, the reversal of racial hierarchies opened the door to a similar reversal of gender relations. *Cleopatra Jones* (1973) depicted a world turned completely upside down, in which special agent Cleopatra (played by six-foot-tall model Tamara Dobson) goes up against white drug kingpin "Mommy" (Shelley Winters). In this world, the men are virtually all degenerates no matter what side of the law they are on; the racist cop, who is in league with Mommy, is the worst of the lot. (Aside from being corrupt and bigoted, his essential depravity is revealed when he is shown sneaking into a porn theater to watch *Deep Throat* during his off-hours.) Cleopatra wins by having a kick-ass sense of style and— with the help of her training in martial arts—by kicking ass.

The proto-feminist consciousness of *Cleopatra Jones* and of the Pam Grier vehicle *Coffy* may have reflected an effort to respond to mounting criticism of the genre and its rather primitive gender politics as well as its perceived glorification of pushers, pimps, and gangsters. By 1973 this reaction against blaxploitation had mobilized leaders of the black community, including the NAACP, which threatened boycotts and helped form the Coalition Against Blaxploitation (CAB) with the intention of creating a rating system for black movies. Amid a climate of intensifying debate about porn films, such proposals raised predictable howls of censorship. In the end, it was not so much CAB's calls for self-policing on the part of black filmmakers as Hollywood's recovery at the box office that brought about the demise of blaxploitation. By 1974 the film industry—less dependent on the genre for profits—was reverting to traditional formulas.

The problem, as the genre's defenders pointed out, was that the guardians of black culture offered few viable alternatives to the sensationalistic fare or the pulsing, James Brown–composed soundtrack served up in a film like *Black Caesar*. Fred Williamson, the film's star, explicitly rejected moral uplift as the rationale for his films and likened the reaction against them to that against *Deep Throat*. The few black films that did try to offer moral uplift could hardly compete at the box office with the likes of *Cleopatra Jones*. And as for genuinely political films, the problem, of course, was that any film that refused to pull its punches risked being yanked from theaters.

By all accounts, this was the case with a film that ranked as easily the year's most inflammatory, *The Spook Who Sat by the Door*. The desire on the part of black audiences for more militant heroes culminated with this remarkable political thriller, based on the 1969 novel of that name by Sam Greenlee and directed by Ivan Dixon. In it, Korean War vet Dan Freeman becomes the token black in a CIA that is forced to integrate in order to meet new hiring quotas. Freeman is a variation on the Manchurian Candidate who, while outwardly docile, devotes himself to mastering the dark arts of the spy trade. He eventually quits the CIA and returns to Chicago to organize a black insurrection, making use of the knowledge he has absorbed at the very heart of the white power structure.

Where Tommy Gibbs, the protagonist of *Black Caesar*, guarantees the Mafia that in return for giving him Harlem, he will keep the ghetto quiet—"and not just Harlem, but Philly, Chicago, L.A."—Dan Freeman does the opposite, organizing and unleashing a wave of uprisings in these very same cities. *Spook* justifies its incendiary narrative by playing on a potent motif of black racial paranoia: the notion that whites seek to establish control of the ghettos through heroin, a process analogized to slavery. Through his organization the Cobras, which includes several Vietnam vets, Freeman concentrates on recruiting and organizing the inner city into paramilitary units. The shooting of a black youth by a cop is the spark that ignites the resulting race war and gives the signal to a scenario that comes straight out of J. Edgar Hoover's fevered brain: precisely coordinated armed insurrection carried out by black militants in cities across the nation. Once the National Guard is brought in, guerrilla war breaks out in the streets of Chicago, and the movie ends with the president declaring a state of national emergency.

Spook was strong medicine. Clinical in its storytelling, the film offered a virtual primer on urban guerrilla warfare. Indeed, so alarming was its story of armed uprising that, according to some accounts, the distributor, United Artists, was pressured by the FBI to pull the movie from theaters. Yet although the movie disappeared from screens, the story on which it was based seems to have found a strange echo in the history of the Symbionese Liberation Army. Shortly after the SLA's first action in late 1973—in which it assassinated a black Oakland school official designated as a race traitor—the *Times* ran a piece speculating that the group may have borrowed its name from Greenlee's novel, which includes a mention of the term "symbiology," apparently derived from "symbiosis." Apart from any value that the SLA may have found in the book's treatment of guerrilla warfare, it may also have adopted its symbol—the seven-headed cobra—from the name of Freeman's commando unit, the Cobras.

The Law of the Jungle

If blaxploitation, despite Williamson's disclaimers, referred to something beyond its own considerable entertainment value, then it was— as musician Curtis Mayfield, composer of the soundtrack for *Superfly*, argued—to the all-too-real crisis of the nation's inner cities. By the early 1970s the preeminent symbol of this crisis was the South Bronx, to which the *New York Times* devoted a lengthy four-part series in January 1973. Concentrated within this neighborhood, whose borders were defined by the East River to the south and Robert Moses's Cross-Bronx Expressway to the north, the article found a "jungle stalked by fear," a veritable breeding ground of urban pathology.

So all-pervading was this sense of pathology that it seemed to defy every effort at amelioration. In a city whose welfare caseload had tripled during the sixties, the South Bronx represented a particularly extreme example of the deep inroads social programs had made into the fabric of the inner city. Forty percent of its four hundred thousand inhabitants were on welfare, and countless federal dollars, aid programs, and housing programs had been lavished on the neighborhood. All this assistance, however, had done little to reverse the tide of urban blight or the flight of the white middle class. Unemployment stood as high as 30 percent, and much of the area's housing stock had fallen into an appalling state. After the city had spent $2.8 million to renovate nine tenements on Fox Street in Hunts Point in an effort to provide low-cost housing, the project was quickly invaded by gangs and drug addicts and then burned. "It was almost as if," noted the *Times* article in a revealing comment, "a hard-won clearing in the jungle had been inexorably reclaimed by the undergrowth." Consciously or not, the evocation of the failed project in the South Bronx invited comparison to the failed project in Vietnam, a comparison Martin Luther King had already drawn in the mid-1960s when he criticized the tendency to send inner-city youth to fight for rights in Indochina that they were denied at home.

With federal and city assistance making little dent in the sicknesses plaguing the neighborhood, its inhabitants increasingly turned to forms of self-governance. The rubble-strewn, graffiti-splattered streets of the South Bronx had been carved up by Puerto Rican gangs who made their homes in abandoned and burned-out buildings. What distinguished these gangs from their predecessors of the 1950s and 1960s was their rejection of heroin. Some of the gangs took credit for driving pushers from their neighborhood streets and for enforcing a kind of vigilante justice on dealers who tried to encroach on their turf. A still more radical response to the problem of drugs could be found in the neighborhood's major health care institution, Lincoln Hospital, where some doctors and other personnel had succeeded in taking over a wing of the hospital. These health care activists, who were concentrated in the hospital's detox unit, sought to turn addicts from drugs to political action, using a Maoist-tinged pamphlet titled *The Opium Trail: Heroin and Imperialism* to awaken their patients to the notion that revolution represented the best form of therapy.

In the end, the *New York Times* series concluded, the prognosis for the South Bronx was bleak. "The South Bronx is a necropolis—a city of death," the head of one neighborhood health clinic stated flatly. "There's a total breakdown of services, looting is rampant, fires are everywhere." The prevailing metaphor was that of a malignant condition ("blight") whose spread now threatened to engulf neighborhoods to the north. That the progress of this condition had advanced to the point of becoming seemingly irreversible pointed to an inescapable conclusion: that further massive infusions of government funds were incapable of reversing "the complicated social and economic pathology of an area in which civilization has virtually disappeared." This note of surrender was further reinforced by drawing attention to the darkening fiscal realities of 1973, specifically to Nixon's impending plans to slash domestic budgets. In an ominous sign of things to come, the Nixon administration had announced a freeze on all public housing that winter. Increasingly, the article noted, state and city governments frustrated by the intractable problems of the inner city were shifting scarce public resources to middle-class areas whose inhabitants had grown resentful of the largesse bestowed on the poor. Mayor Lindsay was quoted warning that "the South Bronx is certain to be one of the areas hardest hit by the President's decision to impose austerity on domestic programs, presumably in order to pay the brutal costs of a senseless war."

In this Darwinian climate, the failure of the Fox Street housing projects took on heightened significance. As the *Times* put it: "The Fox Street experiment now stands as a disfigured symbol of the difficulties of social engineering." None other than Robert Moses, the master builder who had loomed over all public works projects in New York City for decades, and whose Cross-Bronx Expressway was frequently blamed for the area's current deterioration, pronounced the death knell for the South Bronx. It must be conceded, proclaimed Moses, "that this Bronx slum and others in Brooklyn and Manhattan are

unrepairable . . . They must be leveled to the ground." It was a
sentiment shared by many who felt that such neighborhoods should
simply be burned down, though none, perhaps, went as far as Nixon
himself: "Goddamn New York," he stated in one of his Oval Office
rants, adding that it was filled with "Jews and Catholics and blacks
and Puerto Ricans." There is, he continued, a "law of the jungle, where
some things don't survive . . . Maybe New York shouldn't survive.
Maybe it should go through a cycle of destruction."

A Cycle of Destruction

Throughout the winter and spring of 1973, as the economic picture
darkened, Nixon began dismantling the social programs of the sixties.
Lyndon Johnson's death on January 22 acquired an eerie symbolism as
his successor announced a series of dramatic new policy shifts that
meant the end of his two most significant legacies: withdrawal from
Vietnam, followed shortly by the government's announcement that it
was beating a strategic retreat from the War on Poverty. Nixon's 1974
budget, announced in 1973, featured deep cuts in a wide range of
government programs. The housing freeze was followed by proposals
to cut or eliminate entirely one hundred programs, affecting everything
from funding for education and hospital construction to urban renewal. This was coupled with a rhetorical assault on the pathologies that
these programs had allegedly unleashed: permissiveness and dependency; a decline of personal responsibility; the breakdown of the moral
fabric of American society. Making a philosophical virtue out of
economic necessity, Nixon tagged Johnson's Great Society as a failed
utopian experiment in social engineering. At the same time, beset by a
growing public relations nightmare as the Watergate scandal deepened, Nixon sought to shore up his standing among that portion of his
constituency—the so-called silent majority—that had grown increasingly resentful of government programs for the poor. Following up on
the tough-on-crime agenda of his 1972 reelection campaign, Nixon
announced plans in the winter of 1973 to completely overhaul the

nation's criminal code and asked Congress to restore the death penalty.

This conjuncture of circumstances—post-Vietnam economic downturn combined with a mounting backlash against welfare—would be transformed into a larger social convulsion of far-reaching consequences by the jolt that the Arab oil embargo sent through the world economy. The resulting crisis, which brought to an end the post–World War II economic boom, also effectively ended the age of expansive government that had lasted from 1945 up to the early 1970s. Following close to thirty years of unparalleled prosperity and economic expansion, 1973 ushered in a period of contraction that spelled the beginning of the end of much of what had come to be known as the Great Society. Coupled with another momentous event—the collapse of the gold standard, the financial system that, by tying the value of the dollar to gold, had assured stability in world markets—the result was a period of intense economic uncertainty and restructuring. Out of this crisis would eventually emerge a new form of capitalism, but the immediate effect was a cycle of destruction that for many Americans ended the old expectation of universally rising living standards.

Nowhere were the effects of this shift in the nation's political economy felt more acutely than in the nation's cities. One of the cornerstones of federal policy in the years after World War II had been the GI Bill, which subsidized home mortgages and made student loans available on easy terms to returning soldiers. In effect the GI Bill, by making millions of Americans part of the middle class, represented—without being perceived as such—a form of government-subsidized social engineering. The civil rights movement and Johnson's Great Society tried to extend this project to the blacks who had moved in enormous numbers to the nation's northern cities after the war. Integration had been pursued through a combination of legislation intended to guarantee rights (voting and education) and economic assistance (housing and welfare). But this undertaking ran aground both on the rising costs of the Vietnam War and on a growing backlash from the white middle classes, which as the sixties progressed became increasingly critical of large-scale government efforts to remake American society. Soldiers returning from Vietnam found a greatly diminished version of the GI Bill awaiting them. Earlier social divisions that had been addressed through government programs now seemed increasingly unbridgeable. An urban policy expert cited in the *Times* series on the South Bronx put it this way: "The old concept was that you take a group of people who were very poor and prejudiced against and you add money and create a middle class . . . But what we're seeing now is a tremendous division between those who are making it and those who are left behind."

White flight from the inner city, which had accelerated tremendously during the urban upheavals of the sixties, was now coupled with growing skepticism about government programs and intervention. Nothing did more to fuel both tendencies than the advent of court-ordered busing in the northern states. The Supreme Court decision in the summer of 1973 provoked widespread anger and resistance and ultimately only exacerbated the growing cleavage between the cities and the suburbs, which were exempted from busing by a further ruling handed down in 1974. State and federal governments shifted their resources to the suburbs, while at the same time pursuing increasingly aggressive strategies to maintain law and order in the cities. Municipal budgets, drained by the flight of tax dollars, became inadequate to cope with the mounting problems of the inner city: drugs, muggings, graffiti. Confronted by these problems, Lindsay, who had presided over the largest expansion of city government in New York's history, and who had harbored hopes of national political office, decided in the spring of 1973 against running for reelection.

This turning point from expansion to contraction was linked with a new neoconservative trend in politics. The assault on the welfare state went hand in hand with an increasingly punitive approach to crime. Crime, as leading neocon Daniel Patrick Moynihan put it, was to sixties liberalism as Communism had been to forties liberalism. Neoconservatism as a movement had taken shape around a group of thinkers, influenced by University of Chicago professor Leo Strauss, united by their fierce opposition to Communism. After Strauss's death in 1973, Irving Kristol—who famously defined a neocon as a liberal who had been mugged by reality—inherited his mantle as the movement's leader. The movement crystallized in the new tough-on-crime policy whose signal accomplishment was the Rockefeller drug laws passed in the winter of 1973. These laws imposed harsh mandatory sentencing requirements on courts and stiffened penalties for parole violators. The crisis of sixties liberalism advanced to the point where even in liberal bastions like *The New York Review of Books*, one author—who was critical of capital punishment and mandatory life sentences—nevertheless conceded that he wondered "whether we can still afford to treat our street-corner gunslingers as sociological casualties."

In or About 1973

Earlier in the century Virginia Woolf famously proclaimed that "on or about December 1910 human nature changed." The magnitude of the changes enumerated above has led some commentators to observe that 1973 marked a watershed in culture as well as in politics and economics as significant as the one announced by Woolf. Social critic David Harvey is among those who offer support for this view. In his book *The Condition of Postmodernity*, Harvey identifies the period between roughly 1910 and 1972 as the era of high modernism. One of the fundamental events of this era was the birth of a new vision of the modern city, primarily associated with Le Corbusier and Robert Moses, for whom architecture and urban planning represented the vanguard of a progressive, enlightened form of social engineering that would create a better society. In the post–World War II era, vast new urban renewal projects were undertaken under the banner of this belief. Though admirable in theory, in practice it created a legacy of destruction (symbolized by the demolition of New York's great Beaux-Arts masterpiece Penn Station in 1963) and alienation (epitomized by the ubiquitous housing projects that ringed most major American metropolitan centers).

The year 1972 is often taken to be the moment of the final collapse of this vision, a collapse symbolically brought home by the destruction of the Pruitt-Igoe housing complex in St. Louis. Designed and built in the mid-1950s by architect Minoru Yamasaki, Pruitt-Igoe was meant to offer its inhabitants a clean, modern alternative to the slums. It was influenced by the ideas of Le Corbusier and upon completion became a prize-winning project. By the 1960s, however, Pruitt-Igoe had become a crime- and drug-ridden scourge and a symbol of failure. Rape and robbery were endemic; deliverymen refused to enter the project without guards; and snipers and stone-throwers harassed the police. After several expensive renovations did nothing to reverse the decay of the project, it was eventually scheduled for demolition. When asked their opinion on what to do with its dilapidated structures, the inhabitants of the complex reportedly began to chant spontaneously, "Blow it . . . up! Blow it . . . up!" The government obliged, and according to Charles Jencks, "modern architecture died in St. Louis, Missouri, on July 15, 1972, at 3:32 (or thereabouts)."

In fact, although three of the project's thirty-three buildings were destroyed in 1972, the plan called for the others to be preserved while the new space was turned into a park for the area's remaining residents. Not until August 1973 did the Department of Housing and Urban Development make the decision to demolish the other structures. They lingered on, mostly unoccupied, for another several months before being leveled, lending the area in the meantime "the haunting eeriness of a bombed city." To many commentators the dynamiting of the project exploded modernism's claim to engineer a better society. Pruitt-Igoe's demolition came to be seen as the death of the century's dominant architectural movement, a symbol of blocked change. The event became, in the words of architecture critic Jane Holtz Kay, writing in the *Nation* in the fall of 1973, "this summer's, maybe this decade's exercise in architectural analysis"—a symbol of the crisis not just of modernism but of liberal reform in general. "The high-rise ghetto as bombsite," wrote Kay, "becomes a potent media image," one that invited experts from all walks of life to pick over the carcass of this failure and offer their analyses of where it had all gone wrong.

The tale of what had happened to progressive architecture could be told in the intertwined fates of Pruitt-Igoe and Yamasaki's other notable commission, the World Trade Center's Twin Towers. Yamasaki had long since disavowed his housing project by the time he received the commission to design the world's tallest buildings. The Port Authority of New York and New Jersey, which commissioned the buildings, wrapped the project in the rhetoric of early 1960s optimism: "In a jet age that shrinks the globe, the exchange of new goods—much of it the product of postwar technology—promises to help raise the standard of living of the people of many nations." This rhetoric, as one history of the project puts it, exuded the "technological optimism of the early space age . . . the gravity-defying confidence of early NASA scientists."

Translating this grand vision into striking architectural terms, however, proved a nearly insurmountable task for Yamasaki. Creating a structure that could withstand the wind shear generated at such heights virtually guaranteed that engineering considerations would outweigh design choices. "Big But Not So Bold" was the verdict pronounced by architecture critic Ada Louise Huxtable at the towers' dedication ceremony, held April 4, 1973. In Yamasaki's hands, according to Huxtable, the megalomania of the project had been coupled with a strangely dainty decorative scheme that tried futilely to humanize the structures. The towers were also, as it turned out, the victims of a cruel twist of fate; one month after the dedication ceremony, Chicago's Sears Tower claimed the title of world's tallest building. To add insult to injury, the onset of the oil embargo and the city's financial meltdown conspired to keep much of the center unoccupied well into the late 1970s.

A further taste of which way the winds were blowing in the field of architecture could be seen in the redevelopment plans for Times Square. Developer Peter Sharp, who wanted to erect a building at a site on Broadway between 46th and 45th Streets, turned to architect John Portman, whose recently completed Hyatt Regency in Atlanta had made him a much sought-after figure. The signature feature of Portman's buildings was an elaborate interior space featuring large, soaring atriums dominated by trees, fountains, and glass elevators, coupled with an almost blank exterior. Portman's proposal for the Times Square site, unveiled at a ceremony held at City Hall in July 1973, envisioned a gigantic fifty-six-story, two-thousand-room hotel made up of enormous concrete slabs. Mayor Lindsay announced that the new hotel would be not only the most spectacular hotel in the city's history but "a whole concept of how a city ought to be." Portman himself elaborated by saying that in the past New York had given too much emphasis to welfare and low-cost housing, which didn't pay for themselves, and that the city needed to do more to attract private enterprise. This view was mirrored in the position his building adopted toward its gritty exterior environment: Portman described his building as so "self-contained" that someone could spend three days exploring its atrium and other interior spaces without getting bored; access to the hotel would be restricted by the presence of "control points" at grade level; and those guests who chose to do so would be able to admire the view of Times Square from a sidewalk café in a glass box that would show Times Square "in a protected environment." Portman's answer to the sixties spectacle of street riots, demonstrations, and crime was to create a new kind of spectacle built around extravagant interior spaces. Though architecture critic Paul Goldberger hailed the project for its "science fiction, futuristic" feeling—he called it "Buck Rogers in Times Square"—howls of protest greeted the unveiling of Portman's design that tied it up in courts for years. Upon its completion in 1985, the Marriott Marquis was widely reviled. Its back turned aggressively to the street, it was now described by Goldberger as "an upended concrete bunker."

The Sense of an Ending

In Ayn Rand's novel *The Fountainhead*, architect Howard Roark defends his decision to blow up Cortlandt Homes, a low-cost federal housing project he designed with a fellow architect, by claiming that "no work is ever done collectively, by a majority decision." He goes on: "Every creative job is achieved under the guidance of a single thought . . . An architect uses steel, glass, concrete, produced by others. But the materials remain just so much steel, glass and concrete until he touches them." Although Roark's statement would seem to apply uncannily well to the case of Yamasaki, in reality the heroic aesthetic principle enunciated here was a relic by the time Yamasaki's towers were dedicated. On all sides that year were heard epitaphs for the Roarkian superarchitect. As one reviewer, writing in the *Times*, put it, "One of the casualities of the Sixties was the master builder, the hero-architect of modernism." Urban renewal schemes had given the disciples of Wright, Corbu, and Mies the opportunity to clear away "'blight' to make way for the heavenly city of inspired structural statements ordered by rational master plans." The fatal flaw in such schemes, as critics like Jane Jacobs had been arguing since the early 1960s, was a fundamental misreading of the nature of urban life and what made it work. As Jacobs had shown in her studies of the street life of New York's West Village, what to the modernists had seemed like confusion and disorder could be shown to reveal a hidden order. Blind to such mundane forms of organization, the revolution ushered in by the International Style had degenerated into a kind of design terror, the architectural equivalent of Orwell's *1984*. The definitive statement of this antiplanning backlash would come with Robert Caro's biography of Robert Moses, *The Power Broker*, in 1974, which told a story of idealism gone horribly wrong and placed much of the blame for the problems of neighborhoods like the South Bronx at Moses's feet.

What took the place of modernism was something called "postmodernism": a disenchanted, ironic new sensibility that rejected the machine aesthetic that had dominated modernist architecture and ushered in an era of historical pastiche, a mad proliferation of styles, many borrowed from the past and updated for a new postindustrial society. The publication in 1972 of Venturi and Brown's *Learning from Las Vegas* provided the antimodernist reaction with its manifesto. With their witty rhetorical demolition of the modernist program and their pop sensibility, Brown and Venturi breathed new life into a moribund architectural discourse. Like Warhol, they aligned themselves with Pop against what they called "Abstract Expressionism in architecture." Self-conscious heretics, they celebrated, in an ironic vein that became a signature of postmodernism, the popular vernacular of automobile culture and of the American commercial landscape. They approached Las Vegas as anthropologists and found evidence of a naïve primitive civilization inhabiting a world populated by signs. The commercial strip and its signs were for them a species of found art. Though they conceded that "the order was not obvious," they went on to assert that for those who knew how to read these signs, they were full of meaning.

It was not by chance that Venturi and Brown took their cues from Las Vegas, since it was the fastest-growing metropolitan region in the country, and in this sense was emblematic of the larger cultural shift of this period. Theirs was, in a very real sense, an antiurban sensibility, one that found inspiration in a new landscape of "big spaces, high speeds and complex programs." If modernism was essentially an urban style, then postmodernism—at least in Venturi and Brown's vision—was posturban, or simply suburban. But what exactly did this vision portend, aside from the fact that the nation's political and cultural center of gravity seemed to be shifting away from its traditional manufacturing cities in the Northeast to the new postindustrial suburbs and edge cities of the Sunbelt? Not without some justification were they accused by critics of having capitulated to the "Nixonites and Reaganites"; of giving up not just on the great social project of modernism but on any hopes for reform whatsoever; and thus of acquiescing to the commercialization and privatization that took hold in American life in the 1980s. They themselves argued that it was time to take seriously the aesthetics of Middle America, to give the "silent white majority" a voice.

In a more basic sense Venturi and Brown gave voice to a feeling that the storyline that had sustained modernism since its beginnings had broken down. Though they were sanguine about the future direction of architecture, more pessimistic prognosticators read their book as a symptom not just of the end of modernism but of the collapse of all the grand theories and metanarratives—whether liberal, Marxist, or

Freudian—that had given shape to the modern era. Among the most frequently cited sources for this view was the publication, in 1973, of sociologist Daniel Bell's *The Coming of Post-Industrial Society*. Bell argued that a fundamental mutation in the DNA of American society was under way; he saw a new social order emerging in America, a social order in which basic assumptions about work, class, and ideology were being completely overturned. The most salient feature of this shifting and churning in the tectonic plates of American society was the move away from an economy based on manufacturing to one based on services and information management, in which for the first time in the history of industrial civilization white-collar workers would outnumber blue-collar workers.

While Bell grounded this theory in a belief in the emergence of a new technocratic elite that would steer society, he also expressed, with characteristic neocon ambivalence, misgivings about some of the social divisions he also saw emerging. Most notable among these was a new "adversary culture" of the arts that carried the "flag of anti-bourgeois values" and that mocked the industriousness and self-discipline on which American economic growth had been built. The perception of decline that ran through his book found its expression in a characteristic verbal tic of intellectual discourse that captured the contemporary sense of an ending, namely the widespread use of the prefix *post* to define the current sensibility. As examples Bell cited the following: post-capitalist; post-modern; post-civilized; post-collectivist; post-Puritan, post-Protestant, post-Christian; post-traditional; post-historical.

Bell's book received considerable attention, much of it taking issue with his conclusions while conceding his larger point that American society seemed to be undergoing a paradigm shift. Naomi Bliven, writing in the *New Yorker*, suggested that Bell's analysis was clouded by the fact that he himself remained at heart a traditionalist. A postindustrial society, worried Bell, could not provide a "transcendental ethic," a stable belief-system that helped shape politics and public morality. But, as Bliven pointed out, modernism had always been about breaking up and recombining, as in the celebrated examples of early twentieth century time-and-motion studies and cubism. In alluding specifically to these two breakthrough developments, Bliven touched on precisely that constellation of changes that, according to Woolf, marked the advent of the new modernist sensibility—in its own way, a deeply moral sensibility—that came to its symbolic end with the demolition of Pruitt-Igoe.

An Incapacity for Being Modern

The argument for a new sensibility that emerged in the early 1970s was made most strongly in the field of architecture, where it was linked to a larger narrative concerning a fall from modernist grace into postmodern disenchantment, stylistic promiscuity, and ironic commercialism—a fall, or shift, that Venturi and Brown linked explicitly with the name of Warhol. Modernism's demise could be seen on the one hand in the demolition of Pruitt-Igoe, a development, incidentally, that suggested that talk of leveling the South Bronx was not mere hyperbole. On the other hand it could be seen in the manner in which architects began to embrace a new kind of stylistic vocabulary, more commercial and richer than the stripped-down aesthetic of high modernism. According to Harvey, the social contract that had prevailed during the period from 1945 to 1973 had been maintained at the expense of a certain austerity, a spare, functionalist aesthetic that had created a climate of pent-up desire for something more expressive. Pop, which had emerged in the latter stages of this period and now reigned triumphant, offered a new symbolic excess to replace the old symbolic poverty. Was it merely by chance, wondered Harvey, that the turn to this new symbolic excess coincided with the end of the gold standard—a standard that had undergirded both the stability of the world economic system and, by implication, everything tied to that system?

Modernism's apparent demise, lastly, attested to a significant shift in the nation's cultural and political topography. Whether celebrated or demonized, postmodernism had both its own style and its own geography. Its centers were to be found in Sunbelt cities like Atlanta, Houston, Las Vegas, and Los Angeles, all of which duly became required stops on the itinerary of those in search of the essence of the emerging political-cultural dispensation. Unconstrained by the kinds of limits that, in the older urban centers of the East, had forced growth to occur vertically, these cities had grown outward, horizontally, in ever-widening circles that to the eye of the traditional urbanist looked like unplanned, chaotic development. But just as Jane Jacobs had insisted that urban "blight" concealed its own hidden order, Venturi and Brown insisted on the need to analyze the new urban form hitherto defined, out of ignorance, as "urban sprawl."

Jacobs had been contesting modernism's hegemony over the city since the early 1960s. But to really get a sense of where architecture, and American society with it, was heading, one had to leave the traditional city behind. What Jacobs had done for New York, maverick figures like Reyner Banham now did for Los Angeles and Venturi and Brown for Las Vegas. Indeed, the reports of modernism's demise triggered a virtual stampede westward on the part of architectural critics anxious to find out what the future held for their discipline. *New York Times* architecture critic Paul Goldberger was one of the most well traveled, visiting the Atlanta of John Portman as well as Houston and Disney World. As Goldberger proclaimed rather breathlessly in one lengthy article, it was now Mickey Mouse who taught the architects. From its offices in Glendale, California, where the preliminary plans for EPCOT (the Experimental Prototype Community of Tomorrow) in Florida were currently being drawn up, Team Disney exercised "more influence on the shape America's cities will take than any planners, architects, or urban designers could ever hope to." Trips to Disney World, reported Goldberger, are "suddenly becoming the sort of obligatory pilgrimage for young architects that visits to the great monuments of Europe were for earlier generations." Likewise, Venturi hailed Disney World as "a symbolic American utopia" whose apparent vulgarity architects ignored at the risk of snobbery. What had started as an amusement park in the 1950s had become something far more significant: the repository of a strain of technological optimism that, in this day of oil shortages and environmentalism, was becoming increasingly endangered.

At the same time, other figures began to investigate the customs and mores of those who inhabited these vast edge cities and zones of suburban sprawl. Just as Venturi and Brown treated Las Vegas as ethnographers who'd stumbled on a new civilization, Craig Gilbert, producer of *An American Family*, treated the Louds as members of an exotic tribe inhabiting the affluent suburbs perched in the idyllic coastal hills overlooking Santa Barbara. Gilbert was at pains to establish the show's anthropological credentials, including Margaret Mead's enthusiastic endorsement of the series. Gilbert's condescension and assumption of cultural superiority masked a certain defensiveness, perhaps even a desire for revenge against the Nixonite silent majority entrenched in its coastal wonderland.

One of the most striking testimonials to this new interest in how the silent majority lived came in the form of photographer Bill Owens's book *Suburbia* (1973). Owens worked for a small newspaper in Livermore, California, a Bay Area bedroom community that had undergone explosive growth during the sixties. His book strove to capture on camera the essential mystery of suburban culture that lay concealed behind the apparent blankness of the tract houses, the lawns and swimming pools, the Tupperware and block parties. Many of his pictures portrayed families surrounded by the material trappings of their mobility and success: cars, boats, RVs, and other expensive playthings. Others, however, captured a more eccentric or melancholy aspect of suburbia; in one a divorced woman tends plants in the broken toilet she used as a planter on her carefully manicured lawn.

Many of Owens's photos were accompanied by captions conveying their subjects' views. "I find a sense of freedom in suburbia," as one man put it. "You assume the mask of suburbia for outward appearances, and yet no one knows what you really do." Owens took seriously the sense of liberation—including sexual—sought by the inhabitants of suburbia, even if the captions frequently set up jarring or ironic contrasts with the contents of the photos themselves. In one picture of several couples lounging in a hot tub, their legs collectively rising out of the bubbles in a fashion that evoked synchronized swimmers, the caption read: "We don't have to conform."

It was as though, after the great social and psychological distance traveled by Americans during the sixties, returning to such bastions of normality now revealed them in a new, exotic light. Yet for the most part Owens refrained from the temptation of easy satire that marked most contemporary attitudes toward suburbia. As David Halberstam wrote in his introduction to Owens's book, "Altogether too many social critics . . . mocked the new suburbs, particularly the outward uniformity of the homes, as if that uniformity reflected a spiritual uniformity inside." Whereas Owens, like Venturi and Brown, remained open and generous in his appraisal of the new posturban sensibility, others viewed it through a more paranoid lens. Gonzo journalist Hunter S. Thompson's response to Las Vegas was perhaps the most extreme version: to his fevered mind, "The Circus Circus is what the whole hep world would be doing if the Nazis had won the war. This is the Sixth Reich." Richard Nixon, he wrote, "would have made the perfect mayor for this town."

Even those who did not go quite this far nursed suspicions that the "mask of suburbia" concealed an utterly alien sensibility, one that at best was merely extravagantly banal but at worst betrayed something far more insidious, a secret suburban intolerance, even a kind of fascism. (One of Owens's pictures of two boys dressed in military outfits was accompanied by the caption "We like to play war.") The near total absence of minorities in Owens's photographs was not lost on a *Times* critic who noted that "suburbia seems to function as a means of avoiding the unpleasant, and leading what Madison Avenue has defined as the good life." The critic reacted with horror to Owens's depiction of this "advertisement-derived vision of life": "Life imitating art is one thing, but life imitating the setting and perceptions of some mediocre television sitcom is quite another. You could move the Dick van Dyke show lock, stock and barrel into Livermore, and no one would notice—from either side."

Many of the interiors captured in Owens's photographs do indeed have a somewhat unreal quality. One of his subjects, a woman sitting carefully posed next to her living-room fireplace, is quoted saying, "I get a lot of compliments on the front room wall. I like Italian Syrocco floral designs over the mantle. It goes well with the Palos Verde rock fireplace." Certainly such self-satisfaction could be viewed as the symptom of withdrawal from the real complexities of American society, but it also captured something essential about the current state to which history had delivered Americans. As Janet Malcolm put it in an article in the *New Yorker*, current trends in interior design revealed "our incapacity for being modern." Whereas early modernist architects and designers saw in "the spare, machined geometries of their buildings and artifacts the expression of a new social order," the newly prevailing vogue for a more middlebrow style—which Malcolm labeled "Mediterranean"—suggested that a "retrograde spirit is upon us all." "What," asked Malcolm, "could be more Mediterranean than Mr. Nixon himself?"

In Search of the Silent Majority

Perhaps the clearest sense of the direction in which the country was heading could be found in the president's birthplace, southern California's Orange Country. Home to Disneyland, the world's first drive-in church, and a thriving defense industry, this region experienced some of the most dramatic growth in the entire nation in the years between 1945 and 1970. What had originally been a predominantly rural area had been transformed first into a traditional suburban area and then, eventually, into a new kind of "postsuburban" region—a dynamic economic powerhouse in its own right rather than merely an appendage to Los Angeles. Its growth had been fueled by the development of the defense and aerospace sectors, which, along with the climate and southern California's promise of the good life, had lured hundreds of thousands of people to the area. The defense contractors and high-tech industries that made up the bulk of the region's economy made it a home to countless engineers, researchers, scientists, and skilled workers.

Orange County's growth reflected many of the developments highlighted by Kirkpatrick Sale in his book *Power Shift* (1975), which analyzed the postwar shift in political and cultural importance from the Eastern Establishment to the Sunbelt that had burst into national consciousness with Nixon's election in 1968. The emergence of the so-called Southern Rim as an increasingly important component to be reckoned with in what Sale called "the equations of national power" resulted from the huge population migrations south and the concomitant growth of the nation's military-industrial complex, disproportionately based in Sunbelt states.

By the late 1960s, as its industrial economy was being outstripped by its "informational economy," Orange County was morphing into a postindustrial center, with information management, tourism, and leisure its new economic pillars. The region benefited tremendously from the growth of tourism during the sixties, as more affluence and vacation time combined with the construction of the interstate highway system. One measure of this tourism boom was the rise in sales of RVs between 1961 (83,000) and 1972 (740,000). The Disney fantasylands at either end of the Sunbelt were, as Sale noted, well positioned to take advantage of this new leisure economy.

Not surprisingly, given that Orange County's economic destiny was inextricably bound up with the cold war, it was home to a very conservative citizenry. In the sixties Orange County became a political base for a resurgent grassroots Right organized around some of the most conservative political figures in the country, including Barry Goldwater and Ronald Reagan. Despite being dealt a setback with Johnson's landslide defeat of Goldwater in 1964, this base had been tremendously mobilized by the civil rights movement and the social turbulence of the 1960s. It had played an instrumental role in carrying Reagan to the governor's office in 1966. And in 1968 the New Right got its revenge on the Democrats who had written them off as extremists four years earlier. The archconservative Newport Beach–based Lincoln Club would go so far as to claim that its money got Nixon elected. Having served notice of its new clout, the movement expanded beyond its traditional anti-Communism in the late 1960s to take on the new plagues of liberalism, welfare, and feminism. Politically, the region's greatest success lay ahead with the tax revolts of the late 1970s. Reagan's election as president in 1980 would, as Bruce Schulman puts it, make the political culture of southern California the political culture of the entire nation.

Even after Watergate had dealt the movement an apparently crippling blow, it was able to regroup in the culture wars that crystallized in the early 1970s around abortion, pornography, and homosexual rights. It was in Orange County, in fact, that the landmark case of *Miller v. California* had originated. Defendant Marvin Miller had dabbled in underground publishing for years, at one point making a small windfall on a controversial book of photographs of the Kennedy assassination, including one notorious photo, which later disappeared, of a shadowy figure on the grassy knoll. Starting in the mid-1960s, he had gone into the lucrative business of mail-order smut, building up a mini-porn empire based in southern California. This had eventually brought him to the attention of the federal government, which subjected him to intense harassment, sending the IRS after him, tapping his phones, and serving him with subpoenas. According to author Carolyn See, "At any one time [Miller] might have representatives from the Treasury Department, the Secret Service, the Bureau of Internal Revenue, the Department of Justice as well as state and local police parked in front of his house." Finally one of the brochures he sent out in a mass mailing to advertise his "adult material" found its way to a restaurant in Newport Beach, whose manager complained to the police. Arrested for violating California's antiobscenity law, Miller's case found its way to the Supreme Court, where his conviction was upheld by a 5–4 majority ruling.

Perhaps somewhat more surprising than Orange County's political conservatism was the fact that, despite being closely hitched to the most advanced sectors of the American economy, the region also served as an incubator for a vigorous new strain of prophetic fundamentalism. Notwithstanding Daniel Bell's fears that a postindustrial society might lack the moral touchstones of traditional society, Orange County in the late 1960s and early 1970s gave birth to a fantastic number of evangelical congregations. It was there too that the Jesus movement established its first foothold. Scholar Lisa McGirr has explained the seemingly contradictory appeal of Christian fundamentalism in southern California both as a reaction to the social turbulence of the sixties and as a response to the very conditions that had given Orange County its identity. "This hypermodern environment," she argues, "created ambivalence about the consequences of modernity." The qualities that had made the region so hospitable to economic dynamism—the absence of tradition and cohesion—were precisely those that also made it hospitable to religious fundamentalism. McGirr notes the correlation between apocalyptic prophecy and technology, observing that many prophecy writers were engineers, scientists, and military men. The best-selling book of the 1970s, Hal Lindsey's *The Late Great Planet Earth*, which refracted the cold war through the lens of biblical prophecy, found a highly receptive audience in Orange County, where many of Lindsey's subsequent writings were published by local houses. Lindsey's venture in biblical forecasting predicted that Armageddon was imminent and that it would come in the form of a shattering thermonuclear conflict in the Middle East. Many fundamentalists greeted the outbreak of the Yom Kippur War in October 1973 as the fulfillment of his predictions. It was in that year as well that Trinity Broadcasting Network was founded in Santa Ana by Paul and Ann Crouch and Jim and Tammy Faye Bakker, the so-called "first family" of televangelism.

While the American inner city was now littered with the carcasses of past experiments in public housing, Orange County had emerged as a key experimental station for some of the most significant private initiatives in posturban communities. Among the earliest of these was Knott's Berry Farm, the world's oldest themed amusement park, a place whose archconservative creator envisioned it as a shrine to "the wholesome aspects of an idealized and simpler America." This potent mix of entertainment and conservative ideology was also a staple of the Disney empire, whose landmark Anaheim park (opened in 1955) would later be imitated at the other end of the Sunbelt by the Disney World–EPCOT Center project in Florida, where in November 1973 Nixon would choose to give the press conference at which he famously declared, "I'm not a crook."

Perhaps Orange County's most striking contribution to contemporary ideas about the good life could be seen in the planned development of Irvine. This entity, which was incorporated within the county in 1973, was conceived as the nation's premier master-planned community, a middle-class suburban utopia. It was undertaken by the colossal Irvine Corporation on lands owned by the Irvine family. The tentacular reach of this corporation encompassed virtually every aspect of life in the new city, from the University of California campus opened there in 1965 on lands donated by the Irvine Corporation, to the new Irvine Industrial Park that it created simultaneously.

The Irvine Corporation went to great lengths to ensure architectural, economic, and racial homogeneity, requiring residents to join homeowners' associations that imposed stringent guidelines on those wishing to become the owner of one of the homes that stood in row upon row of identical structures with Mediterranean red-clay roof tile. Unlike earlier federal experiments in social engineering, however, this experiment was yoked to a privatized, highly exclusive vision. Sale read it as symptomatic of a search for an "authoritarian stability" that reflected the rootlessness of the region's inhabitants:

> Conformity is a malady of all suburbs, but the Southern Rim cities, so often little more than concentric suburban sprawls without either a physical or cultural center, so new that they lack the cohesion of tradition and the comfort of convention, are particularly prone to such rigidification. Often they seek to create cohesion and unification where there is no natural reason for it, through the artifice of uniform architecture. In Irvine, California, homeowners must select paint for their houses from a list of 25 approved colors.

Again we see here the easterner's suspicion that these homes nursed a social pathology that helped explain the country's rightward drift under Nixon. Indeed Sale's account closely echoed that of his Cornell University chum Thomas Pynchon in *The Crying of Lot 49* (1966). It is this landscape that Pynchon's heroine, Oedipa Maas, stumbles across in the course of her journey into the labyrinth of her ex-lover Pierce

Inverarity's estate, of which she has been named executor. Crawling with Birchers and other conspiracy nuts, it could not be more psychologically remote from what Pynchon, in an eassy on Watts published in 1966, called—in ironic reference to the Disney empire—"Raceriotland." Arriving in the town of San Narciso—probably modeled on Irvine—where Inverarity had begun his land speculating and laid out the tentacles of his vast holdings, Oedipa notes: "Like many named places in California it was less an identifiable city than a grouping of concepts—census tracts, special purpose bond-issue districts, shopping nuclei, all overlaid with access roads to the freeway." On closer examination, however, the apparent randomness of the landscape revealed a secret order; as she looked down the slope, Oedipa "thought of the time she'd opened a transistor radio to replace a battery and seen her first printed circuit. The ordered swirl of houses and streets, from this high angle, sprang at her with the same unexpected, astonishing clarity as the circuit card had. Though she knew even less about circuits than about Southern Californians, there were to both outward patterns a hieroglyphic sense of concealed meaning, of an intent to communicate."

While Venturi and Brown, and to some extent Owens, remained open-minded in their appraisal of the new Sunbelt landscape, other figures like Sale, Thompson, and Gilbert offered a more paranoid reading that traced the geographic coordinates of the nation's current political crisis. So widely had this paranoid reading come to be shared by 1973 that Carey McWilliams, editor of the *Nation* and a Californian by birth, felt compelled to publish in the *Times* a special plea on behalf of his home state, to defend it against the "libelous notion that the roots of Watergate can be traced to the politics and sociology . . . of Southern California, more particularly Orange County." Yet McWilliams's article only underlined the extent to which, in the tea-leaf readings of the eastern intelligentsia, Orange County had assumed a privileged place as a landscape whose patterns, properly read, might reveal the nation's future.

Conspiracy Nation

> [Expletive deleted]
>
> —Watergate tape transcripts

> I just want to ask you one favor. If I'm assassinated, I want you to have them play "Dante's 'Inferno'" and have Lawrence Welk produce it.
>
> —Richard Nixon, speaking to H. R. Haldeman

NOVEMBER 17, 1973: *During an appearance at Disney World, Richard Nixon goes on national television to defend his actions and urge the nation to put Watergate behind it. He concludes by declaring, "I am not a crook." Three days later a gap of eighteen and a half minutes is discovered on the tape of a conversation between Nixon and H. R. Haldeman on June 20, 1972 (three days after the break-in). Nixon's secretary, Rose Mary Woods, denies deliberately erasing the tape. At the beginning of December White House chief of staff Alexander Haig theorizes that "some sinister force" erased the tape.*

The unraveling of the Watergate cover-up during the winter and spring of 1973, as well as the revelations concerning the dirty tricks department operating out of the White House and the Nixon administration's systematic attempts to undermine the political process, inspired George McGovern to warn that the United States had come "closer to one-man rule than at any time in our history." Throughout that year conspiracies and counterconspiracies multiplied. In Los Angeles the Daniel Ellsberg trial exposed the existence of an elaborate plot, carried out by the Watergate burglars, to discredit one of the main protagonists in the "killing of the father" scenario—the man who had released the Pentagon Papers—including an attempted burglary of his psychiatrist's office in search of potentially damaging evidence of mental illness. Dire warnings from the Left that Nixon was plotting a domestic coup were echoed by allegations of U.S. involvement in the overseas coup that resulted in the overthrow and death of Chilean president Salvador Allende on September 11. Meanwhile, a further rash of conspiracy theorizing seized on the demise of the gold standard in 1973, arguing that a cabal led by the Rockefellers had orchestrated this development in an attempt to extend its hold over the world economy.

The deep psychic shock waves caused by the end of the 1960s and Watergate led to paranoia and demonology on both the Right and the Left. The resulting impulse toward conspiracy theory found its ultimate literary expression with the publication in the spring of 1973 of Thomas Pynchon's novel *Gravity's Rainbow*. The novel's first sentence announced the imminent arrival of a rocket whose origins, trajectory, and final destination provided the book's central plotline. Seven hundred pages later, after a wild excursion through twentieth-century history, the reader was finally deposited in a movie theater on Melrose Avenue in Los Angeles, presided over by an unshaven, unsavory figure named Richard Zhlubb, a thinly veiled version of Nixon. In the ultimate paranoid closing of the circle, the rocket's final destination was revealed to be the reader-moviegoer's seat. *Gravity's Rainbow* examined the consequences of the discovery that Americans were no longer on the right side of history—no longer among "the Elect," as Pynchon's novel had it—and it tapped into a rich new strain of paranoia in the national imagination that after 1973 became a dominant trope of American culture.

State of Siege

The so-called "third-rate burglary" that ultimately brought down Richard Nixon began innocuously enough. When on June 17, 1972, five men were arrested in the national headquarters of the Democratic National Committee at the Watergate complex, there seemed at first little reason to believe that the fallout from the arrests would extend further than the two men, E. Howard Hunt and G. Gordon Liddy, who were soon discovered to be the burglars' handlers. Even after it became clear that Hunt and Liddy were no rogue agents but were operating out of the White House and had connections to the Committee to Re-Elect the President, popularly known as CREEP, the silence surrounding the incident remained all but impenetrable. *Washington Post* reporters Carl Bernstein and Bob Woodward encountered repeated stonewalling in their efforts to follow the money trail that linked the burglars to the president's men, and they were able to keep the story alive only with the help of their source Deep Throat. The cover-up remained intact through the election, as Nixon won a landslide victory against George McGovern, and continued to hold through the end of the year.

Only in the winter of 1973, as the first convictions were handed down in the trial of the burglars, did the wall of silence begin to crumble. First burglar James McCord began to talk, followed, after the onset of the televised Watergate hearings on May 18, by White House special counsel John Dean. Then, with one shocking revelation following another in rapid succession, the dark underworld of the Nixon White House was exposed in all its ugliness to an appalled and fascinated public. The unraveling of the cover-up made clear that Watergate itself was merely part of a much larger web of dirty tricks; that the so-called Plumbers arrested in the Democratic National Committee offices were simply one arm of a many-tentacled operation engaged in an extraordinary array of sabotage, electronic surveillance, and psychological warfare—in short, as Woodward and Bernstein put it in their account of the story, *All the President's Men*, "a grand conspiracy to subvert the electoral process." The gradual widening of this conspiracy would eventually extend from Liddy and Hunt to the nation's highest offices, including former U.S. attorney general John Mitchell; acting FBI chief L. Patrick Gray; White House chief of staff H. R. Haldeman; and finally to the conspirator-in-chief himself, Richard Nixon.

When, in an interview with Senate investigators in early July 1973, Nixon aide Alexander Butterfield revealed the existence of a secret Oval Office taping system, the president's fate was sealed. Though the final drama over the tapes would drag on for another year—with Nixon resorting to desperate stratagems to stymie the special prose-cutor's request to turn them over—by the time he made his appearance at Disney World in November 1973, pleading for understanding, all but his closest supporters were abandoning him. The Nixon presi-dency staggered on until the following August, when, rather than suffer the indignity of impeachment, Nixon finally resigned from office. His successor, Gerald Ford, issued an official pardon in Sep-tember 1974.

Ford's pardon of Nixon was intended to close the book on Water-gate. Yet many questions remained. Perhaps the biggest of them concerned motive. Why, given the extent of Nixon's lead in the polls in the summer of 1972, and the magnitude of his final victory over McGovern, had White House operatives been engaged in their dirty tricks campaign? Answers to this question remained murky. Never-theless, as the administration underwent its meltdown, a picture emerged of a presidency in the grip of an elaborate paranoia. One strand in the complex history that produced Watergate extended back to the administration's early years in the late 1960s, when a siege mentality began to overtake the White House in response to the public outrage unleashed by the revelation of its secret bombing campaign against Cambodia. Other strands reached back into deeper layers of cold war history and into the president's own tendency, ever since he first gained notoriety in the Alger Hiss case, to see conspiracies everywhere. This tendency was exemplified by Nixon's statement to Haldeman, made following publication of the Pentagon Papers in the *New York Times*: "We're up against an enemy, a conspiracy. They're using any means. We are going to use any means. Is that clear?" The directive Nixon issued to his top aide set in motion the hidden chain of events that led to the Ellsberg break-in and ultimately to Watergate.

Nixon was by no means alone in his dark obsessions. A general climate of paranoia permeated the White House from which few were immune. His aides compiled an "enemies list" of those believed to be conspiring against the White House—ranging from Jane Fonda and John Kerry to Andy Warhol and football star Joe Namath—and mobilized federal agencies, including the IRS and the FBI, on behalf of the administration's counterattack. Henry Kissinger personally authorized the wiretapping of numerous government officials and journalists suspected of having a hand in the leaks leading to the disclosure of the secret bombing campaign in Cambodia. As the media frenzy surrounding Watergate intensified, ever more extreme measures were contemplated.

Nixon had a famously embattled relationship with the media going back to his televised debates with Kennedy in 1960. His sweaty, sallow appearance in these debates, which contrasted unfavorably with his opponent's cool demeanor, had in the minds of many observers—including the candidate himself—cost him the election. From this point onward, as Joe McGinniss wrote, Nixon was afraid of television, half-suspecting "that it was an eastern liberal trick." Yet Nixon's relation to TV was far from one of simple antagonism. On the contrary, he was very much a creature of the new televisual age of politics. From early in his career Nixon was surrounded by men from the worlds of advertising and public relations. His "Checkers" speech of 1954, delivered to the largest TV audience hitherto, had saved his career from scandal. And in the run-up to the 1968 election, Nixon assembled a highly media-savvy team to help him overcome his image problems. One of the blueprints for this team was Marshall McLuhan's *Understanding Media*, which was distributed to the members of Nixon's staff and guided their efforts to alter the chemistry between their candidate and the American voter. A central feature of this campaign was its reliance on McLuhan's notion of the global village: the new immediacy, "heightened emotionalism," and "susceptibility to rumor" of the audience created by the electronic media. It was to this audience that Nixon's image-handlers sought to address their candidate's message, bypassing the print media that they regarded as biased against their candidate. By the time of the Republican National Convention in Miami that crowned Nixon's 1972 reelection campaign, this team's mastery of the medium was complete. Reporting at Miami, Norman Mailer described Nixon as "the first social engineer to harness and then employ the near to illimitable totalitarian resources of television."

Nixon's distrust of the print media was greatly intensified by the leaks that plagued his administration from the outset, first with the published stories of the secret bombing campaign in Cambodia and then with the Pentagon Papers. His response was to declare an all-out war against the organs of the press, authorizing IRS audits, wiretaps, and break-ins into the apartments of journalists seen as harboring a particular bias against him. This culminated in the White House counterattack against the "media conspiracy" allegedly orchestrated by the *Washington Post*'s Watergate coverage. This counterattack had both its public and its hidden faces: while the White House press office sought to discredit the *Post* as elitist, it also explored other means of silencing the press. As Woodward and Bernstein recounted, by May 1973 Deep Throat was warning that "everyone's life was in danger." In his memoir, Gordon Liddy later claimed that he had openly advocated the possibility of assassinating columnist Jack Anderson.

In attacking the media, the White House tapped into a broader middle-American resentment of the liberal elite. Senator Robert Dole responded to one *Post* story concerning Haldeman's role in the management of a secret White House slush fund for dirty tricks by suggesting collusion between the *Post* and the McGovern camp: "There is a cultural and social affinity between the McGovernites and the *Post* executives and editors. They belong to the same elite; they can be found living cheek-by-jowl in the same exclusive chic neighborhoods, and hobnobbing at the same Georgetown parties." Haldeman himself offered the purest version of the White House demonology concerning the Eastern Establishment and its alleged media control. In an interview in 1973, Haldeman—whose "great dream" was reportedly to become head of the Disney empire—alleged that "somewhere in the jungle labyrinth of Manhattan Island there is a secret nerve center where, every Sunday afternoon, an enormously powerful group of men gather to decide what the Eastern Establishment media line . . . will be."

Dirty Tricks and Psy-War

The administration's attack on the media was simply one facet of a much larger campaign of what Liddy called "intelligence-gathering and disruptions operations" directed against a diverse enemy composed of antiwar activists, Black Panthers, internal defectors like Ellsberg, and finally the leaders of the Democratic Party. As Woodward's source Deep Throat revealed, virtually every organ of the federal government was involved in this campaign, from the Justice Department and the FBI to the IRS and the CIA. When the increasingly embattled White House encountered resistance from the now-ailing J. Edgar Hoover, who died in the spring of 1972, it unleashed its own team of professional conspirators. Many of them had ties to decade-old CIA covert operations against Castro. One Watergate burglar, asked his profession at the arraignment following arrest, answered simply: "anti-Communist." It was one of the strange ironies of this campaign that it relied so heavily on dedicated cold war operatives at the very moment when Nixon himself was taking historic steps—seen by many archconservatives in his party as the ultimate apostasy—to improve relations with both the Chinese and the Russians.

Dirty tricks—or "rat-fucking," as its practitioners called it—were also part of the modus operandi of the so-called USC Mafia (Dwight Chapin, Ron Ziegler, Gordon Strachan, Bart Porter, Donald Segretti) that CREEP unleashed against the opposition. Here lay another of the ironies disclosed by the Watergate scandal: the strange combination of piety and utter amorality that seemed to coexist in many of the president's men. In his review of Woodward and Bernstein's book, syndicated columnist Garry Wills dwelt at length on the seeming contradiction of a White House occupied by straight arrows who attended prayer meetings and yet would stop at nothing to sabotage their opponent: "These new Children of God . . . were genuinely righteous, and censorious, and prudes—which puzzles many now, when we know they were crooks, too. This was an administration with an equal fondness for Billy Graham and for break-ins." The transcripts revealed the strange spectacle of a president for whom it was apparently normal, on a Sunday morning, to leave "the East Room for the Oval Office to intermit prayer-breakfasting with rat-fuckery." Wills's explanation for this schizoid behavior was to suggest that there was a tendency among any sort of "spiritual elect" to operate by its own laws. The Nixon White House, presided over by its "Ratfucker-in-Chief," represented "the dingy new Kingdom of Heaven," whose commandments were: "Seek and you shall find; ask, you will be answered; break and enter, and it shall be given to you."

A further set of disclosures led to the exposure of Hunt's campaign of "psy-war" against the administration's enemies. This included the so-called "Canuck letter," a forged letter containing slurs against U.S. citizens of Canadian origin, whose publication in a New Hampshire newspaper derailed the candidacy of Democratic front-runner Edmund Muskie. It also included the campaign of sabotage conducted against McGovern's running mate, Thomas Eagleton, which the administration had a hand in as well. Deep Throat informed Woodward that the White House had fed the press information that Eagleton had received electroshock treatment for depression on a number of occasions in the early 1960s. These revelations forced Eagleton out of the race and inflicted further damage on McGovern's already-troubled campaign.

Most emblematically this campaign of psychological warfare included the break-in into the office of the psychiatrist who was treating Daniel Ellsberg, in search of evidence of drug-taking, marital infidelity, or mental illness that could be used to discredit the man who had leaked the Pentagon Papers to the press. It was Nixon's fury over the publication of these classified documents that led to the increasingly extreme measures he authorized against the administration's enemies, including the formation of the so-called Plumbers unit to halt further leaks—defined by Liddy as "disclosures of the private acts of government." In itself, however, the release of the Pentagon Papers did more damage to his Democrat predecessors Kennedy and Johnson than to himself, since they detailed the steps by which those two presidents had enmired the United States in Vietnam. It was the violation of the secrecy principle that drove Nixon—himself an obsessively secretive man—into a frenzy and led simultaneously to the seeking of indictments against Ellsberg and his "co-conspirators," as well as information that could be used to smear Ellsberg. When the break-in yielded nothing useful, the Plumbers turned to the CIA, prodding one of the agency's psychologists to produce a psychological profile that showed Ellsberg to be motivated by oedipal aggression against his father and the president.

As Ellsberg would later recount in his memoir *Secrets*, the steps that led him to violate the principle that Nixon sought so desperately to uphold represented the culmination of a lengthy personal evolution. Ellsberg's story was that of a cold warrior who came to question all of the orthodoxies he had once accepted, a true believer who became a dissident. The road that led him ultimately to the Pentagon Papers began in the late 1950s, when he was hired by the Rand Corporation, a think tank with ties to the Pentagon. His arrival there coincided with the Sputnik scare. Assigned to study the military's "nervous system" and to game out various Strangelovean nuclear war scenarios, he later moved to Washington to become a Pentagon employee entrusted with a high-level security clearance. At this post he was uniquely well positioned to observe the process that led to the deepening U.S. involvement in Vietnam. The next six years were ones of intense personal conflict for Ellsberg as he became increasingly torn between his loyalty to the "sacred code of the insider" and his growing disenchantment with the war. Finally this true believer in the principle of secrecy took the steps that—with the aid of marathon Xeroxing sessions—finally resulted in public exposure of the deceptions of two administrations and brought down the wrath of a third on his head. The trial of Ellsberg and his codefendant Anthony Russo collided with

Watergate on April 27, 1973, when the judge in his case received information from the Watergate prosecutor that Hunt, Liddy, and three Cubans had burglarized the offices of Ellsberg's psychiatrist. Three days after Americans learned of the Plumbers' existence, Nixon announced the bombshell resignations of his two closest aides, Ehrlichman and Haldeman.

The trajectory traversed by Ellsberg—from true believer to dissident on trial—coincided with the fifteen-year period following Sputnik's launching during which the global village was born. The televised Watergate hearings represented the culminating event of this process. As McLuhan would argue, one effect of the imagined intimacy of the media age was the erosion of traditional notions of privacy and secrecy: "TV brings the outside into the intimacy of the home, as it takes the private world of the home outside into the forum." In McLuhan's eyes, Ellsberg's release of the Pentagon Papers was part of this paradigm shift, insofar as it revealed the powers that new equipment like Xerox machines placed in the hands of ordinary people and of the press. Nowadays, wrote McLuhan, espionage "has become the largest business in the world, and we take it for granted that the modern newspaper depends on 'bugging' the whole community. In fact, we expect the press to 'bug' the world and to challenge and penetrate all privacy and identity, whether private or corporate."

If Nixon was one of the chief architects of this new assault on privacy, then he also became its most sensational victim. According to McLuhan: "A spectacular paradigm of the information revolution has been developed for the world at large by the Watergate affair . . . The Watergate affair makes it quite plain that the entire planet has become a whispering gallery, with a large portion of mankind engaged in making its living by keeping the rest of mankind under surveillance." The resulting dream of transparency, as Don DeLillo suggested in *Great Jones Street* (1973)—which relates its protagonist's efforts to escape the media empire controlled by the shadowy corporation Transparanoia in order to recover some semblance of privacy—bred conspiracist thinking.

The administration's well-orchestrated attack on the privacy of public figures would eventually come back to haunt Nixon, making him a casualty of the "psy-war" his own men had unleashed. This became manifestly clear as, with the unfolding of the Watergate scandal, the press engaged in increasingly open speculation about the mental stability of the nation's leader. This speculation was further fueled on July 4, 1973, when Arnold Hutschnecker, the Pavlovian-minded psychiatrist who was believed to have treated Nixon on several occasions in the 1960s, published an op-ed piece in the *Times* in which he advanced the notion that the nation's political leaders should be required to submit to psychiatric evaluation before taking office. Hutschnecker's role in Nixon's life had been the subject of potentially devastating leaks during the 1968 campaign. Now, without mentioning Nixon by name, Hutschnecker etched for the whispering gallery's benefit a profile of a deeply paranoid leadership, hinting that the "totalitarian" methods employed by members of the administration stemmed from deep-seated psychological disturbances. Much of the cold war, he speculated, might have been avoided if not for the "irrational fears of imaginary attacks" of the nation's leaders, which caused them "to plot holy wars in the name of self-defense." This piece echoed an earlier editorial of Hutschnecker's that had appeared in the wake of the Eagleton scandal, in which he had originally broached the idea of requiring candidates for high political office to undergo psychiatric evaluation. Again, while the topic was ostensibly Eagleton, and Nixon's name was scrupulously avoided, the implication that there were serious questions concerning the mental stability of the country's sitting president was impossible to avoid.

These questions only intensified as the year wore on. By late fall, the signs of strain in the president were unmistakable. Hutschnecker later felt compelled to deny that Nixon had suffered a nervous breakdown during his last year in office. Clearly, however, the pressure of repeated demands to hand over tapes was taking its toll. The night he put the nation on nuclear alert in response to threatened Soviet troop movements in the Middle East, Nixon told Kissinger that his enemies were pursuing Watergate "because of their desire to kill the president. I may physically die." Fantasies of death may also have dictated his choice of entertainment. Two days after the nuclear alert, on October 27, Nixon watched the movie *Fail-Safe*, a thriller about impending nuclear war whose final image is that of a mushroom cloud.

Certainly the most sensational aspect of the breakdown of traditional notions of privacy in the Watergate affair—one scarcely hinted at by McLuhan—was revealed in the Nixon tapes. Nixon's victimization, like that of the Louds, was largely self-inflicted, the result of his own bugging of himself. As Alexander Haig suggested in proposing his "devil theory"—that a "sinister force" had erased several minutes of one of the crucial tapes—the technologies of mechanical reproduction seemed to have taken on an uncanny life of their own in the president's case. By the end, Nixon himself saw the tapes as the "enemy within." Thanks to the subpoenas issued by the Watergate prosecutor, Nixon's secret and compulsive recording of himself and others came eventually to overshadow even the Pentagon Papers and the Watergate hearings for the glimpse they offered of the inner workings of power. Beyond his involvement in the cover-up, the tapes revealed the true scope of Nixon's plotting and his paranoia. They seemed to lay bare, in a quite unprecedented fashion, the "real Nixon." So closely identified did the man and the tapes become that Barry Goldwater, invited to a White House dinner in November 1973, was left with the impression, after listening to a strung-out and rambling president, of a "tape with unexpected blank sections."

With their ubiquitous "expletive deleteds," the tapes also revealed Nixon's predilection for X-rated language. In the privacy of his office, obscenities poured forth from the presidential mouth, revealing a most undecorous side to a man who, amid the scandals engulfing his administration, had tried to maintain a public image of personal rectitude. It was in this sense not purely by chance that *Post* managing editor Howard Simon code-named Woodward's anonymous source Deep Throat. As this name intimated, Watergate was a kind of pornography, a scandalous glimpse into a world normally veiled in elaborate secrecy and denial. Similarly, the trial of Ellsberg and Russo became likened by one commentator to an "obscenity trial," an "inquisition into the meaning, use and control of a sacred, unspeakable text" that exposed the secrets of an "obscene cult"—the cult of secrecy that Ellsberg had exposed. Russo's wife, Katherine Barkley, sat through the trial proceedings taking notes for what she promised would be an exposé of the "pornography of power" and the "sexist implications of the war in Vietnam and the court system." The whispering gallery was also a kind of peepshow.

This became particularly clear in the interest aroused by the figure of Deep Throat. From his first public appearance in the pages of *All the President's Men* to his smoke-enshrouded presence (played by Hal Holbrook) in the film of the book, to the years of silence that followed, this figure excited fevered speculation concerning his identity and his role in the Watergate drama. The recent, somewhat anticlimactic revelation that he was FBI man Mark Felt, passed over for promotion to bureau director following Hoover's death—a slight that Nixon, for one, thought made him a likely suspect—have laid to rest some of the most overheated of these speculations. They have done nothing, however, to diminish Felt's role in playing another version of the secret agent of history. Yet Deep Throat alone could not bring down Tricky Dick. It took the tapes to accomplish that. Nixon's voice-activated system, which recorded absolutely everything, made his downfall a public spectacle that turned America into a nation of voyeurs. Nixon's recording system was in this sense his own Deep Throat.

The Stalking of Richard Nixon

The paranoia that pervaded the Nixon White House was matched by that of the New Left movement that the administration perceived as its chief enemy. During the early years of the Nixon presidency, the antiwar movement was subjected to ongoing harassment, surveillance, and infiltration, much of it illegal, as the Supreme Court ruled in 1972 in taking a stand against what it called a "national seizure of para-noia." FBI moles, it was suspected and later confirmed, sought to disrupt the movement's activities by planting in its midst agents provocateurs who pushed for greater militancy and violence, thereby justifying the repressive measures brought down on the movement. Prior to Watergate, however, the Left's suspicions concerning these tactics were chalked up by most liberal commentators to unjustifiable paranoia.

The shocking revelations of 1973 changed all this, confirming even the wildest of the Left's scenarios involving the White House and the FBI. With Watergate providing vivid proof of crimes it had been denouncing for years, New Left paranoia became generalized and its picture of Nixon as conspirator-in-chief widespread. Yet to those on the Left who expected a new, more favorable political dispensation to emerge from Watergate, the scandal's denouement proved a bitter disappointment. This denouement was seen as less a triumph than a failure of the system, a premature closing of the book on a still-emerging story of a deeply corrupt power structure. The unseemly haste of Nixon's pardon was interpreted as a continuation of the cover-up, evidence of high-level deal-making that suggested bigger conspiracies at work. The role of Deep Throat invited particularly elaborate speculations concerning Watergate's real meaning, suggesting evidence of a behind-the-scenes power struggle that the Sturm und Drang surrounding Watergate had kept obscured, perhaps deliberately so.

Insofar as it offered a new belief-system for the skeptical, conspiracy theory filled a particular function at this moment of crisis in American history. Paranoia thrives when conventional ways of knowing and ordering the world have broken down, when, epistemologically speaking, everything is up for grabs. The decade-long assault on the institutions and symbols of political authority that had begun with the Kennedy assassination and that finally ended with Nixon's resignation left a void in American society. Into this symbolic power vacuum rushed conspiracy theory, with its perverse fantasy of all-powerful yet invisible authority. The conspiracist response elucidated the crises in American history through recourse to deep-structural economic, psychological, and even metaphysical—as in the growing popularity of UFO-based conspiracies—causal systems.

As New Left member Sidney Blumenthal wrote in 1976, the new popularity of conspiracy theory "is probably based, in part, on the decline of the student radicalism of the Sixties. Thousands (if not millions) of young people, radicalized in varying degrees, are currently unconnected to social movements but have not discarded their critical perspective . . . Conspiracies against progressive leaders and movements are easy notions to grasp . . . They also partially explain present despair; the reason the hopes of the '60s were not realized was because a group of people at the top made sure they were dashed." The breakdown of what Blumenthal called "the civics textbook catechism" had left the American public profoundly skeptical. He cited the energy crisis as a case in point: according to one survey conducted in August 1974, 88 percent of the public believed that the crisis was caused by oil companies conspiring to raise prices.

One of the most probing efforts to construct a sociological profile of the forces at work behind Watergate was that of New Left member Kirkpatrick Sale. In a lengthy May 1973 article in the *New York Review of Books*, Sale advanced the theory of a second or shadow government operating behind the scenes at the highest levels. Nixon's power base, according to Sale, was found in the Sunbelt region that extended across the southern half of the country from Florida to California. Relying on a distinction that former SDS president Carl Oglesby had made between the new-moneyed "Cowboys" of the southern States and the "Yankees" of old eastern money, Sale provided a detailed anatomy of the "unofficial but very important nexus of power behind the acknowledged civics-textbook institutions." Culturally this region was characterized by Protestant fundamentalism, anti-Communism, and patriotism; economically it was tied to the postwar growth of the defense, aerospace, oil, and leisure industries. Nixon was a consummate product of this new configuration of power, and the Watergate scandal, in Sale's reading, represented a Yankee counterattack. Yet whatever comfort liberals might have derived from the downfall of the Nixon administration was misplaced, Sale argued, since the clout of this region was likely to grow in the future, as evidenced by the recent "oil crisis."

Sale would later elaborate this analysis of the nation's power structure at greater length in his 1975 book *Power Shift*. Responding to criticisms of his earlier article, he declared flatly that "the idea of a Southern Rim is not . . . a mere paranoid's invention." In Sale's account, the story of the Nixon presidency had been that of a war between the Eastern Establishment and the Sunbelt. Sale cited John Ehrlichman's claim that leftover New Dealers were conducting a "kind of internal guerrilla warfare against the President," as well as a March 1973 Oval Office conversation with John Dean in which Nixon dismissed the Watergate scandal as the last gasp of a beaten "Establishment"—the liberal elite, the media, the eastern political class that Nixon felt himself to be at war with. Sale himself could not help wondering whether there was some truth to Nixon's dark suspicions— whether the unraveling of the Watergate cover-up might not have been orchestrated by a CIA that was still an establishment stronghold. Was it even possible, he wondered, "that a wider conspiracy was at work, an entangled affair that might have involved the Rockefeller interests in New York, the Yankee bastions like the CIA and the Justice Department bureaucracy . . . as well as other individuals?"

For commentators of this period, Watergate became a kind of Rorschach test, inviting them to project a variety of melodramatic narratives on to its web of intrigue. For Garry Wills, it was the tale of a criminal enterprise masked by outward religiosity—one that found a cinematic echo in the conclusion of *The Godfather*, in which scenes of Michael Corleone devoutly presiding over his son's baptism are inter-cut with scenes of his assassins meting out their ruthless vengeance against his enemies. For Sale, it was the tale of the Cowboy-Yankee power struggle—a power struggle that took on distinctly paranoid overtones, even if Sale was at pains to deny them. For still others on the left, Watergate became the occasion for conspiracy-mongering of a still more baroque kind.

Most tantalizing of all the prospects opened up by Watergate was the possibility of a connection to the Kennedy assassination. The tenth anniversary of the assassination that year became the occasion for all manner of interest in the circumstances and unanswered questions surrounding it. In November 1973 Quadrangle Books, the publishing arm of the *New York Times*, came out with *Nov. 22, 1963: You Are the Jury*, by David Belin, junior counsel for the Warren Commission. Belin's defense of the Warren Report's lone gunman theory was favorably reviewed in the *Times* on November 18, 1973, shortly before the anniversary of the assassination. According to the Freudian view favored by the *Times*, Lee Harvey Oswald had committed an act of "symbolic parricide"; subsequent conspiracy theorizing simply served as a defense against the realization that "we all want subconsciously to kill our fathers." Such explanations did little to satisfy the conspiracy-minded; on the contrary, they only inflamed the paranoid imagination with visions of a larger cover-up, something that in any case took little doing in a context in which Warren Commission member Gerald Ford—author of one of the key texts of the lone gunman theory, *Portrait of an Assassin*—was soon to become president and pardon a predecessor whom many, as we shall see, suspected of having his own ties to the Kennedy assassination.

Further inflaming the paranoid imagination was the new availability of bootleg copies of the sacred text of Kennedy assassination buffs, the Zapruder film. In 1973 film technician Robert Groden, who had worked in the lab that analyzed the original print and covertly made a copy of it, showed his enhanced version of the film to an audience at the newly formed Assassination Information Bureau, a Boston-based organization founded by former SDS members. Assassination conspiracists dissected the Zapruder film frame by frame in search of evidence contradicting the lone gunman theory. Such efforts found adherents at the highest levels; shortly before his death in January 1973, Lyndon Johnson gave an interview in which he suggested that his predecessor had died as the result of a conspiracy.

Linking Dallas and Watergate held out the possibility of finding a master key to the traumatic decade framed by the two events. For those who had long believed that the Warren Commission had whitewashed the real story behind Dallas, the presence of Hunt and the Cubans in the Watergate burglary was the crucial fact. It seemed to suggest a link between the disastrous Bay of Pigs misadventure, a failed coup attempt; subsequent CIA plotting against the president who had "betrayed" the plotters; the Warren Commission cover-up; and Nixon's attempt to stage his own domestic coup with the help of these same plotters. The key figure was Watergate mastermind Howard Hunt, who had participated in the Bay of Pigs and who moonlighted by writing spy novels in his spare time. Hunt's involvement proved a boon to conspiracy theorists, as did the CIA ties of several of the Cuban burglars. One commonly imputed Watergate motive was the White House's desire to steal information in the Democrats' hands concerning Nixon's involvement in Castro assassination attempts. Jack Anderson, whom Liddy had toyed with killing, was reportedly breaking the Cuba story at the time of the break-in.

Another author tracing the connections between Dallas and Watergate was Peter Dale Scott, who published an article on his investigations in the left-wing *Ramparts* in November 1973. Scott identified the Bay of Pigs fiasco as the key to the conspiracy. It was Kennedy's "betrayal" of Hunt and his fellow CIA plotters, followed by his apparent moves to begin withdrawing American troops from Vietnam, that made him the target of a shadowy cabal of reactionary and virulently anti-Communist forces. Nixon's ties to those same anti-Castro elements went back to his tenure as Eisenhower's vice president, when he'd been involved in the initial stages of the planning for the Bay of Pigs. These operatives, who had expertise in planning coup attempts on foreign soil, had then served as key figures in the Nixon White House, where they had been engaged in efforts to stage a domestic coup. The dirty tricks had come home to roost.

As Steve Weissman, the editor of the book *Big Brother and the Holding Company: The World Behind Watergate* (1974), in which Scott's article was reprinted, put it, "the anti-Ellsberg operation looked like something the CIA does overseas." With good reason, in Weissman's mind: Hunt and the Cubans responsible for it had had years of experience planning such operations outside the country. Weissman's book, which included contributions by Noam Chomsky and Kirkpatrick Sale, represented the fullest attempt to detail the elaborate network of connections that tied the Nixon White House to the "Cowboys," organized crime, and rogue elements in the CIA.

Another contributor to this collection was Donald Freed, a member of the left-wing organization Citizens Research and Investigation Committee. Freed's article alleged that the real motive behind Watergate was the planting of evidence that would implicate the Democrats in a series of violent acts that the White House's dirty tricks specialists were planning to stage, with the help of provocateurs, at the Republican National Convention in Miami. This violence would then be used to justify declaring a state of national emergency and to stage a coup d'état.

An earlier stage of this elaborate plot, Freed argued, had involved the attempted assassination of George Wallace, a figure whose growing following on the Right posed a threat to Nixon's reelection prospects. Arthur Bremer, an unemployed, mentally disturbed man had fired several shots at Wallace as he left a campaign rally in Laurel, Maryland, on May 15, 1972. Though he survived, the shooting left Wallace paralyzed and forced him to withdraw from the presidential campaign; in the election the following year, Wallace's supporters endorsed Nixon over McGovern in large numbers. Following the attempt, Bremer immediately became the object of intense speculation, as both the Left and the Right replayed the lone gunman debate that had surrounded Lee Harvey Oswald. Freed argued that the left-wing pamphlets found in Bremer's apartment after the attempted assassination had been planted there, probably by Hunt acting at the behest of Nixon aide Charles Colson, and that Bremer had in fact been tied to right-wing figures with links to CREEP.

Freed's speculations were not confined to the printed page. A playwright, he cowrote the story that became the basis for one of the most explicit exercises in conspiracy-mongering ever committed to screen, 1973's *Executive Action*. (Freed also wrote the screenplay for Robert Altman's *Secret Honor* and served as a consultant on Oliver Stone's *JFK*.) Its release timed to mark the tenth anniversary of Kennedy's death, this film starred Burt Lancaster and Robert Ryan as the leaders of a right-wing cabal of military and industrial interests who orchestrate the Kennedy assassination with the help of rogue FBI and CIA agents. This group wants Kennedy out of the way before he can follow through on what they believe is a plan to lead a Black Revolution, sign a test ban treaty with the Russians, and pull American troops out of Vietnam. Oswald, according to this scenario, was merely placed at Dealey Plaza to serve as the dupe. The film details the elaborate steps taken to create a left-wing cover for Oswald, tying him to causes like Fair Play for Cuba. A key part of this plan involved the use of techniques like cropping and doctoring photos to forge an identity for Oswald that would throw up a smokescreen around the conspiracy and eventually lead the Warren Commission to its lone gunman theory. The plotters' use of techniques of mechanical reproduction documents the ease with which the historical record can be manipulated, falsified, and rewritten. This lurid exercise in Cowboy demonology ends with a coda in which the audience is informed that eighteen witnesses to the assassination, whose pictures are flashed on-screen, all died under mysterious circumstances between 1963 and 1973.

Executive Action's coda provided the point of departure for a similarly inspired film that appeared the following year, Alan Pakula's *The Parallax View*. Here the assassination of a telegenic and charismatic presidential candidate, followed by the mysterious deaths of several eyewitnesses, plunges the film's protagonist, a disaffected journalist played by Warren Beatty, into the world of a sinister organization that specializes in political assassination. The Beatty character eventually goes undercover in order to infiltrate the organization, which subjects him to a battery of tests to determine his aptitude for the kind of work that the Parallax Corporation specializes in. One of these includes a *Clockwork Orange*–like sequence in which Beatty is forced to sit through a montage of violent images that includes repeated shots of Nixon. Here too, as in *Executive Action*, we encounter a comment on image culture that raises several questions: is the Beatty character undergoing psychological testing? or is he being programmed? Hired by the organization, Beatty finds himself at the film's end set up, Oswald-like, as the dupe for yet another assassination; as Fredric Jameson has noted, he ceases to be the rebel figure he believes himself to be insofar as "his oppositional impulses have become the very instruments of the conspiracy." The film concludes with a Warren Commission–like group issuing their finding that the gunman acted alone.

The political thriller genre received yet another airing that year in Costa-Gavras's *State of Siege*, a film that managed both to foreshadow U.S. involvement in Chile and to suggest parallels to a White House under siege. Its depiction of the tragic logic behind targeted assassination as a technique of guerrilla warfare made this film highly controversial and brought charges of anti-Americanism down on the director. Based on an actual incident that had occurred in Uruguay in 1970, the film details, with clinical precision, the events surrounding the kidnapping of an American official whose position with the Agency for International Development (AID) provides cover for his work in training Latin American police forces in the art of torturing political prisoners. In the end the American is killed and unceremoniously left to be found by the police as a message of the power of the urban guerrillas the Tupamaros.

In drafting the screenplay Costa-Gavras received assistance from Franco Solinas, who had also cowritten the screenplay for Gillo Pontecorvo's 1966 film *The Battle of Algiers*—described by Pauline Kael, in her review of *State of Siege*, as "probably the only film that has ever made middle-class audiences believe in the necessity of bombing innocent people." It was perhaps in anticipation of some such message that the film's premiere, scheduled for early April at Washington, D.C.'s Kennedy Center, was canceled by George Stevens, director of the American Film Institute, on the grounds that it "rationalized an act of political assassination." Indeed, the film's reverberations were many, both foreign and domestic. It had been shot in Chile, where Costa-Gavras had struck up a friendly relationship with President Salvador Allende, who would be killed six months after the film's release in an American-backed coup. As Kael put it, the film was an object lesson in the complicity by which all Americans were entangled in the repressive politics of Latin America that had brought on both the

terrorism of the Tupamaros and the extreme countermeasures employed against them.

Indeed, just prior to the film's release, the nature of this entanglement had been at the heart of the inquiry into the role of U.S.
multinationals in the internal politics of Chile conducted by a sub-
committee of the Senate Foreign Relations Committee. At stake were
allegations, published the previous year by columnist Jack Anderson,
that ITT had been conspiring with the CIA to block Salvador Allende
from assuming power in 1970. (It was Anderson's article on this
conspiracy, which had reportedly compromised the identity of a CIA
agent, that led to Liddy's proposal to assassinate him.) Following
Allende's victory, Chilean right-wingers had approached Nixon crony
Pepsi-Cola chairman Donald Kendall for help in organizing a coup.
Though help was denied at the time out of fears that it might backfire
like the Bay of Pigs, by the late summer of 1973 the necessary forces
had aligned themselves for Allende's violent overthrow. The success of
the American-backed coup attempt that occurred on September 11
meant among other things that Chile, which had been abandoned by
American corporations in the wake of Allende's 1970 election, was
once again reopened for business, with the Rockefeller-backed Council
of the Americas assuming a leading role.

According to Kael's logic, Americans were equally implicated in the
rise of domestic extremism—precisely the point argued by those
members of the New Left who stressed connections between the
apparatus used in Chile and that used at home against the antiwar
movement. In the summer, former Kennedy speechwriter Theodore
Sorensen penned an article for the *Times* linking *State of Siege*'s
reception to the current political climate: "One insidious result of
the Watergate affair is the temptation it offers to believe the worst
about every government agency." While trying to clear AID of the
film's allegations, Sorensen nevertheless rejected Stevens's rationale for
canceling the screening, claiming that Kennedy himself would have
appreciated Costa-Gavras's message. Yet Stevens's concerns about the
film's domestic repercussions may not have been entirely misplaced.
According to one account, the members of the Symbionese Liberation

Army, which was forming at the exact moment that the controversy surrounding Costa-Gavras's film reached its height, may have studied the film in the belief that it was a virtual manual on urban guerrilla warfare. Their first "action"—the assassination of a popular black school official in Oakland in November 1973—may have been based on the film.

Right-Wing Conspiracy Theory

The shadow of paranoia that repeated assassinations cast over the national psyche took on elements of farce in the story of would-be assassin Arthur Bremer, whose diaries, published in January 1973 in *Harper's Magazine*, would provide the basis for Paul Schrader's screenplay for Martin Scorsese's *Taxi Driver*. Bremer, these diaries made clear, was a cipher, a blank figure onto which both the Left and the Right could project their competing scenarios. While conspiracy buffs across the political spectrum hinted at dark political machinations, Bremer's diaries traced his own emergence as a kind of assassination buff to sexual issues: "My penis made me do it." Like *Taxi Driver*'s would-be assassin Travis Bickle, for whom "women are all alike, they're a union," and whose sexual problems are displaced into an obsession with guns, Bremer inhabited a psychosexual terrain marked by castration anxiety. On a trip to New York City, Bremer visited an adult bookstore and a massage parlor, where his awkward interactions with his masseuse ended in frustration and humiliation.

Yet Bremer's diaries also revealed a darkly humorous side and an astute sense of the American public's obsession with spectacular crimes. He imagined himself as Alex in *A Clockwork Orange* come to life, but without any "in and out," just "a little of the old ultra-violence." The new conditions forged by the global village, in which the desire for celebrity acquired transcendent power, created a kind of conspiracy between the great criminal and the public, as Bremer intuited. "Hey world!" he writes, "Come here! I wanna talk to you!" He writes deliriously of his desire to commit "the biggest hijack ever" and to start the "next crime binge"—and claims that "the silent majority will back me all the way!" He goes on to speculate that there are probably about "30 guys in prison now who threatened the Pres & we never heard a thing about 'em . . . Maybe what they need is organization. 'Make the First Lady a Widow, Inc.' 'Chicken in Every Pot and Bullet in Every Head, Com., Inc.'" Bremer conjures a farcical populist version of the Parallax Corporation for his brotherhood of would-be assassins. While conspiracy theorists on both Left and Right took for granted the existence of a recognizable and clearly defined "they," Bremer rendered absurd any such assumption.

The diary revealed that Bremer's original target had been Nixon and that he had spent months stalking the president before giving up in frustration at his inability to penetrate the security detail surrounding him. Only then had he turned his attention to Wallace. Yet almost as soon as the first excerpts of the diary were published, questions began to be raised about their authenticity, with many on the Left suspecting that the diaries had been manufactured to provide Bremer with an Oswald-style cover. In fact, given the threat Wallace represented to Nixon's reelection chances, there was some reason to suspect, as Woodward and Bernstein pointed out, that Bremer's attempt on Wallace's life might be the ultimate dirty trick. No less a figure than Nixon himself suspected a Bremer-CREEP connection, according to the *Post* reporters. What seemed certain was that Nixon aide Charles Colson, as soon as news of the assassination attempt came over the wire, cooked up the scheme of sending Howard Hunt to Milwaukee in an attempt to find, or plant, evidence of Bremer's connection to left-wing groups, perhaps even the Black Panthers. According to a release issued by the White House press office only hours after the assassination attempt, literature had been found in Bremer's apartment linking him to leftist causes and possibly even the McGovern campaign. Meanwhile Nixon himself called Mark Felt, who had not yet assumed his role as Deep Throat, to urge the FBI to pursue the case as aggressively as possible to preempt public suspicion of a cover-up.

On the Right, Bremer's supposed ties to left-wing groups quickly became an article of faith. This was especially true among the members of Wallace's American Party, whose leadership following the assassination attempt was taken over by Congressman John Schmitz of Orange County. The archreactionary Schmitz came forth with what he claimed was conclusive evidence that Bremer was part of a conspiracy to kill Wallace. The evidence, according to which Bremer had attended SDS meetings in Milwaukee, was cited by Schmitz as part of a pattern linking Bremer to the other assassins of the sixties: "Oswald, Ray, Sirhan, Bremer—they're supposed to be mixed-up loners. But you look into their background and you find that they aren't loners at all . . . And whether they're from the Fair Play for Cuba Committee or SDS, they've got one thing in common— they're all out of left field."

In placing the American Party's hopes for presidential office in the hands of Schmitz, the Wallace assassination attempt opened the national political arena to the authentic voice of John Birch–style paranoia. As the *New York Times* put it in a lengthy article that ran two days before the 1972 election, the American Party ticket appealed to people who believed that the republic was threatened by a con-spiracy masterminded by "fat-cat financiers" in league with Russia and China and shielded from public view by the press. When in 1964 historian Richard Hofstadter published his celebrated essay "The Paranoid Style in American Politics" in *Harper's Magazine*, he was referring chiefly to right-wing paranoia of the type exemplified by the supporters of Barry Goldwater, who went down to a defeat of historic proportions at the hands of Lyndon Johnson that year. Hofstadter's anatomy of this movement located its major raison d'être in a sense that America had taken a disastrous wrong turn at some point early in the twentieth century. "The modern right-wing," he wrote, "feels dispossessed." Recent historical developments had greatly exacerbated this sense of dispossession: "Events since 1939 have given the con-temporary right-wing paranoid a vast theater for his imagination . . . the theater of action is now the entire world." In Hofstadter's analysis, the basic tenets of right-wing thought could be distilled to: (1) the existence of a conspiracy to undermine capitalism, beginning with the income tax amendment to the Constitution in 1913 and culminating with the New Deal; and (2) the infiltration of government as well as the apparatus of media and education and other major institutions by a network of Communist agents. This infiltration had advanced so far that it was no longer possible to distinguish between the two major parties or their candidates, both of which were in thrall to the forces of "world socialist government."

Tracing the ultimate origins of this vision back to the millennial sects of the eleventh to sixteenth centuries and their megalomaniac view of themselves as members of an elect, Hofstadter established a lineage of the modern right-wing paranoid. American Party leader John Schmitz became the standard-bearer for this constituency in the 1972 election. Although he fared miserably in the election—losing, as he put it humorously, "by a mere 44 million votes"—Schmitz used his moment in the national limelight to great effect. Sounding as if he had just stepped out of the pages of *The Crying of Lot 49*, he tirelessly promoted his view that recent world history could be explained in terms of a conspiracy. A former Marine Corps instructor who had then become a history professor at Santa Ana College in the heart of Orange County, Schmitz was a long-standing member of the John Birch Society. His bible was a book titled *None Dare Call It Conspiracy* (1972), written by Gary Allen and Larry Abraham, with a foreword by Schmitz. Essentially an updated version of the John Birch Society's *Blue Book*, this turgid tract—which the publisher claimed had sold more than 5 million copies—analyzed the forces conspiring to impose a socialist system on the United States. "There is a conspiracy," claimed Allen at the news conference at which Schmitz declared his candidacy, "to set up a one-world socialist government through which 'they' will control the world." Though the scope and shifting nature of this conspiracy was so complex that it required charts, diagrams, and membership lists (of, for instance, the Council on Foreign Relations, a favorite *bête noire* of the far right) simply to illustrate its vast contours, at its heart stood one constant: the Rockefeller family, who had allegedly financed the Bolshevik Revolution and now "regulated" President Nixon.

It was Nixon, in fact, who represented the primary target of Schmitz and Allen's ire; McGovern, in their eyes, was merely a Nixon stooge. Though at first he had been a fellow traveler of the Right, the accommodations Nixon had found it necessary to forge with the Eastern Establishment in order to resurrect his political career, as well as his increasingly pragmatic views on Russia and China, had alienated the Far Right. Like the Birchers' *Blue Book*, which had identified Eisenhower as a Communist agent, Allen and Schmitz saw Nixon as a kind of Manchurian Candidate. "Since around 1960 or certainly 1962, Richard Nixon has knowingly been an agent of the Rockefeller family, which is the ruling force in the Council on Foreign Relations, which favors a one-world super-state, which they would control." As Schmitz put it when asked who he would support if he were not in the race: "That's a heck of a choice: Nixon, the candidate endorsed by Moscow and Peking; or George McGovern, endorsed by Hanoi and the Manson family." In Schmitz's eyes, the media played a key role in helping cloak the conspiracy. It was, he argued, all part of a Pavlovian process of programming: "Words can produce the same kind of conditioned reflex in people—and politicians have found out that if they say one thing and do another, voters will respond to what they say and not what they do." The media, in Schmitz's mind, made all Americans Manchurian Candidates, brainwashed, programmable. To be initiated into the true knowledge of the conspiracy was, in this sense, to be deprogrammed.

The politically ambiguous appeal of Schmitz's platform, which drew support from disaffected Republicans and Democrats alike, testified to a certain convergence in the paranoias of Left and Right and provided a template for much of the conspiracist thinking that entered American life in the aftermath of Watergate. For those who, like Schmitz, believed that dark forces were behind recent world events, the formation of the Trilateral Commission in 1973 became another rallying point. This multinational organization was composed of leading figures from the worlds of politics, business, and academia whose activities, which remained shrouded in secrecy, lent themselves to fears of a conspiracy with designs on the global financial order. Such fears reached their height in the conspiracy theories surrounding the demise of the gold standard in March 1973, which according to some commentators was orchestrated by the Rockefellers as a way of increasing the value of their worldwide holdings. Maverick economist Peter Beter was a chief proponent of this view, which he laid out in his paper "Conspiracy Against the Dollar." With its focus on the Rockefellers and their minions, Beter's analysis offered something for those on both the Left and the Right, echoing both the world government theories of *None Dare Call It Conspiracy* and the Yankee-Cowboy scenario advanced by Sale and company.

Learning to Love the Rocket

Nineteen seventy-three's ultimate exercise in conspiracy theory arrived with the year's major publishing event: the appearance of Thomas Pynchon's long-awaited third novel, *Gravity's Rainbow*. By the time it reached bookshelves that spring, seven years had elapsed since the publication of Pynchon's previous novel, *The Crying of Lot 49*, and ten years since the publication of his first novel, *V.*, in 1963. His career thus exactly spanned the period from the Kennedy assassination to Watergate, during which he became the preeminent novelist of the "paranoid style." Yet even as his literary reputation grew, Pynchon had maintained an almost complete public silence. Virtually nothing beyond a few sketchy biographical facts was known about him. In his review of *Gravity's Rainbow*, the *Times*'s Christopher Lehmann-Haupt dwelt repeatedly on the mystery of Pynchon's identity. Even while shedding superlatives on the novel, Lehmann-Haupt felt compelled to mention several times that nothing was known of its reclusive author. The seven-year period between his second and third novels had been accompanied by a "long silence—no surfacing, no interviews, no rumors, no word." Similarly, *Times Book Review* editor Richard Locke noted the contrast between the author's fetish of privacy and the era's growing preoccupation with celebrity: "As the sixties carried on, Pynchon remained silent; his aversion to publicity (no photographs, no bio, no interviews) was at odds with the times." The near-universal acclaim that greeted *Gravity's Rainbow* was thus accompanied by the critics' palpable sense of excitement, tinged with regret, at the author's perverse refusal to play the game of public relations.

The novel itself plays tricks with many of the reader's conditioned responses. *Gravity's Rainbow* poses quite formidable problems of interpretation. Its multiple plots and subplots and its overwritten language provoke a tendency to overreading that becomes analogized to the clinical condition of paranoia. Yet even while it invites the possibility of a paranoid reading, it also continually turns this impulse back on the reader, repeatedly reminding him or her of the false solace that lies in such a reading. The reader's absorption in the plot (in both senses of the word) is depicted as the product of a desire to find a master key to that plot, a master key ultimately imagined to be in the author's possession—precisely what the novel, and Pynchon's own silence, frustrates.

Ostensibly the novel is concerned with a twelve-month period at the end of World War II, from the fall of 1944 to the fall of 1945. The actual sweep of the narrative is far broader, however, encompassing the entire twentieth century up to the early 1970s and taking in everything from the German occupation of southwest Africa and the battlefields of World War I to the films of Fritz Lang, Pavlovian theory, and the operations of a handful of gigantic cartels. The action begins in war-torn London and then moves to what is referred to in the novel as "the Zone": the ravaged landscape of Germany in the war's immediate aftermath. At its heart are the efforts of various figures to determine the whereabouts of a rocket designed in the war's latter stages by German scientists. Among these rocket-hunters is one Tyrone Slothrop, an American officer whose fate is mysteriously intertwined with that of the rocket. The uncanny event that sets the narrative in motion is the exact correspondence between the sites of Slothrop's sexual encounters and the locations in London hit by German V-2 rockets—a correspondence that, as Slothrop learns, makes his own past a product of the same technology that produced the rocket. This technology is itself the spawn of an unholy alliance of forces, a vast cartel that, at certain points in the novel, is linked with the German chemical concern IG Farben and at others with GE, Standard Oil, and other firms. Confronted with the discovery that he has served as an experimental subject for this cartel since his childhood, Slothrop undergoes a process of psychic decomposition that ultimately renders him merely a site for multiple forms of determinism operating on the self. These include gravity itself, as well as, on a psychological level, the Calvinist doctrine of the elect and the preterite—the chosen and the passed over—and Pavlovian stimulus-response theory.

The novel—which mobilizes a prodigious range of information on rocket science, chemistry, statistics, neuroscience, linguistics, and other disciplines—constructs a plausible narrative of twentieth-century history as global conspiracy; at the same time it also continually proposes an alternative scenario in which conspiracy theorizing represents merely a compensatory effort to impose meaning on a mass of events that have no inner connection. The novel expertly mixes historical fact—such as the Americans' postwar recruitment of German rocket engineer Wernher von Braun to their own rocket program—with more speculative excursions into the historical record to produce a highly unstable narrative. So tightly woven and densely layered are its many plots, and so formidable is the range of knowledge marshaled in the book, that the reader's interpretive instincts are soon overwhelmed. In the end, the process of trying to find the crucial connections that will help decipher the plot becomes analogized to the Pavlovian conditioning that has linked Slothrop's erections to the rockets' sites of impact. Readerly "paranoia"—reading for the plot—is a programmed response, for which the book offers a form of deprogramming.

In his review of Arthur Bremer's diary, Garry Wills dwelt on the predilection of the assassination buff—whether "Bircher" or "leftist"—for conspiracy theory. Even a figure such as Bremer, according to Wills a loser obviously unfit for a role in any plot, invited wild speculation along Oswaldian lines. Wills identified this reflex as a conditioned one, one of "the mind's tricks, trying to soothe itself with patterns": "Better evil plotters with a plan than random evil in the universe. Polls reveal a perverse wish to believe in plots—not for paranoid titillation, but for solace." It is precisely this impulse that Pynchon's novel places in question.

To the extent that, in Pynchon's account, the paranoid derives perverse consolation from his belief-system and learns even to love it (in the Kubrickian sense), then *Gravity's Rainbow* hints at an explanation for the dark state of mind to which the 1960s had delivered Americans. In a number of ways that go beyond the Left's constant comparison of Nixon with Hitler, the novel maps postwar Germany onto post-Vietnam America. One set of coordinates has to do with Slothrop's Harvard classmate Jack Kennedy and the shadow cast by his assassination over the sixties. In an extended surrealistic sequence that Slothrop dredges from his subconscious under the effects of sodium amytal, he finds himself in the bathroom of Boston's Roseland Ballroom along with a black shoeshine boy named Red— actually the young Malcolm X, another assassination victim. Slothrop loses his harmonica down the toilet, and diving in to retrieve it, he encounters during his passage down the Roseland's plumbing identifi- able traces of his classmates' excrement encrusted along the sides of the pipes. These include Kennedy's, who Slothrop remembers as athletic and likable, though "daffy" about history: "Jack . . . might Jack have kept [the harmonica] from falling, violated gravity somehow?" That Kennedy's assassination, aside from ending any hope that he might "violate gravity," also provoked a crisis of historical consciousness is spelled out later in the novel in a sequence involving a Weimar-era séance held by people who are trying to communicate with the spirit of Germany's dead former foreign minister Walther Rathenau. Himself, like Kennedy, the victim of an assassination—in his case, by far-right- wing forces in the early Weimar period—Rathenau, a Jew, is imagined as a figure whose martyrdom makes him the bearer of insights into the real operations of power and history that are disguised by the official textbooks. "The moment of assassination," we are told, "is the moment when power and the ignorance of power come together." The truth about such moments is repressed in the official history; real history is "at best a conspiracy, not always between gentlemen, to defraud." Rathenau ultimately pronounces to the gathering that "all talk of cause and effect is secular history, and secular history is a diversionary tactic."

One of the possibilities that thus plagues many of the novel's characters is the end of history, an apocalyptic scenario that bears an obvious relation to fears—or as Kubrick would have it, love—of a rocket or missile but at the same time relates it to the breakdown of historical cause and effect. That this breakdown may be a relatively recent phenomenon is the conclusion suggested by the novel's final pages. Here the reader is abruptly torn out of the landscape of postwar Europe and deposited in contemporary America, where he finds himself in the company of one Richard Zhlubb, night manager of the Orpheus movie theater on Los Angeles's Melrose Avenue. With his permanent five o'clock shadow and his habit of "throwing up his arms into an inverted 'peace sign,'" Zhlubb stands in for the foremost representative of the paranoid style that entered postwar American life, Richard Nixon. The loss of historical consciousness becomes a function of image culture—specifically that of the movies—and its rewriting of the past.

Here too the novel returns to the harmonica motif, first introduced in the Roseland Ballroom sequence. Zhlubb, we are told, has come out against harmonicas and their users, who represent what he calls—here playing on Nixon's fondness for invoking the so-called silent majority, the American *Volk*—a "small but loud minority." Embarking on a drive in his black Volkswagen (the Nazis' "people's car"), Zhlubb and his reader-passenger soon find themselves being swarmed by cars carrying harmonica-players. "Relax," says the sinister Zhlubb. "There'll be a nice secure home for them all, down in Orange County. Right next to Disneyland." This line is accompanied by canned laughter, and the passenger/reader realizes that the VW's glove compartment contains an entire library of similar tapes. Morbidly, Zhlubb then slips into confessional mode:

I have a fantasy about how I'll die. I suppose you're on *their* payroll, but that's all right. Listen to this. It's 3 a.m., on the Santa Monica Freeway, a warm night. All my windows are open. I'm doing about 70, 75. The wind blows in, and from the floor in back lifts a thin plastic bag, a common dry-cleaning bag: it comes floating in the air,

moving from behind, the mercury lights turning it white as a ghost
. . . it wraps around my head, so superfine and transparent I don't
know it's there really until it's too late. A plastic shroud, smothering
me to my death.

Most disturbing about the death wish shared here is the implication
that emerges from the novel's conclusion, as the rocket stands poised
to crash down on the moviegoer-reader, that it is not Zhlubb's alone
but is shared by all. The paranoid belief-system is simply another
variant on this death wish, insofar as it is based in a secret pleasure at
one's own persecution, real or imagined. This notion is basic to
Pynchon's understanding of the seductions of conspiracist thinking.
Zhlubb's death wish represents nothing other than a variant on the
pleasure in self-destruction that runs through the whole novel. The
sexualized rocket technology around which the plot exfoliates conveys
Pynchon's fascination with the obscene, pornographic qualities of
power.

The novel's conclusion thus contains an implicit commentary on the
end or failure of the sixties. What Pynchon offers is an explanation for
the seemingly unfathomable paradox that lay behind Watergate: the
fact that institutions were toppling yet somehow remained more firmly
in place than ever. Out of this paradox came the endless spirals of
Watergate-era conspiracy theorizing. Yet to those tempted, as many on
the Left were, by the belief that, as Blumenthal put it, "the hopes of the
1960s were not realized . . . because a group of people at the top made
sure they were dashed," Pynchon poses the darker possibility that
those hopes had been sabotaged at some far more elemental level.
What the final scene of the novel depicts is the possibility of viewing
death, including one's own, pleasurably, as a form of entertainment.
This may take any number of different forms: love of the bomb, in the
Strangelovean sense; the Stockholm syndrome; the feverish excitement
attending fundamentalist end-time scenarios; Jong's confession that
"every woman loves a fascist"; Nixon's fantasizing of his death;
Warhol's experiencing of his own assassination attempt as a movie.
Each, in the end, shares a similar logic of complicity.

This logic is finally related to the reader's situation at the novel's end. It is not by chance that Pynchon's final scene is set in a movie theater in the world capital of cinema, given that one of the chief forms of control exercised by the novel's various conspiratorial "theys" has to do with the transformation of life and history into celluloid imagery. The sense that behind what passes for official history is another kind of history, that official history is a diversion, a mass entertainment, emerges in the end as the novel's most basic form of paranoia. This is driven home when the reader finds himself sitting in a movie theater at the novel's end, presided over by Zhlubb/Nixon (a harbinger of former actor Ronald Reagan's election at the end of the 1970s as president), on the receiving end of the rocket that originated in the rubble of postwar Europe and now is about to land on his head.

Epilogue

Reality, you're hard to find.

—Fragment of a poem by SLA member Gelina

AMERICA IN 1973 was a starkly altered place from the country of a decade earlier. Ten years of deeply unpopular war, civil unrest, assassination, and cultural transformation had produced a society that bore little resemblance to pre-Vietnam America. To the POWs, who'd missed out on much of this decade, the experience of returning was one of intense culture shock. Even those who had lived through and welcomed many of the changes of the sixties bore the scars of a time during which social and personal breakdown had become increasingly interwoven. This was especially true after the series of shocks that jolted America in 1973. By the end of that year the institutional failures of American society routinely evoked expressions of systemic, perhaps irreparable crisis. And yet the remarkable thing was how quickly the nation reconstituted itself, and, moreover, did so along lines that reflected continuity with the deepest myths of the American past. By the end of the decade, the country had elected a president, Ronald Reagan, who was both an avowed enemy of sixties campus radicals and an unreconstructed cold warrior, and for whom the POWs became exemplary figures around whom to reconstruct the old narratives of national heroism and virtue.

No better example of the way in which American society absorbed the crises of the sixties and prepared itself for the Reagan eighties can be found than in what is perhaps the definitive story of the seventies, the kidnapping of Patty Hearst. In this lurid saga, all the crisis narratives of 1973 came together in the most distilled possible form. On the one hand, the SLA represented the final spasm of the 1960s— their first action, carried out in the fall of 1973, was an assassination. On the other, they helped usher in a new kind of spectacle, equal parts reality and pseudo-event, that laid the groundwork for the media world we inhabit today.

Patty Hearst Superstar

By 1973 the sixties New Left had come apart at the seams, consumed by internal conflicts, harassed by federal agents, its members imprisoned, gone underground or into exile. Nixon's reelection, followed by the Paris peace accords, closed the book on a movement whose hopes for remaking American society had been bitterly disappointed. The antiwar movement that had peaked in 1970 was, by 1973, dead, and not even Watergate seemed capable of injecting new life into it. Only in a few enclaves was the revolutionary dream still being dreamed. One of them was the Bay Area, incubator of the Free Speech movement and of hundreds of minor cults of insurrection. In the spring of 1973 it gave birth to the SLA, the guerrilla organization whose kidnapping and conversion of heiress Patty Hearst into a terrorist became the most sensational success story in the decade-long campaign by radicals to win the hearts and minds of American youth.

The central figure in the SLA was Donald DeFreeze, a black former inmate of California's Vacaville State Prison. DeFreeze's time in the highly politicized California prison system had turned him from a petty criminal into a revolutionary. By the early 1970s this system had grown into the world's third largest (after those of the USSR and China), an "American Gulag" that had become a hotbed of radical inmate organizing. At Vacaville an inmate study group called the Black Cultural Association (BCA) began meeting to read and discuss the texts of black nationalism. The BCA eventually attracted the interest of local activists, many with ties to the Bay Area's largest left-wing group, the Maoist organization Venceremos. Some of these activists attended BCA meetings and offered the inmates instruction in political science, sociology, and other subjects. It was through the BCA that DeFreeze first came into contact with the figures—all white middle-class youths—that would make up the core of the SLA following his escape (under somewhat mysterious circumstances) in the spring of 1973.

Moving to Berkeley, DeFreeze—now calling himself Cinque, after the leader of a nineteenth-century slave uprising—eventually took up residence with a young woman named Patricia Soltysik, who adopted the name Mizmoon. The two of them drew up what would become the SLA Code of War and, together with a tiny coterie of followers, began training themselves in the art of urban guerrilla warfare. The mid-summer collapse of Venceremos, on the heels of so many other New Left organizations, left a void in Bay Area radicalism—a void that would quickly be filled by the superheated rhetoric of the nascent SLA. August 1973 was the key month in the group's gestation: several new members joined, new funding was secured, and, at the end of the month, the group released a communiqué declaring "revolutionary war" on the United States. Then in November the SLA committed its first "action": the assassination of popular black Oakland school official Marcus Foster, on the grounds that a new school ID program he was implementing contained the seeds of incipient "Orwellianism." Foster's killing nearly spelled the end of the SLA; the group was widely criticized by the Bay Area Left for this senseless act, and it might have sunk back into obscurity were it not for its next, and far more sensational, action: the kidnapping of heiress Patty Hearst from her Berkeley apartment on the night of February 4, 1974.

Thus began one of the most extraordinary sagas of the 1970s, Patty's eighteen-month-long journey into the radical underground in the company of Cinque and his followers—Mizmoon, Gelina, Fahizah, Cujo, Teko, Gabi, and Yolanda. Along the way Patty would reinvent herself as the urban guerrilla "Tania" and take part in the armed holdup of a bank in San Francisco. Most of her small band of comrades-in-arms would be incinerated in a house in Los Angeles during a standoff with the LAPD and the FBI, and Patty would spend nearly a year as a fugitive from justice, despite (as later became clear) having been presented with numerous opportunities to escape the SLA's clutches. She became a media celebrity nonpareil and a poster girl for the radical Left, the gun-toting, bank-robbing rebel of middle-American nightmare. Her escapades elicited posturing by high-level officials across the nation, including the governor of California, Ronald Reagan, who expressed a wish that the food distribution program that the Hearst family organized in an effort to win their daughter's release might set off an outbreak of botulism among the state's poor. Finally, following her arrest by the FBI on September 18, 1975, and her subsequent trial and conviction, the saga ended with Patty's reconversion into repentant daughter, "brainwashing" victim, and in a final twist—following a prison term cut short by President Jimmy Carter's pardon—socialite celebrity and occasional actress in camp-master John Waters's films.

Virtually from the moment of her capture, Patty's saga plunged Americans into an extended debate about its true meaning. The Hearst kidnapping quickly took on Rashomon-like contours, providing the perfect screen onto which mid-seventies America could project a virtually limitless array of crisis narratives, including many of those explored in this book: family breakdown, youth in rebellion, psychological fragmentation, the power of the media, and conspiracy theory. So uncannily does the Hearst kidnapping recapitulate these narratives that it is worth examining several of them more closely here.

Reality Programming

Many Americans were inclined to see the Hearst kidnapping saga as an exemplary piece of guerrilla theater. There was much in this story to warrant this label, for however incompetent they were as revolutionaries, Hearst's captors proved extraordinarily adept at orchestrating coverage by a media eager to offer their audiences fresh diversions from Vietnam and Watergate. With their endless communiqués and staged happenings, the "media freaks" (as Patty later called them) who made up the SLA scripted their conversion of socialite into radical as the consummate seventies story—a story they hoped would ultimately succeed where the rest of the radical Left had failed: in mobilizing "the People" against "the fascist state." Yet in their efforts to contest what they saw as a fast-approaching Orwellian future, the SLA wound up making instead a unique contribution to a rather different, more Warholian future.

The SLA saga owed much—perhaps everything—to the new cultural authority of the media. As Abbie Hoffman had recognized, anyone who seriously contemplated social change in modern America had to be as much a media theorist as a committed activist. Much of the success of the antiwar movement stemmed from its exploitation of the media. Arguably, so too did its greatest failure: its fundamental misreading of the American people, that vast new public conjured up by the sixties' spectacle of war and protest—a public that it mistook for a revolutionary agent but that remained, despite everything, largely unreceptive to the New Left's message. The SLA took this error to its furthest extreme. Its entire twenty-two-month-long career was an extended variation on the theme of "the People" and its enemy "the fascist state." These two great figments of the SLA imagination came together in the slogan with which they signed their communiqués: "Death to the fascist insect that preys on the life of the people."

But if they radically mistook the nature and wishes of the people on whose behalf they claimed to speak, the SLA nevertheless succeeded beyond anything contemplated by the Left in capturing the attention of the public that had first tuned in to and had then grown jaded by Vietnam and Watergate. This public was now primed for a whole new kind of theater, something truly histrionic to arouse it from its current state of "image fatigue." This the SLA provided. From their choice of kidnap victim—the daughter of the head of a newspaper empire synonymous with yellow journalism—to their holdup of a bank whose automatic cameras ensured that the event would be photographically recorded, to their later obsession with obtaining a book contract, virtually every move the group made was plotted with an eye on achieving maximum exposure.

But here the basic fallacy in the SLA's relation to the media was exposed. The group imagined itself using the power of the media to contest the false reality purveyed by the apparatus of the state; it sought to confront a nation subjected to Orwellian techniques of mind control with its own imperialist legacy. Patty became the experimental subject for this revolutionary project. Exposing her to the writings of black revolutionaries was conceived as a form of deprogramming that would awaken her from the privileged dream-world in which she had been raised to the true nightmare of American society. Patty, in the SLA's view, suffered from a reality deficit that could be cured only through a program of political education. Ironically, a quite similar line of argument was invoked at her trial by expert witnesses trying to explain her vulnerability to such a program; as one psychiatrist put it, Patty's "reality gap" left her highly susceptible to the techniques of mind control the SLA practiced on her.

Yet if part of what was at stake in the SLA saga was "reality" and Americans' shaky hold on it, the fact remained that the group's symbiotic relationship to the media deeply compromised its own relationship to reality. The SLA themselves were to learn that—as was suggested by the fragmentary written lament discovered in the ruins of the Los Angeles safe house after the firefight in which six of their members died—reality was "hard to find." Nobody suffered more from that deficit of reality they attributed to Patty than the members of this group themselves, and the endless tapes, communiqués, and lists of demands they delivered to the media could not compensate for that. Indeed, they testified to a consciousness of gesture, rhetoric, and delivery that, as the group's actions were transformed into a kind of reality television programming, became ever more histrionic. Even as Patty herself was being turned into a superstar, the "Queen of the SLA," her image emblazoned on posters and T-shirts across the country, the group's leader, DeFreeze, now operating under the title General Field Marshal Cinque, was beginning to succumb to his own star trip. By the end, so dependent had the SLA become on the media to broadcast its mayhem that even when its own members were being killed, the first reaction of the survivors—watching the fatal Los Angeles conflagration on TV in a motel across the street from Disneyland—was to exclaim: "It's live . . . look, it's live."

Ultimately, the SLA found itself entangled within the coils of a fundamental contradiction. The attempt to critique and change capitalism and the media from within was doomed from the outset, not least because the group's wholly unrealistic beliefs concerning the imminence of revolution in American society seem themselves to have been based on media images. On the one hand, their saga, as one observer put it, offered proof that "we live in a global village where black American revolutionaries study *The Battle of Algiers* and SLA members watch the Tupamaros' experience brought to light in Costa-Gavras' *State of Siege*." On the other, the failure of the SLA seemed to reflect the fact that "the guerrilla lessons were transmitted as images, devoid of their day-to-day working reality."

Personality Crisis

At the trial of Patty Hearst, during the Bicentennial year of 1976, the truth of Lester Bangs's observation that America had become less a global village than a global outpatient clinic was made manifest. The trial proceedings were dominated by teams of psychiatrists who, testifying for both the prosecution and the defense, wrapped the story of Patty's conversion from conventional, if highly privileged, teenage girl into urban guerrilla in an elaborate framework of scientific speculation. It was not surprising that psychiatry assumed this role, for this story offered itself up to the American public as the consummate account of snapping: a cautionary tale about the radical transformation of the self under the influence of a powerful cult of personality and action.

On the one hand, experts testifying for the defense likened Patty to a Korean War POW and explained her actions away as those of a victim of brainwashing. Yale psychiatrist Robert Jay Lifton assumed the podium to explain to the jury the Pavlovian basis of Chinese thought reform, and a chorus of other experts chimed in with accounts of how the tactics used by the SLA to bind Patty to the group—physical and psychological deprivation and coercion—echoed those techniques of political reeducation practiced in China. On the other hand, prosecution witnesses dismissed the brainwashing charge as a red herring and described it as tantamount to arguing that Patty's was a case of possession by the devil. One psychiatrist for the prosecution described Hearst as a "rebel in search of a cause" who had willingly embraced the ideology of violent overthrow.

One of the most effective responses to the defense's brainwashing theory came from Patty herself. In the so-called "Tania Interview" included in the communiqué released following the bank robbery, she stated: "What some people refer to as a sudden conversion was a process of development, much the same as a photograph is developed . . . I'd been brainwashed for 20 years, and it took the SLA only 6 weeks to straighten me out . . . I feel the term 'brainwashing' has meaning only when one is referring to the process which begins in the school system, and is continued in the controlled media, the process whereby the people are conditioned to passively take their place in society as slaves of the ruling classes."

Meanwhile, outside commentators drew upon a wide range of contemporary pop cultural references to explain Patty's conversion. According to one account, Hearst was a straightforward case of multiple personalities, of whom the author counted at least four: Patty, Tania, Pearl (the name she assumed on becoming a fugitive), and Pat (the name given her in prison). Other accounts described Patty as a Manchurian Candidate, programmed to do the bidding of operatives under the control of Communist Cuba or China—a charge that deprogrammer Ted Patrick, for one, took seriously when he approached the Hearsts to offer his help. Similar explanations were offered to account for the actions of the other members of the SLA. One former friend of Gelina invoked the specter of alien abduction, suggesting that she had been possessed by a being from outer space. Whether Patty was seen as a POW, a case of multiple personalities, a rebel without a cause, a Communist agent, or demon-possessed, her story became a disturbing object lesson in the new fragility of the

American psyche brought on by a decade of social turmoil and oedipal conflict.

Lost in much of the sensationalism surrounding the charges of Patty's "brainwashing" was the fact that her conversion mirrored—in an admittedly extreme form—techniques widely employed by contemporary consciousness-raising groups. The experiment in personality makeover that membership in the SLA enjoined on all its members had a quite deliberate aspect: all underwent extensive lessons in elocution in an effort to speak like "the People," which consisted mainly of learning to use double negatives and to interject the word "pig" into virtually every other sentence. According to one account, "Nothing so consumed the SLA as personal identity . . . the effort to transform themselves, free themselves from the bourgeois stain." This project encompassed everything from changing their names to giving up all shred of privacy. To all its members, the SLA offered a heroic name and a rebirth: thus Nancy Ling Perry, a former Goldwater supporter from Nixon's hometown, Whittier, California, who had become a topless dancer in San Francisco's North Beach, would be reborn as Fahizah, soldier in the revolutionary SLA. Yet once one embarked upon the project of revolutionizing the self, it became difficult to set limits. In the wake of the Los Angeles inferno, with the group's leader dead, the remaining survivors fell victim to identity politics—the same racial and gender conflicts that had led to the breakup of the New Left. Unable to find a black leader to replace Cinque, and rejecting Teko's attempt to assume the mantle of leader, the SLA women split off to form a feminist study group. By the time they were arrested, the group had all but renounced its revolutionary project.

Conspiracy Nation

Among the competing narratives that emerged to make sense of the SLA saga, conspiracy theories loomed particularly large. Looked at from virtually any angle, this saga sent conspiracy buffs into raptures.

For one thing, the SLA worldview was itself highly conspiracist. In one communiqué Fahizah summarized the group's analysis of recent American history by tracing back the nation's current crisis to the Kennedy assassination: "When I was in high school in 1963–4, I witnessed the first military coup against we the people of this country . . . The coup was simply accomplished by assassinating then-president John Kennedy, and then assassinating any further opposition to the dictator who was to take power: that dictator is the current president, Richard Nixon." In the SLA's view, Nixon had finally eliminated the last vestiges of opposition in what they described as the "corporate-military coup" staged in the 1972 election.

The SLA's own paranoiac tendencies were matched by those of many of the elaborate theories advanced to account for the group's origins and objectives. Both the Right and the Left wove their own variations of this story. Conservatives predictably projected the outlines of a Communist conspiracy onto the SLA. Cinque, they argued, had been controlled by the Chinese and Cubans via operatives in the California prison system, and had been programmed to lead an uprising in the black inner city. This version of the SLA saga incorporated one of the great specters of the time: that of a black army, made up of returning Vietnam veterans or released prisoners, embracing urban guerrilla warfare.

While the Right saw the SLA's creation as the product of a Communist plot, the Left saw it as a "CIA creation gone haywire." According to one prevalent theory, Cinque was actually a black Oswald, another version of the Manchurian Candidate, whose controller was a shadowy figure named Colston Westbrook, head of the Vacaville BCA. Westbrook's alleged ties to the Phoenix program of targeted assassination that the CIA had operated in South Vietnam against Vietcong leaders invited fevered speculation concerning the extent to which the SLA story was overlaid with the unfinished history of the war in Indochina. Cinque, so the theory went, had been conjured up as part of a new phase in the government's ongoing war on radicals, programmed to create a terrorist organization whose actions would bring down government reprisals and justify the creation of a state of siege. His escape from Vacaville had been part of the plan; yet once he had gained his freedom, Cinque had slipped free of his control and, as one author put it, "gone into the revolutionary messiah business for himself." In this variation on the story, the SLA corresponded to a specter of the Left; it saw Cinque as an agent provocateur and blamed his group for the failure of revolution at a moment when the nation—reeling from Watergate and the energy crisis—seemed ripe for radical change.

The Birth of Post-Sixties America out of the Spirit of Stockholm Syndrome

Perhaps the most telling contemporary comment on the Hearst kidnapping saga occurred as the result of a simple juxtaposition of images. In February 1974 *Newsweek* hit the stands with a cover that carried the headline "Terror and Repression" above photos of Patty Hearst and Aleksandr Solzhenitsyn. This was more than a merely chance pairing, insofar as both of these new public figures would become iconically associated with the failure of revolution. The Russian author's recently published *The Gulag Archipelago*, with its portrait of life inside the vast Soviet prison system, would become the definitive account of the final, bitter end of the romance with Communism. To those promising revolution, it offered a bleak warning: the effort to bring down one repressive system inevitably wound up replacing it with another.

The SLA saga offered mid-seventies America both a homegrown variant on the story of failed revolution and a case study in the destructive psychodynamics of radical groups. But it was in the perverse relation between kidnapper and kidnap victim known as the Stockholm syndrome that the lesson of failed revolution achieved its purest metaphoric representation. First identified following a hostage drama that occurred in the summer of 1973, the Stockholm syndrome hinges on the identification or romantic attachment that develops between hostage and captor. What formed the basis of this strange attachment? Was it a way of embracing victimhood? Or did it rather reflect a fantasy on the part of the victim of escape, rebirth, personality makeover? If so, how widely shared was such a fantasy? Certainly it was widespread enough that, as Patty reported in her memoirs, over half of the people in one survey were convinced she had planned her own kidnapping. And one *New York Times* correspondent covering the Hearst kidnapping accounted for her own fascination with the event by confessing that she herself had fantasized about being kidnapped: "I often had dreams of falling in love with one of my captors." Such fantasies suggest something more than a little paradoxical, namely that the intense need to cast off one form of authority was invariably accompanied by an equally intense search for new forms of it.

Thirty years later, the final word on the Hearst kidnapping saga has not been heard. Indeed, we seem to have come full circle: this saga has found new resonance in contemporary American society, as recent novels by Susan Choi and Christopher Sorrentino and a documentary by Robert Stone attest. If for many years it was the Warholian version of the saga that seemed most compelling, now, in the wake of 9/11, it is the other, more Orwellian version—the threat of terrorism, homegrown or otherwise, and the measures adopted by American society to defend itself against that threat—that have taken on new resonance. The story of the Hearst kidnapping is a precursor to those histrionic narratives, with their weird mixture of real and pseudo-event, that define our current media landscape; at the same time, it speaks to a contemporary sense of crisis in American society, a siege mentality that has parallels to the mentality of the unhinged time that produced the SLA. Emerging from the furthest fringes of the movement that had come together to oppose a deeply unpopular war, the SLA assumed the mantle of protest with self-conscious fervor. But from their efforts to arouse "the People," to their obsession with black leadership and their embrace of guerrilla theater, to their final disintegration into gender and identity politics, the SLA wound up replaying the sixties as tragic farce.

Patty, meanwhile, would become a living symbol of the transient nature of the passions that inflamed radicals of that time. Her transformation into poster girl for the Stockholm syndrome offered a comment on the end of the sixties, which sought to overthrow established authority but in the end succeeded only in erecting perverse new forms of it like Charles Manson, General Field Marshal Cinque, and the Reverend Moon. Ultimately this syndrome would provide contemporaries with an explanation for the paradox of Watergate: a decade of oedipal crisis had left the father, or at least the wish for one, as strong as ever. Perhaps, as the authors of one account of the Hearst kidnapping suggest, it took the SLA to restore to the American patriarchy its lost luster. The ultimate beneficiary of this restoration was Ronald Reagan. Governor of California during the Hearst saga, Reagan would be elected president at the end of the seventies on the strength of his promise to bury that decade and the systemic crises it had come to stand for. Yet the crises of the 1970s are not so easily buried; indeed they have reemerged with new intensity in our own time.

Acknowledgments

In the course of writing this book I have rather unceremoniously plundered the books, articles, and other works of many people who have gone before me. I hope they will forgive me for what they may recognize of themselves here, but perhaps even more for what I may have done to distort their own words and ideas. Along the way, I also relied on the help and suggestions of many friends. For their close readings of all or parts of the book, I am especially grateful to Joe DeMarie, John Savage, Willie Neuman, and Marie Sacco. In addition, I would like to thank the following people who helped me channel the 1970s or otherwise offered encouragement or material support: Susan Lehman, Stefan Killen, Susan Jaffe, Adrian H., Kasey Goltra, Deborah Rodgers, Jonathan Lethem, Peter Lang, Gary Wolf, Andrew Hultkrans, Richard Abate, and Kate Lee. I would particularly like to thank Susan Choi for sharing with me her library of books on the Hearst kidnapping. Last but not least, I extend thanks to my editor, Gillian Blake.

Notes

Introduction

1 *Will the seventies never end?* A. O. Scott, "The Boys of Summer, Thirty Years Later," *New York Times*, July 10, 2005.

1 *and the latter by the Right* David Frum, *How We Got Here. The 70's: The Decade that Brought You Modern Life—For Better or Worse* (Basic, 2000), 169.

1 *"un-decade"* Stephen Paul Miller, *The Seventies Now: Culture as Surveillance* (Duke University Press, 1999).

5 *the scope and immediacy of broadcast news* Mark Kurlansky, *1968: The Year That Rocked the World* (Ballantine, 2004), 40.

5 *"a great deal of verisimilitude"* "Talk of the Town," *New Yorker*, December 3, 1973.

6 *by 1972 or 1973 it had completely disintegrated* Paul Berman, *A Tale of Two Utopias: The Political Journey of the Generation of 1968* (Norton, 1996), 95.

6 *"Kim Il Sung, Kim Il Sung, Kim Il Sung"* Ibid., 108.

7 *a new barbecue sauce with the name "Burn Baby Burn"* Rick Delvecchio, "Black Panthers Hot Again," *San Francisco Chronicle*, July 20, 2005. On Frank's views, see his *Commodify Your Dissent* (Norton, 1997).

7 *"other people can live as human beings"* Kurlansky, *1968*, 197.

8 *"we tell ourselves stories in order to live"* Joan Didion, *The White Album* (Simon and Schuster, 1979), 205, 11.

9 *Wolfe, as a straight white man.* Berman, *Utopias*, 119.

9 *What was left to revolutionize after the 1960s?* Ibid., 12.

9 *the central animating force in American life* Robert Brustein, "News Theater," *New York Times*, June 16, 1974.

10 *along with the Manson murders* Didion, *Album*, 47.

10 *"not just visible but were twitching all around"* Lester Bangs, "1973 Nervous Breakdown: The Ol' Fey Outlaws Ain't What They Used to Be—Are You?" in John Northland, ed., *Mainlines, Bloodfeasts, and Bad Taste: A Lester Bangs Reader* (Anchor, 2002), 146.

11 *"most fully embodied in a frenetically twitching nerve"* Lester Bangs, "David Byrne says Boo!" in Northland, *Mainlines, Bloodfeasts, and Bad Taste*, 116.

Fear of Flying

13 *It is not an overstatement* Eldridge Cleaver, *Soul on Ice* (Panther, 1970), 109.

13 *Clemente's body was never recovered* New York Times, January 2, 1973; Kal Wagenheim, *Clemente!* (Praeger, 1973).

14 *the most complete player of his generation* Time, Newsweek, January 15, 1973.

14 *to criticize club owners for failing to hire black managers* Wagenheim, *Clemente!*

15 *"American technological genius"* David Halberstam, *The Best and the Brightest* (Ballantine, 1969), 543.

15 *carrying out antigravity experiments and exploring the feasibility of life in space* Henry Cooper, "A House in Space," *New Yorker*, May 5, 1973.

15 *"return America to world pre-eminence"* Kermit Vanderbilt, "Writers of the Troubled Sixties," *Nation*, December 17, 1973.

16 *"everybody is a member of the crew"* Marshall McLuhan, "At the Moment of Sputnik," *Journal of Communication* 24, 1 (1974): 48–58. This article is based on a speech McLuhan gave in 1973.

16 *"abstract representations of rockets or airplanes"* Thomas Frank, *The Conquest of Cool: Business Culture, Counterculture, and the Rise of Hip Consumerism* (University of Chicago Press, 1997), 61.

16 *It cut flying time between New York and London in half* www.centennialofflight.gov/essay/Social/impact/SH3.htm.

17 *exceeded that in any other industry* Alastair Gordon, *Naked Airport: A Cultural History of the World's Most Revolutionary Structure* (Metropolitan, 2004), 218.

17 *The growing ease of jet travel helped transform the scale of corporate operations* Mark Gottdiener, *Life in the Air: Surviving the New Culture of Air Travel* (Rowman and Littlefield, 2001), 138–40.

17 *the alluring figure of the stewardess* Gordon, *Airport*, 180–84.

17 *"in our national psyche"* Paula Kane, *Sex Objects in the Sky* (Follett, 1974), 13.

18 *debt incurred through purchasing a new fleet of 747s* T. A. Heppenheimer, *Turbulent Skies: The History of Commercial Aviation* (John Wiley and Sons, 1995); Thomas Petzinger, Jr., *Hard Landing: The Epic Contest for Power and Profits That Plunged the Airlines into Chaos* (Times, 1995).

18 *dedicated in the fall of 1973* Gordon, *Airport*, 241–45.

18 *"the biggest public works project since the pyramids"* Molly Ivins, "A Texas Scale Airport," *New York Times*, September 16, 1973.

19 *"Ark films"* Vincent Canby, "What Makes 'Poseidon' Fun?" *New York Times*, January 14, 1973.

19 *"The planet shrinks about as fast as the plane develops"* New York Times, April 20, 1973.

19 *"space-time compression"* Gottdiener, *Life*, 72. See also David Harvey, *The Condition of Postmodernity* (Blackwell, 1989).

20 *took up residence at airports* David Hubbard, *The Skyjacker: His Flights of Fantasy* (Macmillan, 1971), 73–74; Gottdiener, *Life*, 13.

20 *"as well as those who pass through"* Ivins, "Texas Scale."

20 *"the unknown sites that surround our airports"* Robert Smithson, *The Writings of Robert Smithson* (New York University Press, 1979).

22 *"war without death" waged from the air* Halberstam, *Brightest*, 513.

22 *than it had in all of World War II* Frances Fitzgerald, *Fire in the Lake: The Vietnamese and the Americans in Vietnam* (Vintage, 1972), 556.

22 *Americans tended to conceive of history as a straight line* Ibid., 9.

23 *Ray Bradbury, Isaac Asimov, and Stanley Kubrick* New York Times, August 12, 1973.

23 *"please don't let this plane crash"* New York Times, December 16, 1973.

24 *modern economic and political history* Peter Carroll, *It Seemed Like Nothing Happened: America in the 1970s* (Rutgers University Press, 1982), 117–23.

25 *seizing oil fields in the Middle East* New York Times, January 2, 2004.

25 *with the airline industry leading the way* Gottdiener, *Life*, 163; John Ralston Saul, "The Collapse of Globalization and the Rebirth of Nationalism," *Harper's Magazine*, March 2004, 40–41.

25 *"feeling afraid or insecure in the air"* Kane, *Objects*, 11.

26 *"supposed to play is a neurotic one"* Ibid., 78.

26 *"a jolt in its sex stereotypes in 1973"* Ibid., 106.

27 *"the plane was so thoroughly disintegrated"* New York Times, August 1, 1973.

27 *nonstandard air traffic control services* National Transportation Safety Board, "Aircraft Accident Report," Delta Airlines, Douglas DC-9-31, July 3, 1973.

28 *with which we manage our dangerous technologies* William Langewiesche, *Inside the Sky: A Meditation on Flight* (Pantheon, 1998).

29 *Representatives of the Catholic Church later endorsed this view* "A Chronicle of Man's Unwillingness to Die," *New York Times*, January 1, 1973; *Time*, January 8, 1973.

30 *threatened to crash into the center of Athens* Gordon, *Airport*, 233.

30 *in exerting influence on the United States and Europe* Richard Clutterbuck, *Living with Terrorism* (Arlington House, 1975).

31 *Cuba's status as a hijackers' paradise* Ibid., 97.

31 *later turned over to American authorities* Clutterbuck, *Living*, 107–108.

31 *"the intense communicability of the images surrounding skyjacking"* Hubbard, *Skyjacker*, 213.

32 *some fantasy of achieving manhood* New York Times, January 7, 1973.

33 *taking hostages had become the ideal crime of the 1970s* Tom Wolfe, "The Perfect Crime," in *Mauve Gloves & Madmen, Clutter & Vine* (Bantam, 1977).

34 *"may soon have the hearts and minds of his subjects."* Ibid., 161.

34 *"arrested for carrying a gun on a flight"* For details on Trapnell's hijacking and his life, see Eric Asinof, *The Fox Is Crazy Too* (Morrow, 1976); "Wounded Jetliner Hijacker to Be Arraigned Today," *New York Times*, January 3, 1972; "U.S. Hijacking Case Ends in Mistrial," *New York Times*, January 16, 1973; "Sane or Insane? A Case Study of the TWA Hijacker," *New York Times*, January 18, 1973; "Details of '72 Skyjack Attempt Are Related at Second Trapnell Trial," *New York Times*, April 9, 1973; "Skyjacker Is Called Malingerer, but Not Insane, by Psychiatrist," *New York Times*, April 15, 1973; "Trapnell Guilty of Jet Hijacking," *New York Times*, April 17, 1973; "Trapnell Sentenced to Life for Hijacking," *New York Times*, July 21, 1973.

35 *conspiring to undermine the social order Time*, January 29, 1973; *Newsweek*, January 29, 1973.

37 *"the movement of citizenry within the body politic?"* Hubbard, *Skyjacker*, 49.

37 *"makes them celebrities too"* Hubbard, *Skyjacker*, 215–19.

40 *"get away with his undaunted criminal behavior by feigning insanity"* *New York Times*, July 8, 1973.

40 *copies* of The Fox Is Crazy Too *and Hubbard's* The Skyjacker Lincoln Caplan, "The Insanity Defense," *New Yorker*, August 2, 1984.

40 *in an effort to free him from prison New York Times*, May 26, 1978, and December 22, 1978.

42 *"when I began my analytic adventures some thirteen years earlier"* Erica Jong, *Fear of Flying* (Signet, 1974), 1.

Reality Programming

45 *"blew up on our doorstep"* Lance Loud, obituary in *Los Angeles Times*, December 25, 2001.

45 *"experiences that affect all of us"* Jeffrey Ruoff, *An American Family: A Televised Life* (University of Minnesota Press, 2002), 97.

46 *no longer held* Ibid., 113.

46 *would not live happily ever after Newsweek*, March 12, 1973.

46 *a majority of women were working outside the home* Bruce Schulman, *The Seventies: The Great Shift in American Culture, Society, and Politics* (Da Capo, 2001), 161.

46 *she was no longer* Betty Friedan, "Up from the Kitchen Floor," *New York Times*, March 4, 1973.

47 *"abolish the family"* Joan Didion, *The White Album* (Simon and Schuster, 1979), 111.

48 *"being an agent of social control"* *New York Times*, December 16, 1973.

48 *than Americans were killed in Vietnam* Peter Carroll, *It Seemed Like Nothing Happened: America in the 1970s* (Rutgers University Press, 1982), 27.

48 *"healthier with that division ended"* New York Times, January 24, 1973.

48 *a prime symbol of male potency* Time, January 29, 1973.

49 *either first run or in the rerun* New York Times, August 21, 1973.

49 *"the management of an unstable personality"* Anthony Summers, *The Arrogance of Power: The Secret World of Richard Nixon* (Penguin Books, 2000), 96.

50 *the president had a clean bill of mental health* New York Times, July 4, 1973.

50 *"if a U.S. president suffered a mental breakdown"* Summers, *Arrogance*, 456. See also Fred Emery, *Watergate: The Corruption of American Politics and the Fall of Richard Nixon* (Touchstone, 1994), 408.

50 *family recipes in her responses* New York Times, February 15, 1973.

50 *preferred having dinner with their family to going out to parties* Summers, *Arrogance*, 271.

50 *"their President's very sanity"* Ibid., 440.

50 *"the Nixon marriage was considered fair game by some"* Julie Nixon Eisenhower, *Pat Nixon: the Untold Story* (Simon and Schuster, 1986), 392, 404.

51 (*Some estimates were as high as $17 million*) Ibid., 386.

51 *"had created a monster"* Summers, *Arrogance*, 347.

51 *"accepting it 'as part of the surroundings,' as he expressed it"* Eisenhower, *Pat Nixon*, 307.

51 *"Nixon would begin declaiming"* Summers, *Arrogance*, 348.

52 *"not the Richard Nixon the family saw every day"* Eisenhower, *Pat Nixon*, 409.

52 *"like private love letters, for one person only"* Summers, *Arrogance*, 347.

52 *the awesome new cultural authority it had come to enjoy* David Greenberg, *Nixon's Shadow: The History of an Image* (Norton, 2003), 192.

52 *the most believable form of major media (over newspapers and radio)* New York Times, April 3, 1973.

53 *"Facts no longer enjoy any privilege over various renderings of them"* Harold Rosenberg, *"The Art World,"* New Yorker, March 17, 1973.

53 *of a model postwar family* Greenberg, *Shadow*, 19.

54 *a TV spectacle seen by 60 million viewers* Summers, *Arrogance*, 326.

54 *he succeeded only in looking stiff and awkward* Greenberg, *Shadow*, xxix.

54 *similar kind of public adulation* Emery, *Watergate*, 18.

54 *portrayed him as a giant penis and testicles* Greenberg, *Shadow*, 117–18.

55 *far-reaching revisions to the old social contract* Lynn Hunt, *The Family Romance of the French Revolution* (University of California Press, 1992).

55 *"as the tumbrels deposit their victims before the guillotine"* Greenberg, *Shadow*, 181.

55 *"Television's first 'real family'"* New York Times, February 15, 1973.

55 *were watching* An American Family Pat Loud, *Pat Loud: A Woman's Story* (Coward, McCann and Geoghegan, 1974), 212.

56 *"the politics of everyday life"* Ruoff, *Family*, 15.

59 *a historic turning point from expansion to contraction* Ibid., 61.

60 *"to perform on a stage before other concerned eyes"* Margaret Mead, "As Significant as the Invention of Drama or the Novel," *TV Guide*, January 6, 1973.

61 *their future careers as media celebrities Time*, February 26, 1973.

62 *fall from a state of innocence* Anne Roiphe, "Things Are Keen but Could be Keener," *New York Times*, February 18, 1973.

62 *the more unsettling artifact created in* An American Family Anne Roiphe, "The Waltons" *New York Times*, November 18, 1973.

62 *"without his knowledge"* Abigail McCarthy, *"An American Family* and the Family of Man," *Atlantic Monthly*, July 1973.

62 *"you can become famous for being just what you are" Time*, February 26, 1973.

63 *"They had always thought of themselves as a family show"* Roger Rosenblatt, "Residuals on an American Family," *New Republic*, November 23, 1974.

64 *"tiny, enclosed fraternity of private men elected by no one"* Greenberg, *Shadow*, 146.

65 *"It's not what's there that counts, it's what's projected"* in Joe McGinniss, *The Selling of the President 1968* (Trident, 1969), 31.

65 *"we had emerged from the Garden of Eden"* in Greenberg, *Shadow*, 143.

65 *"the least authentic man alive"* Garry Wills, *Nixon Agonistes* (New American Library, 1970), 140.

65 *The major networks followed suit* Emery, *Watergate*, 359–60.

66 *a husband and a wife* Ibid., 361–68, 379.

66 *revenge from the increasingly beleaguered president* Greenberg, *Shadow*, 171, 176.

66 *the tapes would reassure him of his reality* Shana Alexander, *Anyone's Daughter: The Times and Trials of Patty Hearst* (Viking, 1979), 22.

66 *"survive a public reading of private conversations?"* Eisenhower, *Pat Nixon*, 409.

67 *a "sacrificial spectacle"* Jean Baudrillard, *Simulacra and Simulation* (University of Michigan Press, 1994), 28.

67 *Bill had begun to find her too sexually aggressive, emasculating* Loud, *Story*, 191.

68 *he wished he'd thrown his kids' TV sets into the Pacific Ocean* Ruoff, *Family*, 107.

69 *"some socialized way of looking at things" New York Times*, January 13, 1973.

69 *"I've acquired a real self just by being on Channel 13"* Loud, *Story*, 15.

69 *"the image of family life they saw on the screen"* Ruoff, *Family*, 14.

69 *"I had," she wrote, "been programmed for marriage"* Loud, *Story*, 45.

70 "*It was vast, cosmic*" Ibid., 72–74.

70 "*a kind of permanence or reality if they're on TV*" Ibid., 92.

70 "*Once in the air, I can't turn back*" Ibid., 223.

70 *a hero in the gay community* Ruoff, *Family*, 127.

71 *a gradual shift in the American media* Ibid., 104.

72 *the former Superstar died in her sleep* Jean Stein and George Plimpton, *Edie: An American Biography* (Knopf, 1982), 410–14.

73 "*He was always parental*" http://www.pbs.org/lanceloud/lance/warhol.html.

75 *the society of the simulacrum* For Baudrillard's analysis of the series, see *Simulacra*, 27–30.

76 *the "greatest miniseries ever"* Julia Phillips, *You'll Never Eat Lunch in this Town Again* (New American Library, 2002), 151.

76 *television could effect real change* Greenberg, *Shadow*, 176.

Operation Homecoming

77 "*The name of the game is air*" Robert Jay Lifton, *Home from the War: Vietnam Veterans: Neither Victims nor Executioners* (Simon and Schuster, 1973), 329.

77 "*you know all is lost*" Stephen Rowan, *They Wouldn't Let Us Die: The Prisoners of War Tell Their Story* (J. David Publishers, 1973), 35.

80 *feeling like a stranger in his own home at times* New York Times, April 23, 1973.

80 "*It's like we've been asleep for seven years*" Time, February 26, 1973.

80 "*most everybody is divorced*" Rowan, *Die*, 97.

80 "*I'm going to start a new life*" New York Times, February 20, 1973.

81 "*weakness in the national character*" Craig Howes, *Voices of the Vietnam POWs* (Oxford University Press, 1993), 174.

81 *the new cynical attitude toward government* New York Times, February 8, 1973.

81 *Nixon's visit to China, women's liberation, race relations, and drug use* New York Times, April 26, 1973.

82 "*die for the principle of anti-Communism*" Frances Fitzgerald, *Fire in the Lake: The Vietnamese and the Americans in Vietnam* (Vintage Books, 1972), 565.

82 *the World Trade Center, blaxploitation films, and Andy Warhol* Time, February 19, 1973.

82 *they retreated into a "zombie reaction"* Time, February 19, 1973.

82 *plagued POWs following the Korean War* New York Times, June 2, 1973.

82 "*another tragic victim of the war,*" *observed one family acquaintance* New York Times, June 4, 1973.

83 *worse than anything he'd endured in camp life* Howes, *Voices*, 145.

83 *the* Times *predicted more to come* New York Times, March 6, 1973.

83 *in the process of obtaining a divorce New York Times*, June 2, 1973.

83 *"most shocking to me is the sexual revolution"* Ibid.

84 *"the figure of an unfaithful, defiant, or simply different woman"* Howes, *Voices*, 145.

84 *"the wives have been running things for so many years"* Zalin Grant, "We Lived for a Time Like Dogs," in Various Contributors, *Reporting Vietnam: American Journalism 1959–1975* (Library of America, 1998), 342.

84 *"a filtering screen between the press and the story"* New York Times, February 20, 1973.

84 *"buffer between past trauma and future shock"* Newsweek, February 19, 1973.

85 *denying charges that the POWs' appearances had been scripted New York Times*, March 3, 1973.

85 *"a giant propaganda and psychological campaign prepared by the Pentagon"* New York Times, February 27, 1973.

85 *"the most enthusiastic of American warriors"* New York Times, February 20, 1973.

86 *violated the sovereign air space of North Vietnam to bomb civilian populations* Howes, *Voices*, 42.

86 *the Geneva Conventions did not apply to these prisoners because it was an undeclared war* Rowan, *Die*, 170.

87 *"This shows how humane and just they are" was one POW's comment* New York Times, March 30, 1973.

87 *"a better understanding of why we were fighting the war"* Rowan, *Die*, 180–81.

87 *to manipulate public sentiment about the war New York Times*, April 30, 1973.

87 *saw it "second-hand"* New York Times, June 3, 1973.

89 *he was "appalled" by Nixon and Watergate New York Times*, July 15, 1973; Howes, *Voices*, 119, 217–18.

89 *"if there's such a thing as brainwashing, the military does the best job"* New York Times, July 15, 1973.

90 *"the POWs in that conflict were traitors"* John McCain, "How the POWs Fought Back," in *Reporting Vietnam*.

90 *the "secret agent of history"* J. Hoberman, *The Dream Life: Movies, Media, and the Mythology of the Sixties* (New Press, 2003).

91 *vulnerability of U.S. soldiers to Communist mind control techniques* Howes, *Voices*, 166.

91 *a failure of childhood and adolescent training Time*, February 19, 1973; Howes, *Voices*, 17–18.

91 *had finally broken him, just as it did the rest New York Times*, March 30, 1973.

92 *the same treatment as the Korean War POWs Newsweek*, February 5, 1973.

92 *he had acted drugged to discredit his own statements New York Times*, March 5, 1973.

92 *"the most pro-VC of all POWs"* Howes, *Voices*, 58.

92 *statements critical of "U.S. imperialist aggression"* George Smith, *POW: Two Years with the Vietcong* (Ramparts, 1971), 180.

92 *"If it wasn't brainwashing then what was it?"* Smith, *POW*, 304.

93 *"hate program" designed to make him despise the Vietcong.* Ibid., 120–21.

93 *"Would it be so twisted that I would become a Communist . . . or a vegetable?"* Howes, *Voices*, 147.

93 *a form of "reverse brainwashing"* New York Times, April 30, 1973.

94 *tinged with sexual perversion* Ibid.

94 *they had suffered homosexual attacks in the camps* Howes, *Voices*, 136–37.

94 *a "constellation of masculine attitudes founded on being tough and tight-lipped"* Lifton, *Home*, 238.

94 *"We will win this war on the streets of New York"* Howes, *Voices*, 247.

94 *force them to appear on television* Ibid., 60.

96 *to stalemate the peace talks for four more years* H. Bruce Franklin, *MIA, or, Myth-Making in America* (L. Hill Books, 1992).

96 *"the U.S. had gone to war to retrieve them"* Jonathan Schell, *Time of Illusion* (Knopf, 1996).

97 *a pseudo-event staged to make Nixon look tough* Rowan, *Die*, 167–68.

97 *by the end of the war an estimated 10 million Americans were wearing them* H. Bruce Franklin, *Vietnam and Other American Fantasies* (University of Massachusetts Press, 2000), 184.

97 *"still listed as missing and unaccounted for"* Newsweek, February 26, 1973.

98 *"Vietnam is the shared crime that has turned our country into . . . a pact of blood"* Cited in Peter Carroll, *It Seemed Like Nothing Happened: America in the 1970s* (Rutgers University Press, 1982), 90.

98 *"I was happy to bring the boys home"* Time, February 26, 1973.

98 *"the president who had negotiated their release"* New York Times, May 25, 1973.

99 *helping American society periodically purge itself of moral decay* Richard Slotkin, *Gunfighter Nation: The Myth of the Frontier in 20th Century America* (HarperPerennial, 1992).

100 *"almost painless conquest of an inferior race"* Fitzgerald, *Fire*, 491–92.

100 *the administration's insensitivity to their hardships* New York Times, March 28, 1973.

101 *Several pilots refused to participate in the Christmas bombings* Franklin, *MIA*. See also Marilyn Young, *The Vietnam Wars 1945–1990* (HarperCollins, 1991), 279.

102 *"sign and referent have scarcely any proportionate relation at all"* Slotkin, *Gunfighter*, 621–62.

102 *"saturation bombings of civilian areas with minimal military targets"* Robert Jay Lifton, "Heroes and Victims," *New York Times*, March 28, 1973.

102 *"extraordinary American technological and military superiority"* Lifton, *Home*, 158.

103 *"get a big kill ratio in Vietnam"* William Gibson, *Warrior Dreams:*

Paramilitary Culture in Post-Vietnam America (Hill and Wang, 1994), 23.

103 *"media freak grunts"* Michael Herr, *Dispatches* (Vintage, 1991), 209.

103 *"the WWII style immortal pilot-hero?"* Lifton, *Home*, 354.

103 *a new spiritual elect, reborn, phoenixlike, from the ashes of the war* Howes, *Voices*, 157.

104 *"This is a false ending"* Lifton, *Home*, 445.

104 *until all thirteen hundred men still missing in Indochina had been accounted for* New York Times, February 20, 1973.

104 *"virtually a national religion"* Franklin *Vietnam*, 172.

104 *"second only to religious symbols such as the cross or Star of David"* Franklin, *MIA*, 8.

105 *POWs were still being held in Indochina* Franklin, *Vietnam*, 197.

106 *rewriting it as a story of trauma inflicted on America* Franklin, *MIA*, 8.

107 *taking back all the symbolic territory that had been lost in the late 1960s and 1970s* Gibson, *Dreams*.

108 *the reluctance to project its military power abroad* Franklin, *Vietnam*, 29.

108 *"the hold of the Vietnam syndrome over our national consciousness"* New York Times, November 11, 2003.

108 *the assassination of U.S. congressmen was discussed* E. J. Dionne, "Stooping Low to Smear Kerry," *Washington Post*, April 28, 2004.

109 *"huge collective nervous breakdown"* Herr, *Dispatches*, 71.

109 *"implanting cultural memories"* Michael Janofsky, "McCain Fights Old Foe Who Now Fights Kerry," *New York Times*, February 14, 2004.

109 *as a way of inflicting damage on Bush* Anthony Kaufman, "Conspiracy Leery," *Village Voice*, July 26, 2004.

109 *elevated by* New York Daily News *to Rambo-like status* New York Daily News, August 29, 2004.

110 *to work on the political campaign of a family friend* New York Times, August 29, 2004.

110 *"we are stuck within our circle"* Edward Said, *Culture and Imperialism* (Vintage, 1994), 27.

110 *as part of a pattern of growth and decay* Fitzgerald, *Fire*, 11.

Personality Crisis

111 *"I wanted to see what everyone was throwing up about"* Cited in Pauline Kael, "On the Future of Movies," *New Yorker*, August 5, 1974.

113 *"in case you literally let it gush out"* Tom Wolfe, "The Me Decade and the Third Great Awakening," in *Mauve Gloves & Madmen, Clutter & Vine* (Bantam, 1999), 117.

113 *"on a scale without parallel in any country in history"* Ibid., 126.

114 *"people with steady incomes and stable lives were abruptly stripped of livelihoods and identities"* Flo Conway and Jim Siegelman, *Snapping:*

America's Epidemic of Sudden Personality Change, 2nd ed. (Stillpoint, 1995), 304. On the relation between technological change, economic insecurity, and the preoccupation with identity, see David Harvey, *The Condition of Postmodernity* (Blackwell, 1989), 87.

115 *"taught to hate their parents and to obey the cult leaders blindly"* Ted Patrick, *Let Our Children Go!* (Dutton, 1976), 107.

115 *converted him from a police critic to a police supporter and a Republican New York Times,* July 8, 1973.

116 *his antisocial tendencies.* Patrick, *Let,* 182.

116 *offered their home to Patrick's team of deprogrammers Newsweek,* March 12, 1973.

116 *their parents therefore had no legal authority over them* Conway and Siegelman, *Snapping,* 71.

116 *"our nation is going to be controlled by a handful of people"* New York *Times,* March 5, 1973.

117 *"their Bibles in one hand and their muskets in the other"* New York *Times,* March 31, 1973.

117 *responding with a "loud purring noise"* New York Times, July 31, 1973.

118 *"They're teaching this in all the universities"* New York Times, August 4, 1973.

118 *"The next one they're going to have to deprogram is me"* New York *Times,* May 7, 1973.

119 *"televised nationwide in front of millions of people"* Patrick, *Let,* 131.

120 *"which only complicated my task"* Ibid., 145–46.

120 *"I think we could all use a lot of it"* Ibid., 151.

120 *"It made me dizzy to look at them"* Ibid., 39.

121 *"the same as the one the North Koreans used on the POWs"* Ibid., 20.

121 *a "secret hell" controlled by Satan New York Times,* October 7, 1973.

121 *ordering his followers to attend anti-Nixon rallies as counterdemonstrators* Conway and Siegelman, *Snapping,* 27.

121 *Members were told to suppress all sexual impulses New York Times,* September 16, 1974; Conway and Siegelman, *Snapping,* 23.

122 *"in the manner of Kamikaze pilots shouting Banzai"* Patrick, *Let,* 12.

122 *that had entered the vernacular as "brainwashing"* Conway and Siegelman, *Snapping,* 86.

122 *"many of our POWs were subjected to intensive political indoctrination"* Patrick, *Let,* 238.

123 *"a big black gorilla in tight leather pants"* Ibid., 257.

123 *parallels between the SLA's tactics and those of Chinese thoughtreformers* Conway and Siegelman, *Snapping,* 229–30.

124 *"They're still programmed to what he told them"* Patrick, *Let,* 281–85.

124 *"the two are interconnected aspects of the same problem"* PublicEye.org.

125 *had been brainwashed and programmed by the KGB to assassinate Marcus* Dennis King, *Lyndon LaRouche and the New American Fascism* (Doubleday, 1989), 25–31.

125 *an ominous voice saying, "Raise the voltage"* New York Times, January 20, 1974.

125 *what he himself was subjecting his followers to* King, *LaRouche*, 30.

126 *"You know the whole nation of Red China is under ESP mind control"* New York Times, July 27, 1974.

126 *intense brotherhoods like the Moonies, the Children of God, and the Manson family* Shana Alexander, *Anyone's Daughter: The Times and Trials of Patty Hearst* (Viking Press, 1979), 22.

126 *"That accounts for the success of the Moonies"* Ibid., 374.

127 *"We [parents] may in fact have driven them into madness"* Anne Roiphe, "Struggle over Two Sisters," *New York Times*, June 3, 1973.

128 *"God will make it perfect, so there will be no more sin"* Flora Rheta Schreiber, *Sybil* (Warner Books, 1973).

129 *"rapidly passing into contemporary folklore"* D. W. Harding, "Crazy Mixed-Up Kids," *New York Review of Books*, June 14, 1973.

130 *tried to record his late mother's voice on tape* Peter Biskind, *Easy Riders, Raging Bulls: How the Sex, Drugs, and Rock 'n' Roll Generation Saved Hollywood* (Simon and Schuster, 1998), 219.

131 *remains within the postwar liberal therapeutic framework* Ibid., 223.

131 *a movie about a girl being tortured* New York Times, January 13, 1974.

131 *six people who'd seen the movie had wound up in psychiatric hospitals* New York Times, January 27, 1974.

132 *"just like in* The Exorcist*"* Patrick, *Let*, 244.

132 *the graphic nature of the images provided by these special effects* Kael, "Back to the Ouija Board," *New Yorker*, January 7, 1974.

132 *a ghastly image of "self-inflicted abortion"* Biskind, *Easy Riders*, 223.

132 *seemingly the only institution whose authority had survived the sixties* Kael, "Ouija," 60.

132 *"sow doubt, confusion and horror among onlookers"* New York Times, January 13, 1974.

133 *" 'my little Susie—famous forever'?"* Kael, "Ouija," 61.

133 *NORAD denied detecting any such movements* New York Times, October 21, 1973.

134 *"No one has ever made those fellas welcome"* Ibid.

134 *the president had gone mad* Fred Emery, *Watergate: The Corruption of American Politics and The Fall of Richard Nixon* (Touchstone, 1994), 408.

135 *"they just let a demon's power come in and play over him"* Anthony Summers, *The Arrogance of Power: The Secret World of Richard Nixon* (Penguin, 2000), 318.

136 *"some kind of disaster judgment of God is to fall because of man's wickedness"* New York Times, December 24, 1973.

Warholism

139 *"a magazine of nothing but taped interviews"* Andy Warhol and Pat Hackett, *Popism: The Warhol '60s* (Harcourt Brace Jovanovich, 1980), 291–92.

139 *reinvented by 1973 as a leading chronicle of celebrity culture* Victor Bockris, *Warhol* (Da Capo, 1997), 370.

139 *figures such as Tab Hunter and Truman Capote* Jean Stein and George Plimpton, *Edie: An American Biography* (Knopf, 1982), 196.

139 *"we begin to be puzzled about what is really the 'original' of an event"* Daniel Boorstin, *The Image: A Guide to Pseudo-Events in America* (Vintage, 1992), 19.

140 *"was all over New York in 1973 and 1974"* Bob Colacello, *Holy Terror: Andy Warhol Close Up* (HarperCollins, 1990), 193.

141 *"make it all right to be stylish and irresponsible again"* Ibid., 6.

141 *"We were,"* wrote Colacello, *"letting [our readers] into the party"* Ibid., 252.

141 *Americans' skill at seeing through the tricks of image culture* David Greenberg, *Nixon's Shadow: The History of an Image* (Norton, 2003), xxi.

141 *"only a fantasy woman in the first place"* Andy Warhol, *The Philosophy of Andy Warhol (From A to B and Back Again)* (Harvest, 1977), 54.

142 *"not a train wreck or earthquake, but an interview"* Boorstin, *Image*, 11.

143 *"People need glamour and frivolity for their fantasies"* *Interview*, July 1973.

144 *"couldn't decide any more if they were really having the problems or just performing"* Warhol, *Philosophy*, 26.

144 *"but with the fascination of eavesdropping"* Mary Harron, "Pop Art/ Art Pop: The Andy Warhol Connection," in Barney Hoskyns, ed., *The Sound and the Fury: 40 Years of Classic Rock Journalism* (Bloomsbury, 2003), 369.

144 *Bob Colacello became Bebe Rebozo* Colacello, *Terror*, 75.

144 *"Everyone should be bugged all the time"* Bockris, *Warhol*, 370.

144 *wallpapered with his Campbell's Soup Cans* Warhol, *Philosophy*, 13–15.

144 *"especially after Valerie Solanas was let out of prison in 1971"* Colacello, *Terror*, 75.

145 *"He got very scared after that for a long time"* Stein and Plimpton, *Edie*, 412–13.

145 *"Will someone want to do a 1970s remake of shooting me?"* Warhol, *Philosophy*, 84.

145 *investigating Warhol's 1972 tax returns* Colacello, *Terror*, 75, 164.

145 *"people like [wealthy collectors Gunther] Sachs and Stavros [Niarchos] too"* Ibid., 111.

146 *"ended with Andy Warhol as its regent"* Norman Mailer, *Marilyn: A Biography* (Grosset and Dunlap, 1973).

146 *"The void, he observed, 'got filled with Warholism'"* Amy Newman, "An Art World Figure Re-emerges, Unrepentant," *New York Times*, September 3, 2000.

146 *"The 70s are very empty"* Warhol, *Philosophy*, 26.

146 *"the pale, soft-spoken magical presence, the skin and bones . . ."* Ibid., 10.

147 *described the incident in his memoir* Forced Entries Jim Carroll, *Forced Entries: The Downtown Diaries 1971–1973* (Penguin, 1987), 53–54.

147 *"It was just as if I was watching another movie"* Kenneth Goldsmith, ed., *I'll Be Your Mirror: The Selected Andy Warhol Interviews: 1962–1987* (Carroll and Graf, 2004), 219.

148 *"What I liked was chunks of time all together, every real moment"* Warhol and Hackett, *Popism*, 110.

148 *"like a thin man in black leotards"* Stein and Plimpton, *Edie*, 182, 243.

149 *"a ghost of myself in the future"* Ibid., 414.

149 *"the fascism of shrinks and sanatoria, drugs and doctors"* Robert Mazzocco, "Dancing on the Titanic," *New York Review of Books*, February 7, 1974.

149 *Warhol liked to watch people self-destruct* Colacello, *Terror*, 474.

150 *transformation was what that scene offered people* Classic Albums—Lou Reed: Transformer (Eagle Eye/Pioneer DVD, 2001).

150 *replaced Edie in Warhol's entourage* Stein and Plimpton, *Edie*, 220.

150 *"an audience greedy for more and more geeks"* Lester Bangs, *Psychotic Reactions and Carburetor Dung* (Anchor, 2003), 170.

150 *from pop stars to politics* Ibid., 36.

150 *"the only rock star to write a song about him"* Harron, "Pop Art," 376. Harron overlooks Lou Reed's "Andy's Chest."

151 *the distinction between performer and creation* Jon Savage, *England's Dreaming: Anarchy, Sex Pistols, Punk Rock and Beyond* (St. Martin's Griffin, 1991), 76.

151 *to whet the public's appetite without ever fully satisfying it* Steve Turner, "How to Become a Cult Figure in Only Two Years: The Making of David Bowie," in Hoskyns, *Sound and Fury*, 18–21.

151 *"disappear from public view before interest dies away"* Ibid.

151 *"compelled to commit suicide"* Don DeLillo, *Great Jones Street* (Penguin, 1973), 1.

151 *"living out the fantasy?"* Turner, "Cult Figure," 24–25.

153 *"Stones doppelgängers in drag"* Nina Antonia, *The New York Dolls: Too Much Too Soon* (Omnibus, 1998), 75.

153 *his ongoing repartee with the music press* Ibid., 37.

154 *"enlightened amateurism"* Greil Marcus, *Lipstick Traces: A Secret History of the Twentieth Century* (Harvard University Press, 1989).

154 *a deliberate unlearning of musical reflexes* Savage, *Dreaming*, 82.

154 *that would usher in the later era of corporate rock* Marcus, *Lipstick*, 42, 48.

154 *"the first real sign that the Sixties were over"* Steven Morrissey, *The New York Dolls* (Babylon, 1981).

154 *a reaction to the authenticity and sincerity of the 1960s* Shelton Waldrep, ed., *The Seventies: The Age of Glitter in Popular Culture* (Routledge, 2000), 4, 8, 16.

155 *"seemed like a cruel joke by 1975"* Marcus., *Lipstick*, 45.

155 *"like a used car held together by K-Y and clothes hangers"* Carroll, *Forced Entries*, 116.

155 *"having* ménages à trois *while the Nazis grab power"* Legs McNeil and Gillian McCain, *Please Kill Me: The Uncensored Oral History of Punk Rock* (Penguin, 1997).

155 *"a generalized process for transforming hero into celebrity"* Boorstin, *Image*, 162.

155 *"You can be your own hero"* Clinton Heylin, *From the Velvets to the Voidoids: A Pre-Punk History for a Post-Punk World* (Penguin, 1993), 117–18.

156 *"The art-form of the future is celebrity-hood"* Cited in Heylin, *Velvets*, 240.

156 *"from the ones their parents birthed!"* *Interview*, August 1972, 52.

156 *"movers and shakers of identity crises"* *Creem*, April 1974.

157 *"meanwhile, the girls were looking at us in a trance"* Antonia, *Dolls*, 49.

157 *"Faggot Rock, the music of total drop out!"* Miles, "New York Dolled Up: Glittermania in Gotham," in Hoskyns, *Sound and Fury*, 178.

157 *"a bunch of degenerate queers" at face value* Antonia, *Dolls*, 72.

158 *"his image became self-destructive"* Ibid., 144.

158 *"they were living the movie for real"* Savage, *Dreaming*, 61, 63.

158 *"it's something that we did to ourselves"* Antonia, *Dolls*, 81.

160 *"being connected with the moment"* Stein and Plimpton, *Edie*, 243.

160 *"I always felt I was in a black and white 16 mm film"* *Interview*, October 1973.

161 *"it was now for everyone"* McNeil and McCain, *Please*, 188.

161 *he referred to Warhol's phone-taping as "FBI-CIA art"* Carroll, *Forced Entries*, 31–32.

161 *"we don't all of us want fame"* Ibid., 43.

162 *"I feel a comfort in being alone"* Ibid., 182–83.

Reinventing the Fifties

165 *"We're gonna take over. You're finished"* Peter Biskind, *Easy Riders, Raging Bulls: How the Sex, Drugs and Rock 'n' Roll Generation Saved Hollywood* (Simon and Schuster, 1998), 123.

165 *bottom out at 15.8 million a week in 1971* Ibid., 20.

166 *"They're young . . . they're in love . . . and they kill people"* J. Hoberman, *The Dream Life: Movies, Media, and the Mythology of the Sixties* (New Press, 2003), 168.

166 *the Zapruder film showing Kennedy's assassination* David M. Lubin,

Shooting Kennedy: JFK and the Culture of Images (University of California Press, 2003), 30–31.

166 *countercultural heroes like H. Rap Brown and Franz Fanon* Hoberman, *Dream Life*, 169.

166 *"Do they confer . . . glamour on violence?"* Pauline Kael, "Bonnie & Clyde," *New Yorker*, October 21, 1967.

166 *"might be as potent a drive as sex"* Hoberman, *Dream Life*, 170.

166 *73 percent of the total audience* Kael, "After Innocence," *New Yorker*, October 1, 1973.

167 *its current involvement in Indochina* Biskind, *Easy Riders*, 136.

167 *it allowed him to channel Dean's spirit* New York Times, May 10, 1970.

167 *the old myths of the frontier were all too obvious* Richard Slotkin, *Gunfighter Nation: The Myth of the Frontier in 20th Century America* (HarperPerennial, 1992).

167 *with his "crypto-Western"* The Green Berets Hoberman, *Dream Life*, 210.

168 *"the preeminence of the Western among the genres of mythic discourse"* Slotkin, *Gunfighter*, 627.

168 *helped spirit the fugitive out of the country* Biskind, *Easy Riders*, 271–78.

169 *the most racist state in the nation* Dennis Banks with Richard Erdoes, *Ojibwa Warrior: Dennis Banks and the Rise of the American Indian Movement* (University of Oklahoma Press, 2004), 145.

169 *creation of the Badlands National Monument* Ibid., 146.

169 *"America's latest Indian war"* Slotkin, *Gunfighter*, 636.

169 *"It's like a flashback to Danang"* Banks, *Ojibwa*, 177.

169 *"would have slaughtered us as it did in 1890"* Ibid., 170.

170 *"demonstrated the powerlessness of radical protest"* Peter Carroll, *It Seemed Like Nothing Happened: America in the 1970s* (Rutgers University Press, 1982), 105.

170 *"if I went to Wounded Knee,"* New York Times, March 30, 1973.

171 *"The workers have the means of production"* Dale Pollock, *Skywalking: The Life and Films of George Lucas* (Harmony, 1983), 246.

171 *render the old studio system completely obsolete* Biskind, *Easy Rider*, 434.

171 *a countercultural version of MGM* Ibid., 92.

171 *shut down by its parent company, Paramount* Ibid., 206.

172 *the 1974 grosses were the biggest since 1946* Ibid., 280.

172 *"moral and emotional vacuum at the center of the home"* Ibid., 363.

172 *a wave of "immigrant" films led by* The Godfather Slotkin, *Gunfighter*, 639.

173 *Hopper, with characteristic immodesty, claimed credit* Biskind, *Easy Rider*, 181.

173 *"in the PDR, circa 1973"* Julia Phillips, *You'll Never Eat Lunch in This Town Again* (New American Library, 2002), xx.

173 *celebrating his hundredth birthday that year* Joan Didion, *The White Album* (Simon and Schuster, 1979), 158.

175 "*but where we always were*" Kael, "After Innocence," *New Yorker*, October 1, 1973.

176 "*infantilizing*" *both their artists and their audience* Kael, "On the Future of the Movies," *New Yorker*, August 5, 1974.

176 *put the studios firmly back in the driver's seat* Biskind, *Easy Rider*, 278.

176 "*the corrupt, vigilante form of a* Dirty Harry" Kael, "Future," 43.

176 "*ideals that nourished us in the beginning*" Carroll, *Nothing Happened*, 86.

177 "*began to doubt the premises of all the stories I had ever told myself*" Didion, *White Album*.

177 *proliferation of theme parks and historical preservation projects* Slotkin, *Gunfighter*, 639; James Monaco, *American Film Now: The People, the Power, the Money, the Movies* (Oxford University Press, 1979), 63.

177 "*an imagined past of total harmony*" Robert Jay Lifton, *Home from the War: Vietnam Veterans: Neither Victims nor Executioners* (Simon and Schuster, 1973), 367.

177 *election of an old movie star, Ronald Reagan, as president at the end of the decade* Slotkin, *Gunfighter*, 627, 640.

177 "*on the rubble of the old industry*" Pollock, *Skywalking*, 245.

178 *offered ample opportunity to indulge* Ibid., 28.

178 *did he switch from cars to filmmaking* Ibid., xiv.

178 *the sellout is the "hero-survivor of our times"* Kael, "Innocence," 118.

179 "*from about 1945 to 1962*" Biskind, *Easy Riders*, 235.

181 "*the inaugural film*" *of postmodern nostalgia,* Fredric Jameson, *Postmodernism, or The Cultural Logic of Late Capitalism* (Duke University Press, 1991), 19.

182 "*privileged lost object of desire*" Ibid., 19.

183 "*selling cheeseburgers and root-beer floats*" Carroll, *Nothing Happened*, 129.

183 "*chastened and repaired*" Richard Barnet, "Morality Play" *New York Review of Books*, May 2, 1974.

183 *constituted over half of the filmgoing audience* Kael, "The Current Cinema," *New Yorker*, October 29, 1973.

184 *the guilt of the younger generation's oedipal impulses* Biskind, *Easy Riders*, 363.

184 "*before they became the counterculture*" Kael, "Future," 50.

184 "*the last authentic national folk culture*" *New York Times*, August 5, 1973.

185 *the groups that paid homage to his memory* David Dalton, *James Dean: The Mutant King* (St. Martin's 1974), ii.

185 *some fans paid for the privilege of sitting behind the bloodstained wheel* Steven Morrissey, *James Dean Is Not Dead* (Babylon, 1983).

185 "*the root of the culture of the Sixties and Seventies*" Dalton, *Dean*, iii, 331.

186 "*He's Hidden in a Sanatorium*" Morrissey, *Dean*.

186 *an anthem after James Dean's death* Jon Savage, *England's Dreaming:*

Anarchy, Sex Pistols, Punk Rock, and Beyond (St. Martin's Griffin, 1991), 53.

186 *"a terminal congress of spurting loins and engine coolant"* J. G. Ballard, *Crash* (Picador, 1973), 16.

186 *the fifteen-year period between Sputnik and Watergate* Hoberman, *Dream Life*, xi.

187 *a willing accomplice or a terrorized victim* Jack Sargent, *Born Bad: The Story of Charles Starkweather and Caril Ann Fugate* (Creation Books, 1996).

187 *"with the death of James Dean"* Savage, *Dreaming*, 51.

187 *on the original draft of* Dirty Harry Beverly Walker, "Malick on Badlands," *Sight and Sound* 44, no. 2 (Spring 1985), 82.

190 *"they're more open to things around them, more demonstrative"* Walker, "Malick," 83.

192 *the aura of populist romance that marked Penn's film* Biskind, *Easy Riders*, 314.

192 *"defend the very rules that put and keep them there"* Walker, "Malick," 83.

193 *having it come back as a pop-music ghost* Hoberman, *Dream Life*, 383.

193 *"sort of unanointed royalty who rule by divine right"* Dalton, *Dean*, viii.

194 *"in the academic world, in politics, in the women's movement"* Kael, "Innocence," 49.

Power Shift

196 *further into disrepute* Bruce Schulman, *The Seventies: The Great Shift in American Culture, Society, and Politics* (Da Capo, 2001), 42.

197 *Alfred Eisenstadt's celebrated photograph* James Traub, *The Devil's Playground: A Century of Pleasure and Profit in Times Square* (Random House, 2004), 100–101.

197 *"'You can tell that bastard [Nixon] the war isn't over'"* Robert Jay Lifton, *Home from the War: Vietnam Veterans: Neither Victims nor Executioners* (Simon and Schuster, 1973), 449–50.

197 *"colorful and tasteless as it has always been"* "Talk of the Town," *New Yorker*, December 10, 1973.

198 *one of the most profitable films of all time* New York Times, October 5, 2004.

198 *taken hold among the city's cultural elite* New York Times, January 21, 1973.

198 *if they included the film in their sex education* New York Times, January 3, 1973.

199 *a clitoral was superior to a vaginal orgasm* New York Times, January 21, 1973.

199 *fined the New Mature World Theater $100,000* New York Times, March 4 and March 13, 1973.

199 *the new power of "community" as moral arbiter* New York Times, December 9, 1973.

199 *"even the least spiritual of the guests can see it glitter"* Carolyn See, *Blue Money: Pornography and the Pornographers—An Intimate Look at the Two-Billion-Dollar Fantasy Industry* (McKay, 1974), 118.

199 *"more hostile questions than anyone except perhaps the head of the American Communist Party"* Ibid., 114.

200 *violence would become Hollywood's new pornography* New York Times, December 9, 1973.

201 *in roles designed to reassure white audiences* Ed Guerrero, *Framing Blackness: The African American Image in Film* (Temple University Press, 1993), 73.

201 *"our conditioned susceptibility to the white man's program"* Darius James, *That's Blaxploitation!: Roots of the Baadasss 'Tude* (St. Martin's Griffin, 1995), 5.

203 *reverting to traditional formulas* Guerrero, *Blackness*, 70.

203 *likened the reaction against them to that against* Deep Throat New York Times, March 18, 1973.

204 *pressured by the FBI to pull the movie from theaters* New York Times January 1, 2004.

204 *Freeman's commando unit, the Cobras* New York Times, February 14, 1974.

205 *the fabric of the inner city* Schulman, *Seventies*, 32.

205 *Forty percent of its four hundred thousand inhabitants were on welfare* New York Times, January 15, 1973.

205 *made their homes in abandoned and burned-out buildings* New York Times, January 16, 1973.

206 *"looting is rampant, fires are everywhere"* New York Times, January 15, 1973.

206 *"civilization has virtually disappeared"* New York Times, January 18, 1973.

206 *"the brutal costs of a senseless war"* Ibid.

207 *"They must be leveled to the ground"* Ibid.

207 *"Maybe it should go through a cycle of destruction"* White House Transcript, 1972, cited in www.harpers.org/September11.html.

207 *funding for education and hospital construction to urban renewal* New York Times, January 16, 1973, January 30, 1973, and March 5, 1973.

207 *the moral fabric of American society* New York Times, February 4, 1973.

207 *a failed utopian experiment in social engineering* New York Times, February 25, 1973.

208 *asked Congress to restore the death penalty* New York Times, March 11, 1973.

208 *the old expectation of universally rising living standards* David Harvey, *The Condition of Postmodernity* (Blackwell, 1989), 145, 164.

208 *on easy terms to returning soldiers* Schulman, *Seventies*, 5.

209 *"and those who are left behind"* New York Times, January 18, 1973.

209 *advent of court-ordered busing in the northern states* Schulman, *Seventies*, 57.

210 *"treat our street-corner gunslingers as sociological casualities"* Andrew Hacker, "Getting Used to Mugging," *New York Review of Books*, April 19, 1973.

211 *snipers and stone-throwers harassed the police New York Times*, December 16, 1973.

211 *"Blow it . . . up! Blow it . . . up!"* Tom Wolfe, *From Bauhaus to Our House* (Pocket Books, 1981), 74.

211 *"on July 15, 1972 at 3:32 (or thereabouts)"* Charles Jencks, *The Language of Post-Modern Architecture* (Rizzoli, 1984), 9.

211 *"the haunting eeriness of a bombed city"* New York Times, December 16, 1973.

211 *"becomes a potent media image"* Jane Holtz Kay, "Architecture," *Nation*, September 24, 1973.

212 *"the people of many nations"* James Glanz and Eric Lipton, *City in the Sky: The Rise and Fall of the World Trade Center* (Times, 2003), 37.

212 *"the gravity-defying confidence of early NASA scientists"* Ibid., 5.

212 *"Big But Not So Bold"* New York Times, April 5, 1973.

212 *unoccupied well into the late 1970s* Glanz and Lipton, *City*, 215.

213 *show Times Square "in a protected environment"* "Talk of the Town," *New Yorker*, July 23, 1973.

213 *a new kind of spectacle built around extravagant interior spaces* Harvey, *Condition*, 88–90.

213 *"Buck Rogers in Times Square"* New York Times, August 26, 1973.

213 *"an upended concrete bunker"* Traub, *Playground*, 152–53.

214 *"ordered by rational master plans"* New York Times, December 29, 1972.

215 *"Abstract Expressionism in architecture"* Robert Venturi and Denise Scott Brown, *Learning from Las Vegas* (MIT Press, 1972), 104.

215 *the larger cultural shift of this period New York Times*, April 17, 1972.

215 *took hold in American life in the 1980s* Venturi and Brown, *Learning*, 153–55.

216 *post-traditional; post-historical* Daniel Bell, *The Coming of Post-Industrial Society* (Basic Books, 1973), 51–54.

216 *remained at heart a traditionalist* Naomi Bliven "Who Gets What," *New Yorker*, September 17, 1973.

217 *a climate of pent-up desire for something more expressive* Harvey, *Condition*, 80.

218 *defined, out of ignorance, as "urban sprawl"* Venturi and Brown, *Learning*, xi.

218 *"the great monuments of Europe were for earlier generations"* New York Times, October 22, 1972.

219 *"yet no one knows what you really do"* Bill Owens, *Suburbia* (Fotofolio, 1973).

220 *"as if that uniformity reflected a spiritual uniformity inside"* David Halberstam, Preface, in ibid.

220 *"the perfect mayor for this town"* Hunter S. Thompson, *Fear and Loathing in Las Vegas* (Random House, 1971), 47, 178.

220 *"no one would notice—from either side"* New York Times, June 3, 1973.

221 *"more Mediterranean than Mr. Nixon himself?"* Janet Malcolm, "On and Off the Avenue," *New Yorker*, June 9, 1973.

222 *disproportionately based in Sunbelt states* Kirkpatrick Sale, *Power Shift: The Rise of the Southern Rim and Its Challenge to the Eastern Establishment* (Random House, 1975), 5–6.

222 *take advantage of this new leisure economy* Ibid., 44–45.

222 *its money got Nixon elected* Ibid., 119.

223 *the political culture of the entire nation* Schulman, *Seventies*, 217.

223 *a shadowy figure on the grassy knoll* See, *Blue Money*, 26–27.

223 *"local police parked in front of his house"* Ibid., 15.

223 *the Jesus movement established its first foothold* Lisa McGirr, *Suburban Warriors: The Origins of the New American Right* (Princeton University Press, 2001), 241–43.

224 *"ambivalence about the consequences of modernity"* Ibid., 245.

224 *"aspects of an idealized and simpler America"* Edward Soja, "Inside Exopolis: Scenes from Orange County," in Michael Sorkin, ed., *Variations on a Theme Park: The New American City and the End of Public Space* (Noonday, 1992), 100.

225 *a middle-class suburban utopia* McGirr, *Warriors*, 41.

225 *Mediterranean red-clay roof tile* Ibid., 42.

225 *"a list of 25 approved colors"* Sale, *Power Shift*, 171.

226 *"an intent to communicate"* Thomas Pynchon, *The Crying of Lot 49* (Bantam Books, 1967), 13.

226 *"more particularly Orange County"* New York Times, June 20, 1973.

Conspiracy Nation

227 *"have Lawrence Welk produce it"* Mark Feeney, *Nixon at the Movies* (University of Chicago Press, 2004), 232.

229 *"a grand conspiracy to subvert the electoral process"* Bob Woodward and Carl Bernstein, *All the President's Men* (Simon and Schuster, 1974), 155.

231 *"We are going to use any means. Is that clear?"* David Greenberg, *Nixon's Shadow: The History of an Image* (Norton, 2003), 78.

231 *few were immune* Fred Emery, *Watergate: The Corruption of American Politics and the Fall of Richard Nixon* (Touchstone, 1994), 223, 226.

231 *"that it was an eastern liberal trick"* Joe McGinniss, *The Selling of the President 1968* (Trident, 1969), 33.

231 *a creature of the new televisual age of politics* Greenberg, *Shadow*.

231 *"heightened emotionalism," and "susceptibility to rumor"* McGinniss, *Selling*, 181, 212.

232 *"totalitarian resources of television"* J. Hoberman, *The Dream Life: Movies, Media, and the Mythology of the Sixties* (New Press, 2003), 361.

232 the Washington Post's *Watergate coverage* Woodward and Bernstein, *Men*, 156.

232 *"everyone's life was in danger"* Ibid.

232 *the possibility of assassinating columnist Jack Anderson* G. Gordon Liddy, *Will: The Autobiography of G. Gordon Liddy* (St. Martin's Press, 1980), 208.

232 *middle-American resentment of the liberal elite* Greenberg, *Shadow*, 192.

232 *"hobnobbing at the same Georgetown parties"* Woodward and Bernstein, *Men*, 182.

232 *"great dream"* Anthony Summers, *The Arrogance of Power: The Secret World of Richard Nixon* (Penguin, 2000), 311.

233 *"what the Eastern Establishment media line . . . will be"* Kirkpatrick Sale, *Power Shift: The Rise of the Southern Rim and Its Challenge to the Eastern Establishment* (Random House, 1975), 210.

233 *"intelligence-gathering and disruptions operations"* Liddy, *Will*, 196.

234 *"break and enter, and it shall be given to you"* Garry Wills, "The Kingdom of Heaven," *New York Review of Books*, June 13, 1974.

234 *a number of occasions in the early 1960s* Woodward and Bernstein, *Men*, 133, 316.

235 *"disclosures of the private acts of government"* Liddy, *Will*, 151.

235 *against his father and the president* Emery, *Watergate*, 70.

235 *"sacred code of the insider"* Daniel Ellsberg, *Secrets: A Memoir of Vietnam and the Pentagon Papers* (Penguin, 2002), 268.

236 *his two closest aides, Ehrlichman and Haldeman* Ibid., 444–45.

236 *during which the global village was born* Hoberman, *Dream Life*, xi.

236 *"the private world of the home outside into the forum"* Marshall McLuhan, "At the Moment of Sputnik," *Journal of Communication* 24, 1 (1974): 48–58.

237 *"to plot holy wars in the name of self-defense"* New York Times, July 4, 1973.

237 *to undergo psychiatric evaluation* New York Times, October 30, 1972.

237 *a nervous breakdown during his last year in office* Summers, *Arrogance*, 98.

237 *"I may physically die"* Emery, *Watergate*, 408.

238 *mushroom cloud* Feeney, *Movies*, 286.

238 *"devil theory"* Emery, *Watergate*, 418.

238 *"enemy within"* Ibid., 424.

238 *"tape with unexpected blank sections"* Greenberg, *Shadow*, 258.

238 *"inquisition into the meaning, use and control of a sacred, unspeakable text"* New York Review of Books, March 22, 1973.

239 *"sexist implications of the war in Vietnam and the court system"* New York Times, February 19, 1973.

239 *the secret agent of history* Hoberman, *Dream Life*.

239 *a public spectacle that turned America into a nation of voyeurs* Stephen

Paul Miller, *The Seventies Now: Culture as Surveillance* (Duke University Press, 1999), 300.

240 *chalked up by most liberal commentators to unjustifiable paranoia* Greenberg, *Shadow*, 76.

240 *left a void in American society* Ibid., 97.

241 *"made sure they were dashed"* Sidney Blumenthal and Harvey Yazijian, eds., *Government by Gunplay: Assassination Conspiracy Theories from Dallas to Today* (New American Library, 1976), ix.

241 *oil companies conspiring to raise prices* Ibid., x.

241 *as evidenced by the recent "oil crisis"* Kirkpatrick Sale, "The World Behind Watergate," *New York Review of Books*, May 3, 1973.

242 *"a mere paranoid's invention"* Sale, *Power Shift*, 9.

242 *"kind of internal guerrilla warfare against the President"* Ibid., 237, 4.

242 *"as well as other individuals?"* Ibid., 275.

243 *Oswald had committed an act of "symbolic parricide"* New York Times, November 18, 1973.

243 *"we all want subconsciously to kill our fathers"* Blumenthal and Yazijian, *Gunplay*, 220.

243 *a Boston-based organization founded by former SDS members*, David M. Lubin, *Shooting Kennedy: JFK and the Culture of Images* (University of California Press, 2003), 166.

243 *his predecessor had died as the result of a conspiracy* Hoberman, *Dream Life*.

244 *breaking the Cuba story at the time of the break-in* Summers, *Arrogance*, 413–16.

244 *"the anti-Ellsberg operation looked like something the CIA does overseas"* Steve Weissman, ed., *Big Brother and the Holding Company: The World Behind Watergate* (Ramparts, 1974), 39.

247 *"his oppositional impulses have become the very instruments of the conspiracy"* Fredric Jameson, *The Geopolitical Aesthetic: Cinema and Space in the World System* (Indiana University Press, 1992), 60.

247 *"believe in the necessity of bombing innocent people"* Kael, "Politics and Thrills," *New Yorker*, November 19, 1973.

248 *to block Salvador Allende from assuming power in 1970* Thomas Powers, *The Man Who Kept the Secrets: Richard Helms and the CIA* (Pocket, 1979).

248 *with the Rockefeller-backed Council of the Americas assuming a leading role* Laurence Birns, "The Death of Chile," *New York Review of Books*, November 1, 1973.

248 *used at home against the antiwar movement* Blumenthal and Yazijian, *Gunplay*, 265.

248 *"believe the worst about every government agency"* New York Times, June 24, 1973.

249 *may have been based on the film* Jeff S. Nightbyrd, "Cinque Very Much," in Peter Knobler and Greg Mitchell, eds., *Very Seventies: A Cultural History of the 1970s, from the Pages of Crawdaddy* (Simon and Schuster, 1995), 164.

249 *"My penis made me do it"* Arthur Bremer, *An Assassin's Diary* (Harper's Magazine Press, 1973), 117.

249 *"a little of the old ultra-violence"* Ibid., 104.

250 *"the silent majority will back me all the way!"* Ibid., 118.

250 *"Bullet in Every Head, Com., Inc."* Ibid., 120.

250 *Nixon himself suspected a Bremer–CREEP connection, according to the* Post *reporters* Woodward and Bernstein, *Men*, 326–27.

250 *perhaps even the Black Panthers* According to Liddy, Colson called off Hunt's assignment at the last minute. Liddy, *Will*, 225.

250 *possibly even the McGovern campaign* Woodward and Bernstein, *Men*, 326.

250 *to preempt public suspicion of a cover-up San Francisco Chronicle*, June 9, 2005.

251 *"they're all out of left field" New York Times*, November 5, 1972.

251 *shielded from public view by the press* Ibid.

251 *"the theater of action is now the entire world"* Richard Hofstadter, "The Paranoid Style in American Politics," in *The Paranoid Style in American Politics and Other Essays* (Harvard University Press, 1996).

252 *" 'they' will control the world" New York Times*, August 6, 1972.

253 *"a one-world super-state, which they would control"* Ibid.

253 *"endorsed by Hanoi and the Manson family" New York Times*, November 5, 1972.

253 *designs on the global financial order* Michael Barkun, *A Culture of Conspiracy: Apocalyptic Visions in Contemporary America* (University of California Press, 2003).

254 *increasing the value of their worldwide holdings* Peter Beter, *The Conspiracy Against the Dollar* (Braziller, 1973).

254 *"no surfacing, no interviews, no rumors, no word" New York Times*, March 9, 1973.

254 *"at odds with the times" New York Times*, March 11, 1973.

256 *"not for paranoid titillation, but for solace"* Garry Wills, "An Assassin's Diary," *New York Times*, April 8, 1973.

257 *"might Jack have kept [the harmonica] from falling, violated gravity somehow?"* Thomas Pynchon, *Gravity's Rainbow* (Viking, 1973), 65.

257 *"secular history is a diversionary tactic"* Ibid., 164, 167.

259 *"smothering me to my death"* Ibid., 755–56.

Epilogue

262 *not even Watergate seemed capable of injecting new life into it* Sara Davidson, "Notes from the Land of the Cobra," *New York Times*, June 2, 1974; Vin McLellan and Paul Avery, *The Voices of Guns: The Definitive and Dramatic Story of the Twenty-Two Month Career of the Symbionese Liberation Army* (Putnam, 1977), 30.

262 *"American Gulag"* Shana Alexander, *Anyone's Daughter: The Times and Trials of Patty Hearst* (Viking Press, 1979), 130.

263 *left a void in Bay Area radicalism* McLellan and Avery, *Guns*, 99.

263 *the seeds of incipient "Orwellianism"* Ibid., 68.

265 *its current state of "image fatigue"* Alexander, *Daughter*, 24.

265 *with an eye on achieving maximum exposure* Robert Brustein, "News Theater," *New York Times*, June 16, 1974.

266 *Patty's "reality gap" left her highly susceptible* Alexander, *Daughter*, 168.

266 *"hard to find"* McLellan and Avery, *Guns*, 346.

266 *succumb to his own star trip* Ibid., 306.

267 *"look, it's live"* Patricia Campbell Hearst, with Alvin Moscow, *Every Secret Thing* (Doubleday, 1982), 233.

267 *"devoid of their day-to-day working reality"* Jeff S. Nightbyrd, "Cinque Very Much," in Peter Knobler and Greg Mitchell, eds., *Very Seventies: A Cultural History of the 1970s, from the Pages of Crawdaddy* (Simon and Schuster, 1995), 164.

268 *Patty's was a case of possession by the devil.* Alexander, *Daughter*, 485.

268 *"as slaves of the ruling classes"* Ibid., 65, 219.

268 *Pat (the name given her in prison)* Ibid., 75–76.

268 *he approached the Hearsts to offer his help* Ted Patrick, *Let Our Children Go!* (Dutton, 1976), 281–85; McLellan and Avery, *Guns*, 268–70.

268 *possessed by a being from outer space* New York Times, July 21, 1974.

269 *in an effort to learn to speak like "the People"* Hearst, *Thing*, 299.

269 *"free themselves from the bourgeois stain"* McLellan and Avery, *Guns*, 20.

270 *"that dictator is the current president, Richard Nixon"* Ibid., 175–76.

270 *the "corporate-military coup" staged in 1972* Hearst, *Thing*, 88.

270 *embracing urban guerrilla warfare* Nation, December 17, 1973.

270 *a "CIA creation gone haywire"* New York Times, July 21, 1974.

270 *and justify the creation of a state of siege* Donald Freed, "Operation Gemstone," in Steve Weissman, ed., *Big Brother and the Holding Company: The World Beyond Watergate* (Ramparts, 1974), 99.

271 *"gone into the revolutionary messiah business for himself"* Alexander, *Daughter*, 142.

271 *seemed ripe for radical change* Davidson, "Cobra."

271 *above photos of Patty Hearst and Aleksandr Solzhenitsyn* McLellan and Avery, *Guns*, 22.

272 *convinced that she had planned her own kidnapping* Hearst, *Thing*, 391.

272 *"I often had dreams of falling in love with one of my captors"* Davidson, "Cobra."

273 *it took the SLA to restore to the American patriarchy its lost luster* McLellan and Avery, *Guns*, 39.

A NOTE ON THE AUTHOR

Andreas Killen is an assistant professor of history at the
City College of New York. He holds a Ph.D. from New
York University, where he specialized in modern cultural
and urban history. He is the author of *Berlin Electropolis*,
and his writing has appeared in *Salon* and the *New York
Times Magazine*.

A NOTE ON THE TYPE

The text of this book is set in Linotype Sabon, named after the type founder, Jacques Sabon. It was designed by Jan Tschichold and jointly developed by Linotype, Monotype and Stempel, in response to a need for a typeface to be available in identical form for mechanical hot metal composition and hand composition using foundry type.

Tschichold based his design for Sabon roman on a font engraved by Garamond, and Sabon italic on a font by Granjon. It was first used in 1966 and has proved an enduring modern classic.